An Insider's View of
Sexual Science since Kinsey

An Insider's View of
Sexual Science since Kinsey

Ira L. Reiss

ROWMAN & LITTLEFIELD PUBLISHERS, INC.
Lanham • Boulder • New York • Toronto • Oxford

ROWMAN & LITTLEFIELD PUBLISHERS, INC.

Published in the United States of America
by Rowman & Littlefield Publishers, Inc.
A wholly owned subsidary of The Rowman & Littlefield Publishing Group, Inc.
4501 Forbes Boulevard, Suite 200, Lanham, Maryland 20706
www.rowmanlittlefield.com

PO Box 317, Oxford, OX2 9RU, UK

British Library Cataloguing in Publication Information Available

Library of Congress Cataloging-in-Publication Data

Reiss, Ira L.
   An insider's view of sexual science since Kinsey / Ira L. Reiss.
      p. cm.
   Includes bibliographical references and index.
   ISBN-13: 978-0-7425-4652-3 (cloth : alk. paper)
   ISBN-10: 0-7425-4652-7 (cloth : alk. paper)
   ISBN-13: 978-0-7425-4653-0 (pbk. : alk. paper)
   ISBN-10: 0-7425-4653-5 (pbk. : alk. paper)   OCLC: 623 H2059
   1. Sexology—Research. 2. Sexology. I. Title.
HQ60.R46 2006
306.709'045—dc22

                                        2005033445

Printed in the United States of America

∞™ The paper used in this publication meets the minimum requirements of
American National Standard for Information Sciences—Permanence of Paper for
Printed Library Materials, ANSI/NISO Z39.48-1992.

To Harriet, My Wife of Fifty Years,
Who Has Been the Blessing of My Life

What Could Be

There once was a mythical land of Oz
where everything that could be was.
If only we could see
from what is to what could be.

—Ira L. Reiss

~

Contents

Preface   xi

Chapter 1   Know Your Author   1

  Anti-Semitism in the 1930s   1
  Prostitution and the Depression   2
  Religious Indoctrination   3
  The Double Standard in Sexuality   4
  Anti-Semitism in the Army   5
  A Little Bit of Sex Education   7
  Getting My Degree: Some Key Events   7

Chapter 2   The Antisex Bias of the 1950s   13

  The 1950s Culture   13
  Antisex Bias in Family Textbooks   14
  The Admiral and the College of William and Mary   16
  Questioning High School Students about Sex
    in the 1950s   17
  Publishing on Sexuality in Journals in the 1950s   21
  Trying to Publish My First Book   24
  A Minor Clash with Radio Censorship   28

Chapter 3   What Is This Thing Called Science?   29

  Ancient Roots of Modern Science   29
  The Ethical Side of Science   31
  Political Distortions of Science   32

Advocacy and Science   33
Value Aware, Value Fair, and Premarital Abstinence   34
Linking Personal Values to Personal Assumptions   36
The Tentativeness of Science   37
Summing Up Science   38

Chapter 4   The Sexual Revolution and Sexual Organizations   41

Sexual Standards at the Dawn of the
    Sexual Revolution   41
The Mythical Place of the Pill in the
    1960s Revolution   43
Albert Ellis and the Society for the
    Scientific Study of Sex   47
Richard Green: A New Journal and an
    International Academy   49
Other Sexuality Organizations Spring Forth   50
The Value of Sexuality Organizations   52
Hugh Hefner's Party at the Chicago Playboy Mansion   52

Chapter 5   New Approaches to Sexuality   57

Getting to Know Masters and Johnson: 1962+   57
The Sexual Attitudes Reassessment Movement Begins   61
The New Program in Human Sexuality at Minnesota   62
The New Sexual Dogma: The SAR in San Francisco   63

Chapter 6   Building Explanations of Sexuality   69

The Empirical Basis of the Autonomy Theory   69
Proposition One: Changing Sexual Permissiveness   71
Some Reactions to the Autonomy Theory   74
Why Was Gender Equality and Sexual Pluralism
    So Strong in Sweden?   75
The Swedish Culture in Action at Dalarna   78
A Swedish Panel Discusses Sexuality   79
Historical Factors Promoting Gender Equality
    in Sweden   81
Sweden and Autonomy Theory   82

Chapter 7   Some Clashes of Science, Politics, and Values   85

The Federal Government's Victorian Standards   85
Unveiling the Feminine Mystique: NOW   90
The AMA: Even Doctors Want to Know about Sex   91
Fighting an Obscene Antipornography Bill   93

Chapter 8   An Insider's View of a Major Crisis in SSSS   101
             Wanted: One Gunslinger as President of SSSS   101
             Baptism of Fire: September 1980   102
             Starting the Search for an Executive Director   105
             Denouement in Dallas   106
             April 9, 1981: Decision Day   110

Chapter 9   Exploring Therapy and HIV/AIDS   115
             Sex Therapy: The Program in Human Sexuality   116
             Further Exploration: The Masters and Johnson Institute   118
             Problems with Washington's Disease Fighters   123

Chapter 10   Building a Cross-Cultural Explanation of Sexuality   127
             The Linkage Theory   127
             Defining Sexuality   129
             Social Bonds: Pleasure and Disclosure   130
             Three Universal Societal Linkages to Sexual Norms   132
             Gender Power Differences   132
             Societal Ideologies: Defining Sexual Normality   134
             Kinship and Extramarital Sexual Jealousy   134
             Summing Up the Linkage Theory of Sexuality   136

Chapter 11   Can Sexual Science Really Help with
             Societal Problems?   139
             Early Reactions to HIV/AIDS   139
             Sexual Therapists React to HIV/AIDS   140
             Just How Risky Are Condoms?   143
             Is Abstinence the Safest Strategy?   145
             Sexual Pluralism: The Way to Reduce Our
               Sexual Problems   146
             Sexual Pluralism Theory   150
             Responses to Sexual Pluralism   153

Chapter 12   New Projects and a New Life Agenda   157
             The Governor's Committee on Child and
               Adolescent Sexual Health   157
             Retirement: But Not from Sexual Science   162
             Al Ellis and Rational Emotive Behavior Therapy   164

Chapter 13   Problem Areas in Sexual Science Today   169
             Antiscience: Radical Social Constructionism   169
             The Bush Administration's Hostility to
               Scientific Research in Sexuality   174

Sexnet Debates: Biology versus Social Science 176
The Interaction of Social and Biological Factors 179
Defining Gender Roles 183

Chapter 14   Building a PhD in Sexual Science 187
Some Programs in Sexuality 187
Working toward a PhD in Sexual Science 191
The Essential Elements of a PhD in Sexuality:
Making the Case 192
More Progress toward a PhD in Sexual Science 197

Chapter 15   To the Next Generation of Sexual Scientists 201
The Cultural Wars in Sexuality 201
Sexuality Trends around the World 204
Do Attitudes and Behaviors Correlate? 207
Explaining Trends in Sexuality 209
Future Goals 210

References 213

Name Index 227

Subject Index 233

About the Author 239

~

Preface

For over fifty years, I've been privileged to be a participant in building the field of sexual science, the multidisciplinary field that studies human sexuality. It has been a very exciting, rewarding, and sometimes frustrating experience. I want to share with you some of my critique of this field, but first let me be clear about what I am *not* doing. I am *not* surveying *all* that has happened in our field over the past fifty years. Rather, my critique is based upon my experiences in the field over these decades. So I apologize—up front to anyone in the field whose good work I have not cited. Surely I am not referencing all the good work done in sexual science over the past fifty years. However, I have been in the center of a great many of the interesting and controversial developments in our field, and I know the views and the publications of most of the key people in our field. I would further emphasize that what I have to say is not based only on my recollections or impressions. I am quite aware of the many pitfalls of memory. Therefore, I also checked carefully my annual journal entries, the thousands of letters I exchanged with many of the key people in the field, my own work, and my recent discussions with many people in our field about their current work. I used all these resources to arrive at my interpretations and explanations concerning the field of sexual science as I have experienced it over the fifty years since the death of Alfred Kinsey.

The primary people I am trying to reach are those who have recently finished their education and whose work now requires them to know something about human sexuality. That would include people in a broad array of occupations, such as professors, researchers, social workers, therapists, public health workers, and sex educators. Those in graduate school who are studying in these fields would also benefit by knowing more about my experiences over the last fifty years. What I have to say is relevant today because many of the same issues I confronted are still unsettled. The veterans in sexual science know me quite well, and they may also want to examine my ideas so as to see just where they agree or disagree. In addition, I would very much like to reach those people in the educated public who do not work or study in sexuality but who have a serious interest in understanding more about the scientific study of sexuality.

I have tried to make the book readable for all the above groups. The style I write in is informal, nontechnical, and jargon free. Understanding what I'm saying does not require detailed knowledge about sexual science but simply requires a serious curiosity to learn more about the field. My style should come as a relief to those who are used to reading academic journals. I also avoid footnotes and instead when referring to a source, I simply put the author's name and the year of publication in parentheses. The reader can then go to the references listed at the end of the book and find the full reference. Those of you who wish to go deeper into any of the controversial issues that I discuss can locate key readings in this list of references.

You will find in this book accounts of many of the important controversial disputes that mark the sexual-science landscape of the last five decades. Sexual science has surely not followed a straight upward line from Kinsey to today. The progress is not as much as I would have liked, but nevertheless we have made many impressive achievements. I am an optimist, and my account may reflect some of that optimism, but bear in mind that I am not a blind optimist. Rather, I am an *anxious* optimist, so I do make careful checks on my perceptions and my predictions before I accept them, and especially so before I put them in print.

Many of you may be aware that the beginnings of sexual science date back to the late nineteenth century in Europe—particularly in Germany and Austria and specifically with medical doctors. Starting in the early 1930s, Hitler systematically destroyed sexual science in Germany and elsewhere in Europe. It was Alfred Kinsey who, in the late 1930s, began to lay down the foundation for making America the world center for the study of sexual science. It was Kinsey's scientific work that allowed this shift of leadership from Europe to America. For those who are interested in knowing more about Alfred Kinsey, there are biographies that can be consulted concerning his life (Gathorne-Hardy 2000; Jones 1997).

I pick up the story of sexual science in the early 1950s, when I entered the field—just a few years before Kinsey's death. My explanations center on those aspects of the field with which I was the most involved. My PhD was in sociology, so I have focused heavily on the impact of society on our sexual behaviors and attitudes. However, I have not ignored the role of the psychological and biological sciences. For example, I will comment on the many exchanges I have had with Al Ellis concerning his rational emotive therapy approach to sexuality. I will also comment on debates in our field between those who stress a biological explanation of sexuality and those who stress a social or psychological explanation of sexuality. You will find that my vision in this book is broader than just sociology, as I favor a multidisciplinary approach to the study of sexuality.

I am not one who jumps on bandwagons or joins in the fads and fashions that briefly strut upon the academic stage. Instead, I have worked to develop my own understanding and explanations of the different perspectives in our field. I would add that I don't think you will have any trouble understanding where I am coming from, even if at times you may disagree. If you expect a tabloid portrait of the private sexual escapades of sexual scientists, you will be disappointed. Instead of their personal lives, I stress the professional aspects of the people in our field. My approach in this book is that of a social scientist who holds a broad view of the scientific enterprise. I do my best in this book to discuss the evidence and the reasoning relevant to the evaluation of the ideas that I put forth, and I try to do this in a way that will be clear to the reader.

Of course, there will be those who disagree with my take on how our field has developed and where it is headed today. I learned long ago that accepting the reality of mutual criticism is part of the admission ticket to the study of any scientific field. My overall goal in this book is to portray the very exciting, conflictful, and fascinating developments in sexual science that I have been part of in my lifelong efforts to help build sexual science in our country. I believe you will enjoy my account of this ongoing effort, and I hope you will find it helpful in your own life endeavors.

I want to end this preface by thanking my three readers. Two of them are my colleagues from the Sociology Department at the University of Minnesota: Robert Fulton and Joel Nelson. Both of these scholars gave me the benefit of their thoughtful comments and suggestions. I very much appreciate their time and effort in doing that. But the most important help came from my wife, Harriet, who carefully went over the manuscript and gave me many very valuable suggestions. She has worked with me over the past fifty years on all my books and has coauthored two of them with me. I should add that she is now busily at work on a book of her own, and I am very appreciative of the time she took off to help me. I also want to thank the many sexual scientists who sent me copies of their latest work so that I could be up to date in what I said about them. My thanks also go to Jenn Nemec and Jessica Gribble at Rowman & Littlefield for their very able and professional handling of my manuscript.

Ira L. Reiss
November 14, 2005
Minneapolis, Minnesota

CHAPTER ONE

~

Know Your Author

Knowing something about my personal values will make you better able to judge whether my personal values are biasing any of my perspectives on sexual science. I doubt that anyone can be totally disinterested or value free concerning all the controversial issues in our field, such as those dealing with HIV/AIDS, teen pregnancy, child sexual abuse, conservative versus liberal trends, monolithic versus pluralistic values, and so on. But having values is not the same thing as allowing those values to bias your evaluation of evidence or reasoning. One cannot be avoided, but the other can surely be contained. I will illustrate this difference between values and bias many times in this book. Making my values explicit helps me check my own work more carefully, because it makes me more aware that my personal values can bias my scientific conclusions. I will try to inform you about my values by very briefly sharing some personal experiences in my life before I received my PhD.

Anti-Semitism in the 1930s

I was born in December 1925, during the roaring twenties. My mother and father were loving parents to me, but they didn't get along very well with each other. I was given a good deal of autonomy to run my own life. I believe that one reason for this was that my parents were so busy arguing with each other that they didn't have time to carefully regulate my life. I was closer to my mother, and she was the more expressive and argumentative person in the marriage. My father was a successful businessman who was less argumentative and more of a pragmatist than my mother. Of course, I was bothered by their quarrels with each other, but I really did enjoy having a great deal of freedom, far beyond that of most of my friends. I valued my autonomy then, and I still do today.

Many of my earliest memories of the 1930s involve the virulent anti-Semitism in the world at that time. I am not just speaking of what was happening in Hitler's Germany. I am speaking of what was very much happening here in America as well. I am Jewish, and my public schooling in Scranton, Pennsylvania, was filled with anti-Semitic events. For example, in fourth grade there was a kid who almost every day during recess would come up to me and call me "kike," "moneylender," "Christ killer," and other prejudicial slurs. I would go over to him and call him Hitler, and we would start fighting with each other. The teachers always just told us to stop fighting. They did nothing about the anti-Semitism that they surely heard. I learned that I had to defend myself—not many others were stepping forward to offer help.

Prostitution and the Depression

There were interesting characteristics of the town I grew up in—Scranton, Pennsylvania—that require some explanation. Scranton was a coal-mining town; anthracite (hard) coal and clothing factories were the major sources of employment when the 1930s depression hit. Scranton, like most cities at that time, was in deep economic trouble, and we lived close to poverty for a few years until finally my father's persistent struggles paid off and he was able to establish a small clothing factory. Other entrepreneurial souls in Scranton were founding a different sort of business as their way of surviving the depression years. Houses of prostitution opened. There were scores of them in the alleys behind twelve of the downtown streets. The economic and cultural impact of prostitution on Scranton was dramatic. Prostitution brought in a large amount of money to many parts of the city, and, as a result, the sex industry gained considerable covert political support and thrived throughout the depression years. On a Saturday night, the population of Scranton increased tremendously. Scores of cars came in from New York City, Philadelphia, and elsewhere. The cars were loaded with men eager to "check out the Scranton girls." Sexual services from black and mulatto prostitutes were less expensive than the same services from a white prostitute. The cultural scripts on race, class, and gender for the 1930s and early 1940s were indelibly written into the social and economic structure of Scranton's houses of prostitution.

As noted, the houses brought money into the eager cash registers of the hotels, restaurants, gas stations, and bars. As a young boy, I benefited economically from their existence. No, I did not become a child pimp or a child performer. My part-time role was more indirect than that. It was impossible to grow up in Scranton and not know where these brightly painted "pleasure houses" were located. I recall that when I was about ten years old, cars would stop beside me when I was walking with friends near the downtown area. The male passengers would lean out of the car window and say, "Hey kid, where are the cathouses?" When I gave them directions, the men in the car would usually toss me a nickel or sometimes a dime. I was fascinated by the power of sex to so easily bring so many men, so far from their homes, into an economically depressed coal-mining town. It reinforced the idea to me that there must be something very special about sexuality—something mysterious, powerful, and extraordinarily rewarding.

When I was in high school, I became a customer, and at times I would stay in the parlor after having sex, to talk and get to know the "working girls" better. Many of them were also high school age. They would make it clear in their conversations with each other and with me that they were not going to be like the friends or sisters they knew who worked for years in some factory sweatshop for low pay with nothing to show for it. They had their rationale for what they were doing. There were some avant-garde aspects in Scranton's prostitution system. In order to protect themselves and their clientele, prostitutes offered condoms to all their customers. That was what started me on the road to safe sex decades before condoms became very widely used. Also, the prostitutes were regularly inspected for disease by medical doctors. Many of the girls hoped to earn good money, save it, open up a beauty shop or a dress shop, and eventually get married. I saw some of these same women years later, and only a few had achieved their goals.

Bear in mind that a good deal of the condemnation of prostitution in Scranton was not from people who supported equality for women in society. The rejection of sex without affection, and particularly a negative view of female casual sexuality, underlaid much of the conservative criticism of prostitution. Much of this antiprostitution view seemed based more on a narrow view of what is acceptable sexuality than on a striving for gender equality. In my mind, much of the harm in prostitution is not in the recreational approach to sexuality but in the economic pressures, the gender inequality, the abusive pimps, and the illegality that still permeates the profession.

Religious Indoctrination

There was one influence that my parents made sure I was exposed to, and that was religion. I was sent to Orthodox Hebrew School for two hours every day after public school. I didn't enjoy much of that experience, but it had a significant influence on me. Orthodoxy demands that you accept the Torah—the first five books of the Old Testament—and see them as divinely inspired. However, once you do that, you are encouraged to analyze every word of it and to discuss and argue about conflicting interpretations of passages in the Torah. I enjoyed finding things that seemed incongruent, like the age of Sarah and also of Moses's mother when they gave birth—Sarah was ninety, and Moses's mother was a few hundred years old! But I wasn't a very attentive student in other ways. This disinterest led to a memorable experience with the rabbi.

One day, we were going over a particularly difficult biblical passage, and the rabbi asked the class what the meaning of the passage was. Nobody was coming up with an answer that the rabbi accepted, so I thought I'd take a try at it. I gave my interpretation, and the rabbi walked up to my chair, looked at me solemnly, and then slapped me hard across the face. I was stunned, and I asked him if he had slapped me because my answer was so bad. He said, "No, I slapped you because your answer showed me that you can do far better work than you have been doing all year, and to fail to use the talent God gave you is a sin. I wanted you to know that." That surely was a backhanded compliment. Nevertheless, this experience and others in Hebrew School did teach me a respect for the value of thoughtful inquiry. I still carry that with me.

There was another major input from my religious training. I was given a very restrictive view of sex before marriage. This was at the same time that I was directing cars to the "cathouses," so I was getting in spades the traditional sexual upbringing of the time. I learned that sex was available, but I also learned that it was formally prohibited. This built-in conflict made it likely that people would develop guilty feelings about much of the sex they would experience. This was not an ideal situation and was surely not an easy one to work out for oneself.

By age fourteen, I gave up orthodox religion, and I gradually drifted away from its restrictions. I wanted to go to movies and play football on Saturdays instead of going to a four-hour religious service and then home to study the Torah. But parts of some things stay with you emotionally even if you reject them intellectually. I still like parts of Judaism, and after getting married, Harriet and I joined a Reform Jewish Temple, where you can bring your mind as well as your feelings into the service.

The Double Standard in Sexuality

It should come as no surprise that in a coal-mining, open-prostitution town there would be a powerful double standard regulating sexuality. The prevailing view was that men wanted and needed sex, but women were different, and they should be condemned if they had sex with you. Men were also seen as smarter than women, and that in part justified their greater sexual rights. I'm sure I had internalized some of this, but not anywhere near as much as most of my friends had. After all, I had a mother who was dominant in my parents' marriage, a paternal grandmother who was a feminist pioneer working to give women more equality in Orthodox Judaism, and a sister who was a straight-A student. How in the world could I think women were inferior and didn't deserve equal rights? I felt fine with accepting equality.

I would argue with my high school buddies about the double standard. I tried appealing to their self-interest by advising them that if we wanted to make out with women, we couldn't treat them like they were less intelligent and deserved fewer sexual rights. That was clearly a self-defeating path to take. Why would women have sex with us if we held those views? My friends thought my reasoning was interesting, but it didn't convince any of them to change their views. However, in my personal life with women, my more-equal treatment of them was clearly appreciated. The double standard was to me a prejudice, and one that any self-respecting woman or man should reject. It was in the same category as anti-Semitism and racism. In my experience, women in the 1940s didn't often make their sexual interest obvious until they felt they had a receptive partner who wasn't unfairly judging them. But, once they felt safe, they revealed a good deal about their feelings, sexual and otherwise.

Anti-Semitism in the Army

Another important influence on my values regarding sexuality came from my hitch in the U.S. Army (1944–1946). I turned eighteen in December 1943 and was sworn in the next month. After army testing, I was placed into a unit that was supposed to be sent to college for special training for the intelligence branch of the army. Many of the men in that outfit had already started college when they were drafted, and many came from upper-middle-class homes. Very few came from a coal-mining, open-prostitution town like Scranton. What most surprised me about these men was that, although they were mostly about eighteen to twenty-two years old, many of them were still virginal or had very limited sexual experience. I thought the world was like Scranton, where very few boys passed age eighteen without sexual experience, but I soon learned otherwise. The army changed its plans to send us to college for special training and instead sent most of us for basic training as part of a combat-engineer battalion at Camp Chafee, Arkansas. There we learned how to build and blow up roads and bridges, how to plant and disarm mines, and how to use a wide range of weaponry. Then they sent us overseas to try out our skills against the Nazis. We went to England and then landed in Normandy.

One important and upsetting incident in my army experience was an encounter with anti-Semitism. Anti-Semitism didn't end in public school. It was abundant even in the army during the war. This incident happened in 1944, when our combat engineer battalion was at our port of embarkation (POE) right outside New York, just one day away from shipping out to Europe. We were housed in barracks. I was an eighteen-year-old private, and one of the staff sergeants in our outfit, Sgt. Hubbard, a regular-army man who had been in the army since before the war, came over to me. It was nighttime, and he asked me to get some coal for the stove in our POE barrack. It took a few minutes to get the coal because there were other soldiers ahead of me doing the same thing. I recall what happened then as if it were yesterday. Here's the dialogue, as I remember it, that followed my return with the bucket of coal.

Sgt. Hubbard barked at me, "It took you long enough. You Jews are always slow at helping someone else."

That was too much to take, and I cocked back the bucket of coal and said, "Here, I'll show how quick a Jew can be." I threw the bucket of coal right at him and stood there glaring at him, waiting for his response.

He was furious, and he also seemed very surprised. Much of our headquarters company, including other noncommissioned officers, were there in that barrack, and many of them saw and heard what happened.

Hubbard jumped up and screamed at me, "You know I could have you court-martialed for that. Who do you think you are?"

I replied to him, "Go ahead, report it, and I'll tell them about the Hitler-loving comment you made about the Jews, and we'll see what they do to you."

He was angry now, and he glared at me and said, "I should knock the shit out of you right now."

I shot back, "Do you see me shivering? Come on and try it! Come on!" I was very angry and ready for anything that might happen.

He stared at me, hesitated, and then turned and walked away.

Early the next morning, Lt. Tinsely of our company came over to me. He had been informed about the incident. He asked me if I wanted to put on the gloves in the gym and box with Hubbard. He thought that would clear the air between us. He thought that was important, since we could well be in combat together. By then my anger had turned into disgust and dislike for Hubbard's anti-Semitism. I told Lt. Tinsely that I didn't think boxing would settle anything. I told him that the question between Hubbard and me concerned anti-Semitism, not boxing ability. I told him that I felt strongly that the army was fighting the Nazis and that we shouldn't tolerate Nazi-type prejudices in our own ranks. Lt. Tinsely agreed with me, and that ended the affair. Later that day I was to learn that Sgt. Hubbard was missing. I never heard from him again. He had gone AWOL during the night, and he missed the sailing of our boat to Europe.

A Little Bit of Sex Education

I saw in these better-educated men in my company a chance to learn from them. They were better educated concerning good books, classical music, how to play chess, national politics, and much more. I had something to offer in return. Many of my army buddies noticed that I was more comfortable with women than they were. They wanted to meet women but didn't seem to know what to do. As things worked out, I helped them learn how to meet, talk to, and get involved with women—not by lectures, but simply by going out with them to meet women. And I learned from them about books, music, chess, and much more. I like to think we all benefited from the exchange. My army experience convinced me, more than anything else, that biology is flexible and that learning is very important in shaping our sexual attitudes and behaviors. These army friends were no different than my Scranton friends in their biological inheritance, but they still were a world apart in their sexual attitudes and behaviors.

Getting My Degrees: Some Key Events

After being discharged from the army, I went to college using the G.I. Bill, plus some help from my parents. There were some events in my educational experiences that also highlight my values. One involved a course I took in 1948, my senior year at Syracuse. The professor was adamant that premarital sex was wrong and that it would lead to disastrous outcomes such as disease, pregnancy, social ostracism, and self-condemnation. He asked each of us to analyze premarital sex and write a paper on our own conclusions about its moral worth. I wrote out my more-accepting ideas and shared them with the professor in class as well as in my paper. I tried to explain the basis for my different viewpoint. I gave marital sex a high value, but, unlike the professor, I suggested that it was also morally acceptable to have premarital sex with affection, or just for pleasure. I gave the body-centered sexual relationship a lower rating than the person-centered sexual relationship, but I did not condemn either of them. Then I asserted that the same ethical standards that apply to men apply to women. I explained my reasoning for all of my views in the paper (Reiss 1948). The professor was unconvinced by my arguments. However, writing this paper further clarified to me my own pluralistic and gender-equal values.

I rewrote the paper and showed it to my six roommates. I wanted to get their feedback. I didn't persuade them to adopt my views, but they did tell me that my ideas got them to thinking about the issues involved in judging sexual morality, and they encouraged me to write a book someday about my ideas regarding sexuality. This whole experience was a good one for me, and I see it as the prelude to my lifelong critical analysis of America's sexual beliefs. This paper incident occurred in the same year that the first Kinsey book appeared. I read Kinsey's book on males and thought it was very informative about a wide range of sexual behaviors. I felt that Kinsey's work was helpful in reducing people's guilty feelings about sexuality. This reduction of guilt thinned out the emotions and thereby made it easier for people to think more clearly about sexuality. Reading Kinsey probably would not change people's values, but I believed it would help them better think through and examine their own beliefs.

After graduating from college in 1949, I worked for my dad in his factory. I found the experience unrewarding, and after a year I left to attend Pennsylvania State University to work toward a doctorate in sociology with a minor in philosophy. After receiving my MA in sociology there, I decided to spend my second year taking graduate classes for my PhD at Columbia University in New York. I did not stay, however, because it would take too long to get a doctorate there—an average of eight years at the time. I returned to Penn State for my third and final year of graduate studies. My dissertation experience in this last year in graduate school revealed much to me about the academic world and about my own values, and I'll briefly tell that story here.

I wanted very much to finish my dissertation and get out into the freedom of the academic world, but my dissertation project turned out to evoke quite a bit of conflict in my advisory committee. My dissertation was an ambitious project aimed at comparing the various viewpoints of sociologists concerning how best to obtain the subjective thoughts and feelings of people in a society. I compared the qualitative and quantitative methodological positions on this issue and developed my own perspective. This issue held great interest for me and was part of what was then a widespread debate in sociology about just how scientific sociology could be when studying people's subjective beliefs and attitudes. My dissertation combined my interest in theoretical explanations with my interest in controversial issues. These two areas of interest still rank very high with me.

A heavy dose of departmental politics injected itself into my dissertation project. One of the faculty members on my committee, Walter Coutu, thought he had written the answer to my dissertation inquiry in his book (Coutu 1949). He favored the quantitative approach. I did mention Coutu's ideas in my first dissertation draft, but I did not give them prominence, and I did not endorse them. Coutu seemed bothered by this. However, I strongly believed in my right to academic freedom to make my own judgments about a controversial area. I was soon to find out how academic politics can compromise academic freedom, particularly if you are a graduate student.

My PhD advisor, Arnold Green, was an associate professor. Walter Coutu was a full professor, who in the fall semester would be voting on Green's promotion to full professor. This conflict of interest worried Arnold Green, and he told me that he was hesitant to set up my final oral while my conflict with Coutu was unresolved. However, the conflict with Coutu concerned the heart of my dissertation. I was dealing with the issue of whether, in the study of people's viewpoints, you should give priority to getting at the meaning and significance of people's beliefs or whether you should give priority to the reliability of the techniques used to get at those beliefs. I felt that the significance of *what* was being studied about people's subjective viewpoints was of prime importance, even if the results could not easily be replicated. I did not disregard the value of reliability, but I thought it was of secondary importance. It was this position that was in conflict with the more proreliability views of Walter Coutu. I consulted with another committee member, Seth Russell, the chair of the department, and he advised me to compromise and take a more middle-of-the-road position by assigning significance and reliability a more equal share of importance. In the interest of finishing up in time to take my first job, I modified the final draft of my dissertation and did just that.

But my modification was not enough to end the conflict. Coutu still came down more on the side of the importance of reliability, and he wanted more than equality for his perspective. I was unwilling to move any further from my new position that both significance and reliability are essential and thus are equal in value. I had only a few weeks left in which to schedule my final oral if I was to finish my degree before leaving for my first job. My advisor, Arnold Green, was still unwilling to schedule my dissertation hearing because of Coutu's continuing disagreement with me. I wanted to argue our differences at the final oral, and I asked for that chance. After all, the final oral was officially called a "dissertation defense." I could lose one vote on the committee and still pass if everyone else voted for me. But Green was adamant in his refusal to schedule the final oral. I was getting desperate, but then I thought of a way out of my dilemma.

Since Green respected rank so much, I decided I needed to somehow gain the support of a person who outranked both Green and Coutu. Seth Russell was the chair of the department and was therefore the highest-ranking department person on my committee. But I could not talk directly to Russell about Green's hesitance to set up my final oral without aggravating the intradepartmental conflict further, so I took another path. I spoke to Russell and told him that Green and I had talked about having my oral on the twenty-first of August. I asked him, as chair of the department, for his approval to finalize the date. Russell thought my statement about talking with Green meant that Green had agreed to set up my oral on that date. That was precisely what I hoped my vagueness would accomplish. Russell went ahead and endorsed the date of August 21 for my final oral. It was true that I had talked about the date with Green; I simply neglected to add that Green had not agreed to schedule it then. Desperate times call for desperate measures.

After I spoke to Russell, I proceeded to call Green, and I told him that Russell wanted my final oral to be scheduled on the August 21. I knew that Green respected rank and that therefore he would not deny what he thought were the chair's wishes. Also, because Russell appeared to have made the decision, Green figured that he could not be blamed by Coutu for setting up the final oral, so Green agreed to allow it to go forward. I then called Coutu and told him that Russell and Green had agreed to set up the oral on the twenty-first. He did not object. The rest of my committee accepted the date as well. I had played the cards in the power game and had won the opening round. But what would happen at the oral itself was still up for grabs.

My oral was scheduled at three thirty on Friday, August 21. It was the last day possible for holding an oral before the fall semester. I had to be finished that day if I was to get my degree before leaving for my first job. The oral began with the usual formalities. The difference of opinion with Coutu came out during the oral, but in muted form. Coutu was not as critical as I had feared. Also, Green sought to shift the discussion to areas that would not arouse Coutu's disagreement, and Russell tried to reduce the tension by suggesting minor changes that should be made in the dissertation. Russell had shown support for me throughout my stay at Penn State, and he provided the needed leadership that afternoon to keep the oral on track toward a successful completion. The other four members of my committee expressed support for my dissertation during the oral as well. Then the discussion ran its course, and Green asked me to leave the room so they could decide if I had passed.

When I went out into the hall to await the final decision of the committee, I was very unsure of the outcome. The committee could have decided to ask me to radically rewrite my dissertation, which would have delayed my degree a full year. I very much wanted to start my first job without that burden. Finally, I was called back into the room and was informed that, although I had to make a number of minor changes to the dissertation, I had passed. I was tremendously relieved. I believe Coutu voted to pass me, because he came to the graduate student party that my friends had that night, and he personally congratulated me. So perhaps the problem with my dissertation existed more in Green's anxiety about promotion than in Coutu's disagreement with my position. This experience was an early lesson on the role of power in the realm of ideas. If we want to defend academic freedom, then we had best be aware of the political dimensions that may enter in and corrupt that freedom.

I could go on with much more of my early life, but this should be enough to afford the reader a fair idea of my personality and my values. If you want more, see Reiss 2001a and 2005, and visit my website: www.soc.umn.edu/~reiss001.

CHAPTER TWO

~

The Antisex Bias of the 1950s

The 1950s Culture

Now that you know something about me, let me fill in a portrait of the American sexual culture at the time I entered the academic world in the early 1950s. I'll illustrate the cultural climate of that time by relating a few experiences I underwent as I started to do research on sexuality and to discuss sexuality in more of my classes.

The 1950s was a profamily decade and one that clearly did not approve of sex outside of marriage. The war ended in September 1945, and everyone started to make up for lost time. In 1946, we produced a record crop of babies, who later would be known as the first of the baby boomers. The baby boom lasted until 1964. Despite this family centeredness, there were stirrings in the youth population toward a more gender-equal and pluralistic sexual ethic. Much of this was kept partially underground until the 1960s, but a countercultural sexual view was gaining power among our young people. One very important reason for the increasing acceptance of sexuality was that married, as well as single, women were employed in increasing numbers. When the war ended, our government thanked women for working during the war and then advised them to go home and fulfill their role as wife and mother. But millions of American women did not take that advice, and from 1950 on there was a constant and significant growth in the proportion of women who worked outside the home. Even among women who had preschool-age children, there was a steady increase in the proportion working outside the home, and this was a head-on challenge to traditional family values (Reiss 1971). Our economy was expanding, and we needed women to fill the increasing number of jobs, so this trend was well rooted in the demands of our emerging economy and was very unlikely to change.

In my judgment, the increased economic autonomy for women was a major factor in young women's more-positive attitude toward sexuality in the 1950s. Increasing economic power affords a group a greater sense of entitlement. Also important to keep in mind is that this increasing rate of employment among mothers meant that increasing numbers of children would have greater autonomy to run more of their own lives, and youth autonomy does have a way of increasing acceptance of sexuality among young people. So, at the same time that the mothers of the early baby boomers were being empowered, their children were also being given more freedom. These changes were one of the major roots of the sexual revolution of the 1960s and 1970s, which I will talk about in chapter 4.

In September 1953, after finishing up at Penn State, I took my first job at Bowdoin College in Maine. A clear illustration of America's political values at this time occurred in my interview with the president of Bowdoin College in June of that year. In the midst of that interview, President Coles asked me how I felt about communism. Recall that this was the McCarthy era, and there was a great deal of fear in many colleges and universities of being publicly smeared as a supporter of communism. I didn't want to cave in to such narrow political pressures. I didn't believe the communist threat was real, but I didn't want to lose the job, so I waffled a bit and said, "I am still debating that question, and I haven't reached a final judgment." President Coles seemed to like my vague answer. He immediately confided in me that Bowdoin had planned to give an alumni award to Alfred Kinsey that year, but the worry about public criticism had forced them to cancel their plans. He made it very clear that he personally wanted to give the award to Kinsey, thereby showing me that he saw himself as a liberal, despite his asking me the question about communism. His statement also made me aware that Kinsey had attended Bowdoin and had received his bachelor's degree there in 1916. I got the job, and I was pleased that I now would be at the same college that Kinsey had attended.

Antisex Bias in Family Textbooks

When I was hired, my Sociology Department chair, Burt Taylor, asked me to teach a sociology of the family course. I had never had a course on the family, and I wondered how to go about picking a textbook. I decided that I would look at what the textbooks said about sexuality and judge on that basis. I had read the 1948 Kinsey book on male sexuality and had also just finished reading the 1953 Kinsey book on female sexuality (Kinsey et al. 1948, 1953). In addition, I had read a study by Ernest Burgess and Paul Wallin of one thousand engaged couples in Chicago that analyzed the sexual attitudes and behaviors of these couples (Burgess and Wallin 1953). So I felt that I knew something about the scientific literature on sexuality. Also, I was still single and had my own fresh personal knowledge of sexuality. I examined about twenty family textbooks and carefully read what they said about premarital sexuality.

Almost without exception, the textbooks contained an explicit condemnation of premarital sexual intercourse. This moral position was not backed up by research evidence from any of the studies noted above, and even less so by clear reasoning. The most common statement in these textbooks was that if you had premarital intercourse, the following things would happen to you: (1) you would get venereal diseases, (2) the woman would get pregnant, (3) you would be socially condemned, and (4) you would feel strong and lasting guilt and regret about having had intercourse outside of marriage. The premarital sexual relationship itself was portrayed as exclusively lustful, impersonal, uncaring, and selfish (Reiss 1957).

I was shocked when I read these chapters on premarital sex. This was not acceptable scholarship, and it surely was not social science. Clearly, this was moral advocacy, poorly reasoned, badly researched, and totally uninformed by the scientific work that had been done. It reminded me of the position of my professor at Syracuse in 1948, who had spoken of premarital sexuality as wrong because he saw it as selfish and leading to pregnancy and disease. Neither he nor the textbook authors ever thought of describing types of premarital sexual relationships that would be much more likely to avoid negative outcomes and that might well involve affection.

Now of course there are also many dangerous and damaging sexual relationships, but the important point is that these very negative sexual relationships were clearly not the only type of premarital relationship that was happening in America. There was no discussion of sexual relationships in which the couple uses contraception to avoid pregnancy and disease and in which there are very rewarding psychic and physical outcomes. Those types of relationships were being entirely ignored by the textbook authors. By doing this, those authors were presenting a biased account and were greatly exaggerating the extent of the "inevitable" disastrous outcomes of premarital sexuality. In my judgment, those authors were delivering a sermon rather than a thoughtful and fair-minded analysis of premarital sexuality (Reiss 1956, 1957).

The textbook I chose was the one that just didn't say much at all about premarital sexuality. I thought this would allow me the freedom to bring in my own ideas and go over the research I knew about. The book I chose was a revision by Reuben Hill of a well-regarded textbook by Willard Waller. Waller was a sociologist who in his other books had written with great insight on the family and on divorce. In this particular text, he stressed understanding human relationships more than pronouncing moral condemnations. In my class on the family, I discussed a number of sources of knowledge about sexuality. In addition to the studies by Kinsey and Burgess and Wallin, I brought in studies by Locke and Terman (Locke 1951; Terman 1938). I also brought in a number of plays like Arthur Miller's *Death of a Salesman*, Henrik Ibsen's *A Doll's House*, Tennessee Williams's *A Streetcar Named Desire*, and Eugene O'Neill's *Anna Christie*, as well as novels like Guy de Maupassant's *A Woman's Life*, Aldous Huxley's *Brave New World*, Henry James's *Daisy Miller*, and Arthur Koestler's *Darkness at Noon*. I used these sources to further illustrate in a more qualitative format the crucial points about sexuality that I wanted to make. The students seemed to really enjoy the class. They "wooded" me on the last day of the class. Wooding was a stomping of feet and was the Bowdoin equivalent of strong applause. This was my first class, and of course I was very pleased with their response.

The Admiral and the College of William and Mary

I left Bowdoin in 1955 to teach at William and Mary in Williamsburg, Virginia, and I experienced some different types of academic issues about sexuality. Here's one incident that illustrates some of constraints that existed against teaching about sexuality without the traditional, moral perspective. The president of William and Mary then was Alvin Chandler, a former admiral. One book that I used in my family class was a nineteenth-century novel by Guy de Maupassant entitled *A Woman's Life*. I saw it as a beautiful example of the life many women experienced in the late nineteenth century. It had received much praise over the generations since it was written, and it was now available in paperback. Someone in the class must have complained to President Chandler that it was an obscene book. Chandler encountered me one day as I was walking to my class. He called me over and smiled as he took a paperback copy of the book out of his brief bag, and he said he wanted to ask me something about the book. I asked him what he wanted to know. I have checked my journal entry for that year, and here is my best re-creation of our conversation that day:

"Look, Professor Reiss, on the cover of this book, there is a picture of a woman in a robe sitting on a bed. Isn't this the kind of book that you and I used to read behind the barn?"

He was still smiling, but I wasn't. I replied, "President Chandler, I grew up in a city, and so I don't know anything about barns. This is a classic novel of the nineteenth century. Tolstoy called it the best French novel since *Les Misérables*. It gives the students insight into the life of women in nineteenth-century France."

He looked embarrassed and muttered, "Okay, I just wanted to check it out." He wasn't smiling anymore, and he just turned and walked away. I'm sure he hadn't read anything in the book itself. Chandler wasn't on the favorites list of many professors at William and Mary, and this incident illustrates why. In my mind, he wasn't the best choice to be president of William and Mary.

One thing that helped to make academic freedom work at William and Mary was having a chair that defended your freedom to teach as you thought was best. I discussed this run-in with Chandler with Wayne Kernodle, the chair of sociology. Wayne fully supported me. He told me to teach the way I thought best and not be concerned about such criticism. Things could have been different had I not had such a chair.

Questioning High School Students about Sex in the 1950s

In the fall of 1958, I was asked to teach the yearlong research seminar for sociology majors. All our majors were asked to do a research project of their choosing that displayed their knowledge of how to gather data, analyze it, and interpret it. This was quite a challenge for undergraduates, and I do believe that during those years we produced some of the best-trained sociology undergrad majors in the country. I had a research project of my own that I wanted to get someone to work on with me. In my first book, I had written that a new premarital sexual standard was coming into vogue in America. I called it "permissiveness with affection." This new standard accepted sexual intercourse for those who were affectionately involved with their partner. There were data showing that sexual relations for women were very often tied to love feelings, and that the number of these relationships had grown. We knew from Kinsey and others that many of these women in love relationships did not feel guilty about having sex. But no one had ever measured sexual standards in a precise scientific fashion, so I wanted to get a student to work with me to test out my idea that permissiveness with affection was becoming a popular premarital sexual standard. I planned to use this research for a future book.

Four students from the class volunteered to work with me on this project: Ron Dusek, Martha Fisher, Richard Shirey, and John Stephenson. John was clearly the leader of the group and the one with the best background in sociology. He eventually went on to the University of North Carolina to get a PhD in sociology. Each of these four students worked on the project for about twenty hours every week for the entire 1958–1959 academic year. That is a huge amount of time for students to put into one class when they were carrying a full academic load. I believe their personal interest in the project was one key element in their willingness to devote so much of their time and energy to this research.

I wanted to include in my research the two high schools in Williamsburg. One was all white, and one all black. There was de facto segregation despite the fact that the Supreme Court had outlawed segregated schools back in 1954. I sent the four students to the white high school principal to obtain permission to administer a questionnaire on premarital sexual standards to all the high school students. They came back to me with sad looks and related a tale of failure. The principal of the high school, Mr. Pitts, had turned them down flat. I called and made an appointment to see him. Pitts and I sat down at a small table, and he told me that there would be too many complaints if he ever gave out a questionnaire on premarital sexual standards to the students. According to my recollection and my journal entry for that year, the following dialogue ensued:

I asked him, "How many girls each year get pregnant in your high school?"

He gave me his answer, but he seemed puzzled by the question. I clarified by asking him, "How would you like it if the parents of the girls in your school learned that you turned down a chance to reduce the number of pregnancies that girls in your high school experience? Don't you agree that we must first understand anything that we want to control? I believe that giving out my questionnaire would be a major step toward understanding how to better contain premarital pregnancy."

He got my point and understood that I was saying he would be criticized whichever way he chose to act. However, if he did allow us to give out our questionnaire, I had given him a good defense against whatever criticism might arise. He thought for a moment and then said he would allow us to do our study, but he insisted that I not use the ninth graders and that I study only the tenth, eleventh, and twelfth graders. I agreed to that. I learned from that encounter the importance of showing others how it would be in their interest to cooperate. He was an administrator, not a scientist, and so if he was to cooperate, it was reasonable that he would want to be shown a benefit that was relevant to his responsibilities as principal.

The black high school principal, Mr. Montague, was a friend of my chair, Wayne Kernodle. Wayne was a native southerner but an integrationist, and over the years he and his wife, Ruth, had had Montague to their apartment for dinner a number of times. Such integrated socialization was not common in the 1950s, and so Wayne was a good person to have introduce me to Mr. Montague. Wayne and I went in together to see him and sat down around his desk. Wayne introduced me, and I described my project and asked Montague for his permission to give out the questionnaires. He avoided answering me and instead switched the topic to the politics of the Byrd political machine in Virginia. Wayne joined in that discussion, but I kept trying to get the topic back to my questionnaires.

Then finally it dawned on me that Montague was looking for some sign of where my political views were before he would decide about my project. I then joined the political discussion and said, "Let me share a joke about the Byrd machine that may interest you. I heard that the Byrd machine has become so inbred that it finally produced an idiot—the governor!"

The governor at that time was against integration, and by telling my joke, I made it clear where I stood. The principal turned to me and said, "When do you want to give them out?" Once more, the importance of being aware of people's personal agendas was the key to getting cooperation. The principal had wanted to be sure that I would not use the data to show how "promiscuous" blacks were or to be critical of blacks in other ways. The best guarantee for him was to know my racial values. Coming in with Wayne and telling my joke had given him the assurance he needed. I should add that, of course, the personal agendas of both of these high school principals were shaped by the racist and antisexual culture of the 1950s. For example, if the common culture had seen blacks and whites as equals, and if the culture had also viewed premarital intercourse as acceptable under some conditions, it would not have been difficult to quickly get permission from both principals. But in the 1950s, the broad cultural agenda in Virginia was nowhere near that liberated.

A short time later, I added two Virginia colleges to my study: William and Mary and Hampton Institute. In order to test my ideas about a new emerging sexual standard of permissiveness with affection in all these schools, I needed a well-designed scale that could with reasonable accuracy measure premarital sexual standards. I proposed that we had four basic premarital sexual standards in our country: (1) abstinence, which demanded that both men and women not have intercourse prior to marriage; (2) the double standard, which gave men much greater sexual rights than women; (3) permissiveness with affection, which allowed premarital intercourse equally to men and women if there was strong affection or love in the relationship; and (4) permissiveness without affection, which allowed premarital intercourse equally to both men and women even if there was no affection in the relationship. I felt that the permissiveness with affection standard was increasingly replacing the abstinence standard and was also weakening the double standard.

I consulted with my four students and devised a twelve-item scale that contained several questions concerning a person's acceptance of kissing, petting, and intercourse for men, and a second twelve-item scale that contained the same questions asking about a person's acceptance of these sexual behaviors for women. I saw affection as a key determinant of how both male and female students would answer these questions, so the questions varied the degree of affection, from having no affection to being in love and engaged. All students were given both male- and female-scale questions to answer, so we could measure the presence of a double standard. If my ideas about the major role of affection in the acceptance of premarital sex were correct, then both male and female students should show greater support for having premarital coitus with affection than was popularly believed (Reiss 1964a, 1967, 1998a). If this were the case, it would indicate that the double standard was weakening and that abstinence was losing support as the majority premarital sexual standard.

Early in 1959, the questionnaires were given out to the two high schools and the two colleges. I was of course very eager to see whether the questions formed a valid scale and also to see just what the popularity level of coitus with affection was for both male and female students. It took time for the four student assistants to tabulate the answers of the almost seven hundred respondents. Remember, in 1959 we did not have access to computers to do this. After listing each person's responses to the scale questions, my assistants had to analyze these thousands of responses to see if they were just random responses or if they formed a shared pattern that supported the importance of affection in our premarital sexual standards. I waited to see what they found.

The answer came in early spring of 1959. Harriet and I lived in an apartment just across from the street from the main campus, and one night we heard a lot of noise coming from the campus dorms. We looked out our window and realized that the usual spring panty raid was happening. This involved the male students standing outside the female dorms and yelling to the women to throw out their panties to them. It was a poor substitute for sex, but the symbolism was obvious, and after all, it was spring. We were watching this out our window when the phone rang. It was John Stephenson. He practically screamed into the phone: "They worked! The scales worked! They worked at all four schools! Affection was a key factor at all the schools for both male and female students!" This meant that the scale questions displayed a shared cultural way of being answered that supported my hypothesis that there was indeed, in all four of the schools, support for a premarital sexual standard of permissiveness with affection for both females and males. The phone call from John said that our questions clearly measured premarital sexual permissiveness and supported my major hypothesis. I couldn't have asked for more.

The results were very close to what I had expected. Bear in mind that this was in Williamsburg, Virginia, and the year was 1959. I was sure that the percent who saw permissiveness with affection as acceptable would be significantly higher in places like New York City or San Francisco. Once I published the scale, it was very widely used by researchers in this country and abroad for studying premarital sexuality, and it is still used today (Reiss 1964a, 1998a).

This student research was only the beginning of a major research project that I would develop and analyze in my second book (Reiss 1967). In the next few years, to broaden the student sample, I added two more colleges to my research project: Bard College in New York and the University of Iowa. In 1960, after I left William and Mary and went to Bard College, I applied for and received a National Institute of Mental Health (NIMH) research grant to support analyzing the student sample data. Then, in 1963, I received further NIMH support to add a representative national sample of adults. That was a crucial sample, for if my scale worked on a sample representative of the country, it would validate the scale, and I could check on my ideas about cultural change in America (Reiss 1967). In chapter 6, I will report the exciting results of this national test and present my explanation of what I found.

Publishing on Sexuality in Journals in the 1950s

Another important way to learn about our sexual culture in the 1950s is to examine the reception given to academic publications. In that decade, it was very difficult to publish academic work on sexuality that didn't toe the conservative line. The book publishers and even the academic journals displayed the impact of the sexually conservative climate of the broader adult society. I'll illustrate this point by relating to you my experiences with getting my first journal articles and my first book published.

My first article was an analysis of the double standard in sexuality. I highlighted the internal contradictions and problems within that standard and predicted that it would lose popularity. I wrote the article in the summer of 1954. It was rejected by three journals (*American Sociological Review, American Journal of Sociology,* and *Marriage and Family Living*). It was finally accepted by a woman editor (Kathleen Jocher) of *Social Forces,* and it appeared in the March 1956 issue. I was told by many people that the double standard in sex was not something that could be changed—they felt it was inborn and unalterable. When my paper was finally published, I sent a reprint to Alfred Kinsey, since I knew from reading his two books that he would find my implied criticism of the double standard to his liking. I was pleased when Kinsey responded to my article in a July 14 letter saying that he would "be very glad to take [my] thinking into account as [his] own research deal[t] with this subject." (Almost all the letters I quote can be found in Reiss 2005.) Kinsey had shown his opposition to the double standard by his implied criticism of societies that did not allow the "natural" expression of sexual desire by women as well as men. Keep in mind that Kinsey was a zoologist, and so he was supportive of male-female differences in biology. Nevertheless, he knew about the great diversity *within* each gender, so he did *not* support differences in sexual rights for men and women. I planned to correspond further with Kinsey about my research, but unfortunately he died just one month later, in August 1956.

I had also written a second paper in the summer of 1954. This paper was a direct criticism of the bias against premarital sex in family textbooks. It was more of a frontal attack on the biases in the family textbooks than was my double-standard article. Of course, it grew out of my experiences with family textbooks from when I began to teach at Bowdoin College. The article was rejected by ten journals. What enabled this article to get published was the presence of a new journal: *Social Problems.* It was edited by Jerome Himelhoch, and it was the official journal of the new Society for the Study of Social Problems, which was founded in 1954. The organization was dealing with controversial topics, and I joined it when it began. I presented the ideas of this paper at the 1957 Eastern Sociological Society meeting in New York City. Jerry Himelhoch was there, and he told me that he liked what I had said and wanted to publish my paper. I was very happy to finally have someone say this about my paper. I sent it to him, and within a very short time it appeared in the April 1957 issue of *Social Problems.*

I believe that a good part of the high rejection rate I encountered was because I was saying that a scientific approach to premarital sex would recognize that a good deal of sex is not just lustful and selfish but has a major component of affection and that many young people find that type of sex to be very rewarding. In the mid-1950s, that was not a popular position to take—even if it was true. A few of the responses I received after my article was published underlined this point about our restrictive sexual culture at that time. One came from a well-known psychologist, M. Brewster Smith, who after reading my article wrote to me: "Your point I think is exceedingly sound. I would bet, however, that there are religious and economic pressures that would become sharply visible to an author who acted in terms of the reasonableness of your argument."

Also, Meyer Nimkoff, a well-known family sociologist, wrote to me, praising the article, but he raised what he called a "practical difficulty." He said, "In Sweden, teachers say in public that it is all right for young unmarried couples to have sexual intercourse if they love each other. Do you think American college professors can make such a public statement with safety?"

Actually, all I was saying was that many young people participate in sex that has strong elements of love and affection and that *those people* accept it as morally right—I did not say whether I personally accepted it or not. To be sure, I did personally accept such affectionate sexuality, but that admission was not made in the article. No matter what a professor's personal values are, the important thing to check is that he or she does a fair job in handling and evaluating the evidence that exists. Accordingly, I thought it professionally unacceptable for textbook authors to refuse to recognize what I felt was a major trend in sexuality for young men and women.

The comments made to me by Smith, Nimkoff, and others document that the fear of being thought of as someone who was promoting "sinful" sexuality was surely alive and well among academics in the mid-1950s. Regardless of this, I continued to receive many congratulatory letters. The most satisfying was from Paul Gebhard, who replaced Alfred Kinsey as the executive director of the Kinsey Institute. In July of 1957, he wrote,

> Thank you for your reprint; even before receiving it we were on the verge of writing to you. We read with great appreciation the original article in *Social Problems*, and want to congratulate you not only for the penetrating comments, but also for the common (or, actually, uncommon) sense which was manifest. The hypocrisy which you so effectively spotlighted has always been a source of irritation to us.

Among others who wrote favorable comments was John F. Cuber, a well-known family sociologist at Ohio State University: "I think you have rendered the cause of objective writing in the field of family a worthy and a needed service. . . . Administrative expectations for the teachers of these courses make the world pretty safe for the perpetuation of error."

My two articles were getting me known among those working in the family field, especially among those interested in studying or writing about premarital sexuality in our country.

Trying to Publish My First Book

At the same time as these articles were being published, I had begun working on my first book. In the summer of 1956, with lots of editing and typing by my wife Harriet, I finished a full draft of the manuscript for a book on premarital sexual standards in America. I had earlier sent an outline to publishers, and four of them had expressed interest (Knopf, Random House, Macmillan, and Appleton-Century-Crofts). I sent them the first draft, and they all responded that the book fell in between the trade book and textbook markets, and so they weren't sure they could market it successfully. They also suggested that I cut it down from five hundred pages to three hundred. In the summer of 1957, I did just that and also made up a more detailed outline of the book that I planned to send this time to university presses.

I hoped I would get a more favorable response from the university presses. Unfortunately, the initial responses came in rather negative. For example, one letter from Wilson Follett of the New York University Press said that such a book was not possible "for a society in which the representative people maintain privacy and the people who will talk are not representative." But how could Follett know that "the people who would talk" were *unrepresentative* unless he had some special knowledge about what sexual standards *representative* people believed in? And if Follett had such knowledge, then why couldn't I gain such knowledge? I smelled the same acrid odor of value bias that I had experienced before. One way that some people deal with ideas they don't like is to convince themselves that no one can possibly know such things. Then they don't have to rethink their own sexual values.

The director of the University of Washington Press, W. M. Read, said, "No state university press could do the publishing job because of the nature of the subject." This was a rare admission of the bias that existed in academic publishers concerning sexuality. The University of North Carolina and Yale University both suggested I publish it with a medical publisher—like Kinsey did. It seemed that they thought sex needed a medical prescription before it could be shown to the public. Earlier, Macmillan had referred me to their Medical–Public Health Department, but that department reached a split decision and decided against publication because, as the director, W. Holt

Seale, said, "In sum, the final opinions were that your concepts and theories are at variance with the opinions of modern workers in this field and, therefore, your book would not be accepted as authentic."

Director Seale further recommended that I get the opinion of a marriage counselor like Dr. Abraham Stone or Mrs. Gladys Groves. I never followed these suggestions, because I was writing as a sociologist, not as a medical doctor or a counselor. It seemed Macmillan's medical department wanted to get legitimation from outside of sociology so they could explain to critics why they published a book with such a "radical" thesis about changes in premarital sexuality. The radical thesis was my prediction in the book that permissiveness with affection would become our dominant premarital sexual standard and displace abstinence and that the process would move forward before the end of the 1960s (Reiss 1960a, 235–41). I backed up my prediction by analyzing difficulties in fitting abstinence with the evolving American society. I also brought in research data from a number of major studies and other sources showing that changes away from abstinence were already under way (Burgess and Wallin 1953; Kinsey et al. 1948, 1953).

I did not totally ignore all of the editorial comments I was receiving. After these early 1957 rejections, I went back to the manuscript and revised it further and updated it with more sources and more explanations of my perspective. I then sent the manuscript out again to those few publishers that said they would like to see it. One of those was the University of Chicago Press. In February 1958, they sent me a quote from their anonymous academic advisor:

> The volume is basically propaganda for the new standard of premarital intercourse which he advances. That is one reason why it is not sound scholarship. Since he is not disinterested he tends to slant research findings to substantiate his own convictions. The volume does not come to grips with certain fundamental aspects of sex relationships which he skims over or ignores completely.

I was hurt by their comments. I wondered if Chicago would have even looked for evidence of any "propaganda" if I had come out supporting abstinence before marriage. I doubt it. Most books on sex at this time were doing just that. The dominant mode of thinking is usually taken as accepted wisdom and is not questioned. Chicago never informed me of what "biases" they had found, nor of what "fundamental aspects of sex relationships" I had ignored. They never gave me even one specific example. Could it simply be that I was not presenting the party line and that I certainly was not giving support to personal views of the academic reader? Many people reading my manuscript would conclude that I favored the changes I predicted, or else why would I predict them? That perspective implies that bias determines what trends you predict. If that is really true, then social science is dead.

This is a good time to spell out the very important difference between *values* and *bias*. You can have personal values on an issue and yet examine the evidence fairly, and it is also true that you can be indifferent about an issue and still not do a fair and careful analysis. The key to doing good science is to not allow your values to bias your conclusions. This guideline holds no matter how strongly you feel about what you're studying. So, stating unpopular and unconventional conclusions is not in and of itself evidence of bias, and supporting the conventional view on sexuality is surely not evidence of a lack of bias. The measuring rod should be how carefully, completely, and fairly one examines all the major empirical evidence. That is what makes for sound scientific work, and if you do a careful analysis, then you can prevent your personal values from biasing your conclusions.

In my book manuscript, I concluded that the available research evidence indicated that permissiveness with affection was taking over center stage in premarital sexuality in our country, and I wasn't shy about saying so. I utilized the four best data sources available at the time and presented additional evidence and reasoning to fully check out my predictions (Burgess and Wallin 1953; Ehrmann 1959; Kinsey et al. 1948, 1953; Terman 1938). Is that approach one that displays "propaganda for a new standard"? Or was Chicago's criticism simply propaganda for an old standard?

I was clearly having a hard time getting a publisher. My book wasn't for the mass market. By relying so heavily on evidence and logic, it was too academic, even though it was written in an informal style. Also, as noted above, I took positions against the status quo and predicted radical changes in sexual standards that would begin to clearly take hold before the end of the 1960s. Bear in mind that this was the Eisenhower fifties, the baby boom period, and most adults were centered on their families and not on changes in premarital sexuality. My radical critique and predictions seemed quite out of step with those times. But I wasn't going to give up.

In the summer of 1958, I continued to work on the manuscript. I sent the full manuscript to a few new publishers, but I had no luck with them either. Now, after two years of trying, I had accumulated a total of seven rejections by publishers who read the manuscript: Knopf, Macmillan, Appleton-Century-Crofts, University of Chicago Press, Indiana University Press, Princeton University Press, and Dodd-Mead. I was getting discouraged, but I had a strong reservoir of belief in the value of my message in the book. I paused and remembered that back in October of 1955, the first publisher

I wrote to was the Free Press in Glencoe, Illinois, and they had expressed an interest in the manuscript that I was about to write. But when I started sending out my manuscript, I thought I would first try trade publishers and then the university presses. In February of 1959, I finally followed through and decided to send the manuscript to the Free Press.

Miracle of miracles, they liked it very much. What a pleasure to hear praise from a publisher instead of criticism! Just three months after receiving my manuscript, they sent me a contract. They were an academic-style press but were not tied to any university. They were known for their superb academic quality even though they were a new publishing house. One of their mottoes was "What sterling is to silver . . . ." The director was Jeremiah Kaplan, and he was also highly respected. They had published works by the most famous sociologists of the day—Talcott Parsons, Robert Merton, and others. I felt honored and very pleased to have such a wonderful conclusion to my search for a publisher. After much effort and perseverance, I had broken through the wall of antisex bias in the culture of the 1950s. The public was ready for my book. *Newsweek* magazine, in its October 1960 issue, ran a full-page story on it. Also, the Child Study Association selected it as a book of the year. The book sold over 25,000 copies—a very rare occurrence for an academic book. I was elated.

Then came the academic journal reviews of the book. The review in the *American Sociological Review*—the most prestigious sociology journal—was written by William Kephart, a well-known family sociologist. The review was quite favorable, but with the caveat that I had gone astray in the last chapter of the book: "Reiss apparently lost control of the typewriter [in predicting that] our society will have more or less accepted premarital coital permissiveness with affection" (Kephart 1961).

He was also critical of the fact that I did not "take cognizance of any biologically based differences in sex desire between males and females." But time was on my side. The sexual revolution began in the 1960s, and that fit perfectly with my predictions in the book (Reiss 1960a, 235–41). American sexual culture was beginning a radical makeover. Sexuality was becoming more accepted by young people, and there was a major change toward greater acceptance of permissiveness with affection and more criticism of the double standard and abstinence. I saw sexual standards and behaviors as primarily learned and said so explicitly. The evidence I consulted from cultures around the world and in our own history showed far too much variation in female sexual desire for me to support a position of any immutable difference between male and female sexual desire (Capellanus ca. 1184; Davis 1929; Ford and Beach 1951; Malinowski 1929; Murdock 1949).

A Minor Clash with Radio Censorship

Let me close the chapter with a story of attempted censorship of my words when I was invited to be on a radio talk show to discuss my new book. On December 12, 1960, Mary Margaret McBride asked me to be on her radio show for the full hour on WGHQ in Kingston, New York. Mary was a woman from the Midwest who was well known in the radio business. But, as I was to discover, she was also a conservative. Based on my annual journal and my recollection, here's what happened:

The first thing she said to me was a bit of a shock. "I am sure you realize that our sponsors and much of the audience see discussions of sexuality on the radio as potentially offensive, so I would ask you to please not use the words *coitus* or *intercourse* when referring to sexuality."

I responded, "But you know that I discuss premarital sexual standards throughout my book. How will the listener know if I am talking about petting, masturbation, or other forms of sex unless I specifically say that I am talking about coitus?"

She simply responded to me by saying, "They'll know what you mean. We don't have to be that blunt." I felt that it was not just concern for others that was behind her language etiquette request. She seemed uncomfortable herself with what I was saying to her right then.

I could see that she wouldn't budge from her position, and so I didn't argue further. But when the show began, I used the terms coitus and intercourse as often as I saw fit. At the commercial break, she spoke critically to me and said, "I asked you not to use that language."

I responded, "My first obligation is to clearly communicate my ideas to the listener. I'm sorry if that offends you or others, but I am not using vulgar terms, so I doubt if any reasonable person would object."

She was unfazed by my response and asked me again not to use "those blunt words." But I continued to use them. The show was live, and there was little she could do to stop me. Needless to say, I was never asked back by Mary Margaret McBride, but I felt good about following through on my values. I wanted to be clear about my ideas with the audience, and that was what I was trying to do. Catering to conservative public opinion had never been a high priority with me.

~

CHAPTER THREE

What Is This Thing Called Science?

Ancient Roots of Modern Science

Since this book is about sexual science, I should discuss in some greater detail just what I mean by a scientific approach to sexuality (Reiss 1963, 1993, 1999). I start first with the recognition that all societies that we know about have developed an empirical approach as one of their ways of understanding the world. By an empirical approach, I mean one that respects the importance of observation, experimentation, and reason in understanding the reality of our world. We can see this most transparently in the economic systems of different societies. For example, in hunting-and-gathering societies, we find that careful attention is paid to which hunting techniques have worked in the past and seem most likely to work in the future. In time, a new method of catching game may be proposed and tried out, but if it fails to work well, they'll tend not to use it again. The lives of these people depend on their making sound decisions regarding how to hunt animals and how to gather food, so they rely on observation and experimentation in order to enhance their survival possibilities.

The same would prevail in agricultural societies, where farming techniques have evolved from generations of learning what works best for their soil and climate situation. Surely this is very much the case in our own society, as our mass-production techniques were developed in the manufacture of cars in the early twentieth century. More recently, our culture has now developed computerized programs to handle a great many of the production techniques that formerly were done by people. The observation, experimentation, and reasoning found in all economic systems of the world are also the essential ingredients of all sciences. So, all the key elements of scientific thinking have been with us for thousands of years. Four hundred years ago, the Western world began to develop more rigorous and detailed ways of doing their observation and experimentation, but the basic elements of scientific thinking are a basic part of all human societies (Longino 1990, 2002).

Allow me to add that, of course, all societies rely on other sources of knowledge besides these observation and experimentation approaches. There are religious, philosophical, and political institutions that compete to gain acceptance and power in societies as sources of knowledge. When modern-day science was beginning to make itself felt in the seventeenth century, there were explosive clashes with these other approaches to knowledge. Religion had for many centuries been very powerful in the West as a source of what was accepted as knowledge. Science in the seventeenth century began its dethronement of some of the areas of knowledge that religion had dominated for centuries. The battle is not over. Even today in a number of public school districts, there are disputes between religion and science over the teaching of evolution versus the teaching of more religious explanations of how life developed. Religion still dominates when it comes to concerns that cannot be empirically tested, such as the existence of God, the possibility of an afterlife, and such. But when we try to understand the physical and social world in which we live, science is now the key source of knowledge in most of the Western world.

It was the scientific successes of the last four hundred years that led to a vast increase in the power of the empirical approach, or what came to be called "the scientific approach." Over this entire time span, more sophisticated methods of observation and experimentation were increasingly developed, particularly in the fields that today we call physics and chemistry. From their beginning, the findings of these young sciences turned out to be useful in navigation, in digging wells, in warfare, and in many other ways valued by society. The development of these scientific fields increased our knowledge of the world and our ability to manipulate it. Over the past few centuries, all the sciences have expanded their ability to understand and to predict, and this has increased the public's confidence in the value of scientific explanations.

New scientific fields like biology, psychology, and sociology developed mainly in the last one hundred years or so. Progress in these fields has vastly increased our ability to make our lives safer and healthier. One late-twentieth-century impact of medical science research was the public awareness of the causal link between cigarette smoking and lung cancer. This has led to a large decrease in the percentage of the adult population that smokes—now at an all-time low of about 25 percent. The same impact of science can be seen in our scientific studies that have shown that condoms can greatly reduce the risk of contracting HIV and other sexually transmitted diseases. This has led to a very significant increase in the use of condoms by unmarried people—the rate tripled between the 1970s and the 1990s (Abma et al. 1997). We didn't learn about smoking or condoms by intuition or by ideology but rather by careful observation, experimentation, and reasoning—in other words, by scientific efforts. Science gained in social influence as it produced knowledge that proved to be helpful in people's lives. Especially in a democracy, the number-one reason for the increased power of science is the public's belief in the beneficial value of science in their personal lives. For a science to prosper, it must build up and maintain a public constituency.

The Ethical Side of Science

There is also an ethical side to science that must be acknowledged and understood. After all, science is an institution run by human beings, and so, just as with other institutions like economics, politics, family, education, and religion, it must contain an ethical guide to what is good or bad science. In science, this ethical conception of what ought to be done and what ought not to be done concerns what it is proper to study, the need to do careful research, the importance of valid and reliable measurements, the value of theoretical explanations, and much more. Let me illustrate one important ethical aspect of science by reference to an event that occurred in England in the seventeenth century.

The early physical scientists in the Royal Society of London were making suggestions to the king and to other powerful people about how social life might be improved. The king, the church, and others in power did not like this scientific intrusion into their realm of power, so they met with the scientists and worked out an agreement that came to be called the "Royalist Compromise" (Proctor 1991). The rulers demanded that scientists not become advocates on solving social issues and promised that if they agreed, then the state would fund their research projects.

This seventeenth-century compromise between science and politics indicates that what scientists do can have important consequences for a society. Therefore, those in power seek to restrain science from disrupting or otherwise reducing their political power. In our field of sexual science, it should be obvious that when we study human sexuality, we will be reporting research findings and explanations relevant to how we handle our sexual problems.

We can be sure that such reports will offend some political or religious groups. This was the case in physical science in the mid-twentieth century, when after World War II the government undertook research on the development of a hydrogen bomb. There were physical scientists who said that this sort of work was beyond the acceptable ethics of science as they saw it, and so they refused to participate in the project. Sexual-science projects also involve such ethical choices concerning what is done with the human subjects in research. Most of the social sciences have developed their own ethical guidelines, and our universities have their own guidelines as well. So, whether we like it or not, what we do in all the sciences will often have consequences that will make various groups uncomfortable and other groups comfortable. We need to learn how to handle such situations in ways that we can defend as ethical, but we must always keep in mind that the primary goal of science is to learn more about whatever it studies. So we must learn to resist political pressures that seek to limit our research in order to promote the political goals of various groups.

Political Distortions of Science

The connection between science and the rest of society is a two-way street. The impact goes to as well as from science. What those in power do in politics, religion, economics, and education will often have consequences for those of us working in science. This can be illustrated at the present time by referring to part of the report published by Representative Henry Waxman of California, chair of the Committee on Government Reform Minority Office (Waxman 2003). Representative Waxman objects to the pressure the Bush administration has put on government agencies to change their websites so that they downplay condom safety and report that abstinence-only sex education works very well, despite the evidence against these conclusions (Waxman 2003; Kaplan 2004). Clearly, such governmental action violates the ethical standards of good science. Good science does not alter its findings in order to please politicians.

There is just no possible way for science to do away with such attempts to distort it. Therefore, the important thing that scientists need to do when this occurs is to unite in publicly protesting against such political pressures that would ignore or distort our scientific findings. If we do not resist when politics attempts to distort science, then we may soon find that our science has itself been distorted and greatly weakened. This would surely diminish any public support for our work. If we, as scientists, do not defend our own work, who will? One of the most fundamental scientific values is that our research-

and-theory findings must be accurately presented to the public. Apply this same principle to yourself. Would you just stand by and not protest when someone impugned your personal integrity and distorted the words that you've spoken? To do so would be to allow your position in any society to be weakened, and the same is true with science. Scientific integrity is the issue at stake whenever scientific findings are distorted.

Advocacy and Science

Many sexual scientists would oppose advocating particular solutions to social problems that they have researched. They would say that we ought to do advocacy only as private citizens and not as scientists. I would argue against that "value-free" positivistic perspective. Advocating for the value of a particular solution to a social problem that we have scientifically studied is a very important part of science. Keep in mind that we didn't sign anything like the seventeenth-century Royalist Compromise that I discussed earlier in this chapter. That was a compromise in England made at a time when science was in its infancy. Today, science has the prestige and power to resist such restraints on scientific work. The important point is that if we do not advocate for the solution that we as researchers think is most likely to minimize the problem we have studied, then we are abdicating our decision-making power and handing it over to the politicians.

Do you think doing this is to the advantage of scientific research and progress in containing sexual problems? Do politicians really give their top priority to scientific studies? Do they really know more than we do about resolving a social problem that we have studied carefully? Politicians typically focus on what will get passed and what will get the approval of the constituents who voted them into the legislature. Shouldn't we at least offer the solution that we think will work best and present our case to the public as well as to the politicians? Today there are social-science lobby groups, such as the Consortium of Social Science Associations (COSSA), that advocate for solutions and that fully support our right to present our knowledge and advocate for a solution that we feel will work best. I believe these advocacy groups in social science are a positive scientific development, for they increase our ability to go beyond reporting trends, and they increase our value to the public, who want sexual problems contained. I have no doubt that we as scientists need to be participants in the decisions concerning how to handle social problems. We should shed our fear of being criticized for suggesting solutions and realize that doing this will help solve the problems that concern us all.

Let me present a current controversy that documents how important it is that sexual scientists propose solutions to the sexual problems they survey. In dealing with sex education in the public schools, we can point to the evidence indicating that *comprehensive* sex education that discusses both abstinence and contraception is more effective than *abstinence-only* programs, such as those the government is funding (Kirby 2002). Despite this fact, many politicians still support the abstinence-only sex-education programs that ignore or distort contraception, because they fear losing votes if they don't do this. So we as sexual scientists need to make the public aware of the ineffectiveness of abstinence-only programs and make it clear to everyone that polls indicate that the majority of the American public supports comprehensive sex education. Advocating for the superiority of comprehensive sex education will correct misconceptions held by the public, and also by some politicians. By doing this, we would make the public aware that the supporters of abstinence-only sex-education programs are putting their belief in abstinence as the one moral choice above our ability to better contain pregnancy and sexually transmitted diseases (STDs) in the student population.

One organization that does strong advocacy on this issue is the Sexuality Information and Education Council of the United States (SIECUS). They publish evaluative research on sex-education programs and then lobby for the adoption of those programs that work best. I believe that we as sexual scientists should stand up and object when our research on sex education is ignored or misrepresented. We need to make the public aware of our work if we want to promote effective sex-education programs. We should be doing more than just publishing our findings in obscure and technical scientific journals.

Value Aware, Value Fair, and Premarital Abstinence

In our scientific work, including our scientific advocacy, we need to work hard to avoid bias in our research and in our conclusions. We need to check carefully for evidence *against* what we believe to be true, as well as for it (Popper 1959). One way we do this is by having peer-reviewed journals, where other scientists who may have different values than we do examine our writing and make sure it does not contain any compromises with scientific goals. In addition, since human beings cannot really be value free, we need to ensure that we increase our ability as scientists to be *value fair* and *value aware*. Knowing more about our own personal values will help us be more alert and will minimize the possibility that our personal values may slant our scientific work (Reiss 1993). Trying to be value fair and value aware can help us avoid distorting the evidence so that it fits with our personal values. This is particularly important in sexual science because we are constantly dealing with controversial issues like contraception, abortion, pornography, and many others. In short, by becoming aware of our own values, we can put ourselves on guard against letting them bias our work (Bourdieu and Wacquant 1992). Values that are very widely shared can easily escape our scrutiny, while values that we reject are quite easy to spot. Let me illustrate this by examining the way many Americans view premarital abstinence.

People who argue against making condoms available in clinics for high school students often state that if our young people were abstinent, we wouldn't have to worry about things like HIV infections. They conclude that promoting abstinence is the safest strategy. But is this really the case? The condom failure rate varies from between 1 to 2 percent for married couples who don't want more children to 10 to 14 percent for young teenagers. So, you might jump to the conclusion that abstinence is the only 100 percent safe choice. Many people don't question the logic of this conclusion, but it suffers from a fatal flaw. If you are comparing abstinence vows with condom usage, then you need to measure not only the failure rate of condoms but also the failure rate of abstinence vows. Clearly, many of those who vow to be abstinent until they marry fail to abide by that vow and have coitus.

Another factor to keep in mind is that those who favor abstinence often exaggerate the failure rate of condoms and oppose any discussion of condom use in sex-education classes. That means that if an abstinence believer does have premarital intercourse, he or she will be less likely to insist on condom use and will thus be at higher risk for infection as well as for pregnancy. Researchers have reported that in terms of pregnancy, those females who are supportive of abstinence but who violate their vows are indeed more likely to get pregnant (Brewster et al. 1998; Cooksey et al. 1996; Rostosky et al. 2003). Others have compared STD rates and have found that some who practice abstinence have unprotected oral or anal sex. Such people believe that they are still technically abiding by their abstinence vows, but the STD rate for such abstinence believers has been found to be as high as for those who are having intercourse (Bruckner and Bearman 2005). I would conclude that a fair comparison would find that vows of abstinence break far more easily than condoms do (Reiss and Reiss 1990, 1997). Abstinence is surely not a risk-free strategy. Many who at some point in time wanted to be abstinent fail to do so. So, why is it that so few have challenged the claim that abstinence is 100 percent safe? Of course, it would be 100 percent if people never violated their vows, but even though abstinence programs may delay the onset of coitus, when premarital sex does occur with this group, as I have noted, it is quite risky because it is often without the benefits of contraception.

I believe the reason that challenges to the 100 percent safe claim are rare is that most people have been trained by religion and other sources to value abstinence highly, and so they do not even think about being fair when comparing the risk of vowing abstinence with the risk of using condoms. Here is precisely where the advice to be more value aware would be of immense help. If we carefully check the beliefs and values we hold, we are more likely to become aware of where they can bias the evidence that our sexual science produces. Self-analysis is a major pathway to learning how not to allow our personal values to turn into biases in our work. We can still value whatever we want, but we need to learn not to allow these values to go unexamined when we are doing research and theory in an area in which they are relevant. The ease with which some people genuflect unquestioningly to abstinence before marriage can serve as a warning of how shared values can become blocks to clear thinking about sexuality.

Linking Personal Values to Personal Assumptions

We all have our assumptions about what people are like. For example, we each make assumptions concerning the extent to which people are basically rational or basically emotional. These assumptions about the nature of human beings have been largely ignored in sexual science. I felt that examining this particular assumption could be of great value, so about ten years ago I did a pilot study with a few of my large classes. I developed a questionnaire containing items about the acceptance of a wide range of sexual behaviors, and I also included two questions to get at the students' basic assumptions about the nature of human beings. One question asked the students about the degree to which they endorsed the view that people are basically selective and evaluative in their lives, and the second question asked the students about the degree to which they believed that people are basically emotional and imitative in their lives. The students' answers to these two questions were very powerful predictors of attitudes toward premarital sex, marital sex, extramarital sex, homosexuality, erotica, and more.

I looked particularly at the large number of students who endorsed one of these two questions and rejected the other. This produced two polar types: one accepted selectivity and rejected imitativeness as the basic nature of people, and the second rejected selectivity and accepted imitativeness as the basic nature of people. Those students who accepted selectivity and rejected imitativeness were far more likely to be accepting of all the areas of sexuality than were those who endorsed the imitative view and rejected the selective view. The results were unusually strong. To me, this result indicated that one way people justify an accepting attitude toward sexuality is by endorsing a view of people that assumes that they can be selective and can therefore be trusted to often make reasonable choices. Likewise, the more-rejecting attitudes toward sexuality seem to fit very nicely within the view that people are imitative, and so opening up sexual choices will lead to disastrous outcomes. Just how do these perceptions of human nature get transmitted by our religious, political, economic, educational, and family institutions? Studying such basic assumptions of our thinking can lead us to very useful insights into what shapes our sexual attitudes and behaviors throughout our lives. I would strongly encourage some of you to research this area further. I'm certain that it will be very rewarding.

The Tentativeness of Science

Science is run by human beings, and that means there will be errors made, even when all the safeguards and practices we have to prevent them are in place. So, despite my high evaluation of science, I do not think of it as affording us a complete or *final* proof of anything. Science examines what information is available on a specific area of the world and then devises its explanations for whatever patterns are discovered. Bear in mind that this means that it is always possible that some other scientist may come along and create a "better" explanation of the exact same patterns. The new explanation may be a simpler one, one that predicts outcomes more accurately, or one that fits more easily with other theoretical explanations, and in all these ways, the new explanation would be an improvement. So, over a long period of time, there are but a few explanations that will prevail. I can make this idea of the tentativeness of science clearer by presenting a quote from Albert Einstein and Leopold Infeld (1950, 33):

> In our endeavor to understand reality we are somewhat like a man trying to understand the mechanism of a closed watch. He sees the face and the moving hands, even hears its ticking, but he has no way of opening the case. If he is ingenious he may form some picture of a mechanism which could be responsible for all the things he observes, but he may never be quite sure his picture is the only one which could explain his observations. He will never be able to compare his picture with the real mechanism and he cannot even imagine the possibility of the meaning of such a comparison. But he certainly believes that, as his knowledge increases, his picture of reality will become simpler and simpler and will explain a wider and wider range of his sensuous impressions. He may also believe in the existence of the ideal limit of knowledge and that it is approached by the human mind. He may call this ideal limit the objective truth.

While it is surely important that we keep in mind the tentativeness of the theoretical explanations put forth by scientists, it is also of great importance that we realize that this tentativeness is a strength of science and not a weakness. By opening itself up to new ways of thinking and to better explanations, science encourages change and avoids the hardened dogmas that characterize so many of our other social institutions. Of course there are resistances to change even by scientists. Like most people, scientists can easily fall in love with the explanations they know best, especially with those they have personally created. In such cases, scientists may defend their theories despite strong evidence in favor of an opposing explanation (Longino 2002).

Thomas Kuhn in 1962 suggested that scientists often choose between two competing scientific models or paradigms by choosing the one that best fits with the type of problem they are currently trying to solve rather than by the more impartial standard of comparing the predictive efficiency of one model against the other or the amount of research evidence favoring one model or the other. *Despite this assertion of imperfection, there is in my mind no better way than using observation, experimentation, and reasoning to arrive at the best possible knowledge of an empirical phenomenon.* No human system works without flaws and problems. However, the alternative to science is a world in which dogmas would battle dogmas and in which we would be ruled by rigid ideologies. A good part of our present world is characterized by just such unyielding approaches to knowledge. According to my set of values, a world in which dogma dominates is a poorer world in which to live than the one that science, even with its imperfections, offers us.

Summing Up Science

The portrait of science that I am drawing is of a social institution that is immensely valuable in helping us cope with our medical, technological, social, and personal problems. In this book, I am focused on sexual science, but what I say about science really applies to all science, whether it be physics, biology, or sociology. Science is essential to those who work in the area of sexuality because it is such an emotional area. Without a scientific approach, our field in particular would be dominated by bigots and ideologues. The political powers that be would make up their own "facts" and reality much more so than they do today. By supporting a scientific approach to understanding our world, we strengthen our ability to contain attempts by politicians and others to define the world in ways that benefit them much more than us.

Despite the high value I ascribe to science, I have tried to avoid idealizing it. Skepticism is a major value in all scientific work. One should be skeptical about the methods used to gather data, the measurements involved, the representativeness of the data, and the theoretical explanations that are offered. We do the best science when we look at alternative theories and search for evidence against our own theories. Bear in mind that, as Einstein and Infeld so nicely described in their quote, we can never open up the "watch" and really see what makes it tick. All our explanations remain subject to alteration over time, but that doesn't mean that we can advocate any idea we happen to have—we still rely on evidence, reason, and careful and fair examination of all we do before we even tentatively accept an explanation. There is a reality out there, but it is elusive, and we will never be able to grasp it in its totality. So we had best be cautious in how we describe our world.

Despite all the above qualifications about our theoretical explanations, I would submit that they are the essential ingredient to any advance of a science. Accordingly, we are in trouble if all our sexual scientists present us only with descriptive data about how many people said this or that or did this or that. Certainly, description is an essential part of science, but we must go further and build up our theoretical explanations of why we have found a particular set of responses. As in all science, we in sexual science need explanations for why the "clock" that we are examining seems to work as it does. Science without explanatory theory is simply bookkeeping. Explanations are the crown jewels of science, for they present to our society ways of containing and understanding the many problems that we confront daily. Scientists are supported by major constituencies in society, and we pay them back for their support when we help in the resolutions of our social problems and make our world less dangerous and more rewarding.

~

CHAPTER FOUR

The Sexual Revolution
and Sexual Organizations

Sexual Standards at the Dawn of the Sexual Revolution

Kinsey's first two books were a major encouragement to anyone who wanted to study human sexuality (Kinsey et al. 1948, 1953). My 1960 book was in part my attempt to fill in what Kinsey had neglected (Reiss 1960a). Kinsey focused heavily on the sexual *behavior* of males and females, and there was very little about sexual *attitudes* in his work. I felt that attitudes were a very important part of our sexual life and were significantly related to how we behaved. Think of two different people who have sex: one of them feels thrilled and elated afterward and looks forward to having more sex, but the other person feels degraded and guilty and vows not to repeat the behavior. Putting those two people in the same behavioral category would be a major loss of understanding of sexuality. We need to know about attitudes as well as behavior if we are going to be able to grasp the meaning of sexuality. The same is true in all areas of life. Does going to church indicate the same amount of religiosity for all people who go? Does having a college degree indicate the same level of knowledge for all college graduates? You have to probe into people's attitudes in order to grasp more clearly the meaning of any behavior.

As mentioned in chapter 2, in my 1960 book, I presented what I believed were the four major premarital sexual standards in our society: permissiveness with affection, permissiveness without affection, the double standard, and abstinence. I compared these four standards to see how well or poorly integrated each one of them was with our youth culture and with our basic social

institutions—religious, political, educational, family, and economic. By revealing this comparative integration level, I would discover which premarital standard was likely to dominate in the future. The permissiveness with affection standard came out on balance to be the best fit, and so I predicted
that it would become our dominant premarital sexual standard. I went on to
say that in the 1960s we would experience a rapid change in our premarital
sexual standards that would speed up the ascension of this standard (Reiss
1960a, 239–41):

> It is hypothesized that in the 1960's, [we] will complete the consolidation
> process . . . and also start a more overt, public, and formal acceptance of stan-
> dards which allow person-centered petting and coitus. . . . We may well find
> more and more people being brought up from childhood in accord with these
> more liberal norms. . . . The change in sexual standards not only involves the
> female becoming more permissive but it also involves the male becoming more
> discriminate—it is a dual change in which the male and female are approach-
> ing each other. . . . [The college educated] will set the pace in sexual changes in
> the direction of person-centered sexual behavior. . . . Changes in other institu-
> tions, such as the family and our political and economic establishments . . . will
> probably continue to some extent in the equalitarian direction in which they
> have been headed for the last several generations.

My prediction was right on the money. The seeds of the sexual revolution
were planted in the youth population in the late 1940s, and then, by the
1960s, they had sprouted forth in sexual behavior. This period of rapid
change came to be called the sexual revolution, and it lasted until the late
1970s and then stabilized, with permissiveness with affection being accepted
by the clear majority of our youth population. Let me briefly talk about the
evidence for this period of rapid change.

The best evidence for the sexual revolution in attitudes toward premarital
intercourse comes from representative national samples. My 1963 representative national sample was the first to use a scientifically tested scale to measure premarital sexual permissiveness (Reiss 1967). This was a time when the
sexual revolution was about to dawn in our country. Therefore, the sexual attitudes that were found in this study can serve as a baseline for measuring the
amount of change that occurred as the sexual revolution advanced in our
country. In 1965 and 1970, two other representative national samples were
taken that used questions comparable to mine. All three of these studies were
done by the National Opinion Research Center (NORC), a highly respected
research organization. All three studies asked if premarital intercourse was
acceptable when in love or engaged or under other conditions. The percent-
ages accepting premarital coitus were 20 percent in 1963, 28 percent in 1965,

and 52 percent in 1970 (Reiss 1967; Scott 1998; Klassen et al. 1989). These three national surveys are our best documentation of this period of rapid change in premarital sexual attitudes (Reiss 2001b).

In 1972, NORC started the General Social Survey (GSS) as an annual representative national sampling to measure a wide range of attitudes. The first survey included one question on premarital coitus. The percentage accepting premarital intercourse in 1972 was found to be 63 percent. After this, the rise was much more modest—it was 69 percent in 1975, and by 1978 it was 71 percent (Davis, Smith, and Stephenson 1978). There was not much change after that, and the percentage accepting premarital intercourse in 2004 was 73 percent (Davis and Smith 2004). The key years of the sexual revolution in premarital attitudes, then, would have been from 1963 to 1975—an increase from 20 percent to 69 percent.

In the 1990s, the director of the GSS, Tom Smith, put out a chapter on trends in the acceptance of premarital coitus, but for some unknown reason he did not discuss the results of the 1963, 1965, or 1970 studies, even though they were done by NORC, the same organization that does the GSS studies that Smith now directs (Smith 1994). Instead, for the years before 1972, he presented results from the less-scientific work of media and polling groups. The rapid increase shown in the three representative national samples undertaken prior to the start of the GSS was not even discussed. The changes reported after the beginning of the GSS surveys were relatively minor compared to these earlier changes. Thus, to understand the sexual revolution, you would have to study these three national samples. I have never understood why Smith chose to present polling and media surveys for these early years rather than these three scientific representative national surveys. One could quibble about the exact percentage change or the exact wording of questions, but there is no doubt that these three national surveys present very powerful evidence concerning the most dramatic years of the sexual revolution (Reiss 2001b). In addition to measuring premarital sexual permissiveness, these early surveys contain a great deal of other important information concerning people during the volatile 1963–1970 period of the sexual revolution. These data cannot be ignored by anyone who wishes to learn more about the sexual revolution in premarital sexuality. I urge those of you with an interest in this time period to learn more about the important findings of these surveys (Klassen et al. 1989; Reiss 1967; Scott 1998).

The Mythical Place of the Pill in the 1960s Revolution

Many people think the contraceptive pill was the major reason for the sexual revolution of the 1960s and 1970s. This technological explanation of the sexual revolution disagrees with my explanation of that sexual revolution. I predicted the revolution because of the changes I detected in our basic social institutions, but the media and even many experts supported the pill explanation and convinced many others that it was the key cause of our sexual revolution. A number of writers during those decades pushed this reductionist explanation. Here are the words of historian Bradley Smith:

> The event that was to have the greatest effect upon sexuality in the United States and, ultimately, in the world was the release of the birth control pill. . . . Young women who would never before take a chance on sex with their boyfriends for fear of pregnancy . . . adopted new attitudes toward sex. . . . The resulting freedom changed the sex habits of the nation. (Smith 1978, 232)

Smith is thus arguing that gender equality and autonomy were themselves the consequences and not the causes of the development of the contraceptive pill. In this view, the pill is seen as the central force that produced the sexual revolution and the major gender-role changes in our society. The reasoning here is that, with the pill available, the main factor that blocked women from sexual equality was removed. Sally Olds, a talented and well-known freelance writer, was taken in by this view. She wrote,

> The turbulent 1960s ushered in the sexual revolution. . . . Advances in contraceptive technology made this surge in sexual activity possible, and may even have spurred the entire rebellious era by turning at least one oft-repeated maxim on its head, that "bad" girls were sure to get "caught." (Olds 1985, 104)

We have also had support for this view from the famous sex therapists Masters and Johnson in a 1986 book:

> The pill made premarital sex considerably safer and permitted millions to think of sex as relational or recreational rather than procreative. . . . The availability of the pill provided a sense of freedom for many women and probably contributed more to changing sexual behavior than has generally been imagined. (Masters, Johnson, and Kolodny 1986, 22–23)

Lots of people believe this explanation even today, and it sounds persuasive, doesn't it? But let me discuss the evidence and reasons why it's really not a very accurate picture of what happened.

Those who believe in the revolutionary power of the pill presume that before the sexual revolution of the 1960s, women were ready and willing to have intercourse if only their worries about pregnancy were alleviated. This makes female sexual motivations much like a car with an engine running that is blocked from going forward by only one obstacle, fear of pregnancy—just remove that obstacle, and women will surely participate. I don't believe the fear of pregnancy was the main block to female sexual participation. Such a view overlooks the gender role of women in our society at that time. Women throughout the first half of the twentieth century had been subjected to a restrictive sexual upbringing. Accordingly, they had been programmed by society not to have premarital sex and had been told that if they did they would be condemned.

The Kinsey data, gathered mostly in the 1940s, supports my perspective that fear of pregnancy was not the major reason for low participation by women. The primary reason given by women in the Kinsey sample for restricting their premarital coitus was "moral objections." That was cited as a reason by 80 percent of his female sample, whereas fear of pregnancy was cited by only 21 percent of his sample. In fact, 56 percent of women explicitly said that it was *not* a reason for their restraint. In addition, 32 percent of the women said their lack of sexual responsiveness was a reason for restricting coitus (Kinsey et al. 1953, 344). This lack of primary emphasis on pregnancy as a reason for restraint doesn't mean that pregnancy was not an important concern for women. It surely was a serious concern, but for most women, moral objections that had been drilled into them, particularly by their family and their religion, was by far the more important reason for their reluctance to have sex. Limiting the sexual experience of women gave men more confidence that their girlfriends would be loyal and faithful to them. There was no equivalent necessity for men to afford this confidence about their own sexual loyalty. In effect, this double-standard upbringing was just one of many expressions that showed the power of men over women in our society.

But promoting abstinence for women doesn't stop men from having sex with them. A man would simply persuade a woman to violate her standards and then blame her for the transgression. This practice is the heart of the ancient double standard, and I'm sure it still sounds familiar to many of you. The 1960s sexual revolution did somewhat mute the difference in sexual restrictions between men and women, but it is still very real, even for young women today in the twenty-first century. Unequal and unfair? To be sure, but social customs are not built on the principle of fairness—they are based far more on who has power. Just ask blacks, Jews, Native Americans, Hispanics, Catholics, or any other minority group about that.

Even today, women feel that they cannot be as free as men, for there is still pressure for a woman to avoid the appearance of being too cavalier about sex. We don't live in isolation from our fellow humans. Their opinions of us, and especially the wishes of those close to us, influence us more than does a new contraceptive advance. A changed attitude of acceptance of sexuality among the key people in your life makes it far easier to accept sex than does the advent of a new contraceptive technique, and we know that attitudes were changing in the 1960s and 1970s.

Another way to see the flaws in the pill explanation is to ask yourself this question: If the pill did launch the last sexual revolution, what would you expect to happen? Surely, two decades after the pill launched the revolution, we should find that most women who have started to have premarital coitus would go on the pill or at least use some contraceptive method. But, if that were the case, we wouldn't have the Western world's highest rate of unwanted pregnancy. There is far-from-universal use of the pill by women who engage in intercourse even today. By the mid-1980s, a national study indicated that half the teenage unmarried women starting coitus used no contraceptive method at all, and less than 10 percent were on the pill (Jones et al. 1986). If the pill was the cause of the sexual revolution, wouldn't it be rather widely used some twenty-plus years after it was introduced?

Another very important point to consider is that contraceptive methods are not new. In the eighteenth century, Casanova recommended that lovers use a lemon rind over the cervix to prevent pregnancy. At the 1876 Philadelphia World's Fair, the most popular exhibit was the display of the new vulcanized rubber condom (Reiss 1977). The diaphragm and pessary cap came into use in the 1880s. The condom, if properly used, is quite effective in preventing births (Reiss and Reiss 1997). The British cut their birthrate in half between 1876 and 1936 by using the methods noted here. In our own country, Jews, more than most groups, used condoms to achieve zero population growth rate for several generations. The revolutionaries of the 1960s did not have to wait for the pill. If their upbringing allowed them to use effective contraceptive methods, they had been present for generations.

What women and men needed in order to be sexually freer was a change in the equality and autonomy that our society granted to women. After World War II, women were able to increase their ability to run their own lives. As noted in chapter 2, when the war ended in 1945, many women did not give up the jobs they had taken during the war. Over the next few decades, they began to increasingly enter the labor force. Increased economic power has a way of making people feel more empowered to make their own life choices, including sexual choices. The children of these women, the baby boomers, were also gaining more autonomy because their mothers were employed. I would submit that this major social and cultural change in the autonomy of women and children was the central cause of the sexual revolution that began in the 1960s. Accompanying this increased gender equality was an increasing acceptance by a woman's friends of her right to have sex. This group support is what I see as one key reason why the increase in female sexual permissiveness became a lasting change. Contraceptive advances surely help a sexual revolution, but without societal changes, these new contraceptive techniques are often left unused.

Albert Ellis and the Society for the Scientific Study of Sex

The field of sexual science began in Europe in the late nineteenth century but was destroyed by the Hitler regime in the 1930s. It was at about this time that our country took over the leadership in the study of human sexuality (Brecher 1969; Ellis and Abarbanel 1961; Haeberle 1978; Krich 1965; Money and Musaph 1977). Kinsey began his research in the late 1930s. By the 1940s, Albert Ellis, a New York psychotherapist, began doing his research on sexuality. When I started teaching at Bowdoin College in 1953, I knew I was going to be writing about sexuality, and I searched for others who might also be writing about how we in America handle our sexuality. I found very few social scientists who were studying sexuality in any way, and almost no one who was looking at how our society shaped our sexuality. Then I came across some of the publications of Albert Ellis. In 1954, he published *The American Sexual Tragedy*, which was an indictment of the way our society was handling sexuality. I liked the boldness of his thinking and his focus on how our society impacted on our sexuality. When my first journal article appeared in March of 1956, I sent a reprint to him, and we began a lifelong correspondence. We both agreed that a much more pluralistic sexual ethic than that present in America was what our country needed. However, we differed as to how to encourage such a pluralistic ethic in our society. As a psychologist, Al was focused more on the individual, and as a sociologist, I was focused more on the society. We exchanged many letters, particularly concerning our divergent viewpoints. This exchange has continued right up to the present (Reiss and Ellis 2002; Reiss 2005).

Al and I first met in person in April of 1957. Together with my wife, Harriet, I went to the Eastern Sociological Society meeting in New York, and we arranged to meet Ellis and his wife there after I gave my talk. I was presenting a paper that pointed out the increasing popularity of permissiveness with affection as a premarital standard. In the question period after my presentation, someone in the audience stood up and inquired, "Why do you just talk about the increase in sex with affection? What is wrong with sex without affection?" I looked at the thin bespectacled man who posed this question, and I thought to myself, in 1957, who else besides Albert Ellis would ask such a question? I smiled and asked the man, "Are you Albert Ellis?" He said yes, and the room burst into laughter. That was our first face-to-face meeting and the beginning of a lifelong friendship.

In addition to airing our agreements and disagreements in our letters, Al spoke to me about the need for an organization of the professionals in America who were studying sexuality. Al confided to me that in 1950 he had tried to found such an organization, but Kinsey had opposed doing this, and so Ellis's efforts had come to naught. Paul Gebhard later told me that one motivation for Kinsey's uncooperative response was that he felt that Ellis might start an organization that would compete for research moneys with the Kinsey Institute. Then, in 1956, Kinsey died, and Ellis once more pursued his goal of establishing a national organization of sexual scientists. By then, we were corresponding, and he asked me to join with him and become one of the charter members. I liked the idea of such an organization, for I felt it would promote cooperative scientific efforts and a mutual exchange of ideas among those working in the field. The organization was called the Society for the Scientific Study of Sexuality (SSSS), and there were forty-seven charter members when it was founded in 1957. We held our first meeting in New York City in November 1958. Today, there are about a thousand members, and of the original forty-seven, only Ellis, John Money, and myself remain. Most of the rest have passed away. I believe I was the youngest charter member, being thirty-one at the time the organization was founded. Ellis was forty-four at the time, and he's ninety-two and still active as I write this in 2005.

In December 1959, I arranged to organize a meeting of SSSS on science and values. I put together a panel on this issue, consisting of John Money, Walter Stokes, and myself. John Money was a psychologist in a pediatrics department at Johns Hopkins Medical School. He had written about children born with ambiguous genitalia and was working further on this topic. I had not met him before this meeting. Walter Stokes was a psychiatrist in Washington, D.C., who wrote about sexuality from a therapeutic perspective. I had met him at another conference just a year earlier. Walter Stokes was the person who suggested that I submit my research proposal for my sexual-attitude study to the National Institute of Mental Health. Finding support for sexuality projects in federal government agencies was rare, and so this was very helpful advice.

My "Science and Values" meeting went very well. My ideas about not letting values bias research were strongly accepted by Money and Stokes. In my presentation, I did not endorse a positivist philosophy that required researchers to be value free. However, I also didn't want the newly developing cultural acceptance of premarital sex to become a form of liberal bias. I had

had enough bad experiences with textbook bias, and I wanted to avoid the trap of disguising my own values as scientific facts. We had to treat all value positions fairly. Sexual scientists were not cheerleaders of any subculture; we were analysts and problem solvers for the society. Hugo Beigel, another charter member, liked my paper and published it as the lead chapter in the first collection of SSSS papers (Reiss 1963).

The organization was growing. At the beginning, members of SSSS were predominantly from the New York area, but it wasn't long before they began to come from other parts of the country as well, particularly from California around Los Angeles and San Francisco. In 1965, SSSS began publishing the *Journal of Sex Research* (JSR) as the official journal of our organization. It is the oldest continuous sexuality journal in this country, and it has become one of the premier journals in the area of sexuality. The articles in *JSR* were often written by social scientists, but there were also articles written from medical, biological, and other perspectives. A few years later, our journal got company with the founding of another academic sexuality journal. Here's a part of the story of how that came about.

Richard Green: A New Journal and an International Academy

Richard Green was a psychiatrist who had studied with John Money at Johns Hopkins University. By 1970, he was making his mark in the field with his groundbreaking research on children's sexual orientation at the University of California–Los Angeles (UCLA). It was at this time that I met Richard at a medical conference in Palm Springs, California. After the session one afternoon, he came over to me and started talking about his desire to found a new sexuality journal. He felt that the field was now big enough for that. He wanted to offer a different type of journal than the *Journal of Sex Research*. He wanted a journal that would appeal to a broad array of sexual scientists from many different countries. He wanted me to be on its editorial board. At first I declined, for I was busy helping out with the *Journal of Sex Research*. But Richard promoted his cause every time we spoke, and he stressed that he needed my social-science expertise if the journal was to be successful. He was quite determined and rather convincing, and I finally agreed to be on his editorial board. The next year, 1971, he started the publication of the *Archives of Sexual Behavior*, and today this journal has joined the *Journal of Sex Research* as one of the premier sexuality journals in our country.

Richard had more than a journal in mind. He wanted to found a new sexual-science organization—one that unlike SSSS would be international and would thereby encourage the spread of sexual science in other countries as well as here in the United States. He was able to get fifty-four charter members willing to found the new organization, and by 1974, he had founded the International Academy of Sex Research (IASR) and had made the *Archives of Sexual Behavior* the official journal of the academy. Richard instituted greater checks on academic qualifications before membership was granted. SSSS required a graduate degree, but the IASR also required published research before membership was granted. Currently, it has about three hundred members and meets alternately in the United States and in other countries. There is more of a medical and biological emphasis in the academy's membership than in SSSS, and that can also be seen in its journal.

Other Sexuality Organizations Spring Forth

Another name to add to the list of people who instigated the founding of our oldest sexuality organizations is that of Mary Calderone. I met Mary at the meetings of organizations that focused on scholarly work in the marriage-and-family area. The National Council on Family Relations is the largest and one of the oldest of such organizations. There was also the Groves Conference, which was set up to honor Ernest and Gladys Groves, who had written extensively about the family. I started to go to these meetings in the late 1950s. Since there were no courses in sexuality at that time, the material on sexuality was covered in classes on marriage and the family, so these organizations were relevant to my interests. It was from these family organizations that members for the sexuality organizations were often obtained.

Mary Calderone, a physician, was not primarily interested in doing research and creating theoretical explanations of sexuality. Rather, she wanted to encourage education about sexuality. Mary was at this time a middle-aged woman, and she felt that she would be nonthreatening and would be listened to by the American public. She possessed a great ability to talk openly concerning sexuality with just about anyone and about almost anything. I recall that at one meeting, Carl Broderick and I were in Mary's room on one night of the meeting, and we were discussing problems in the American style of raising children. She told Carl and me how uninformed she had been about female masturbation when she was growing up. She then turned to us and asked us how we had learned about male masturbation. Carl was a Mormon, and I wondered if he was comfortable with her question. But I needn't have worried. He easily relayed to her how he had learned about masturbation. I also responded and told her of my experiences. I did feel a bit awkward in this discussion because Mary was about my mother's age, but she was so natural and relaxed about the topic that it disarmed me. I mention this incident to show that Mary Calderone was a woman far ahead of her time and with an ability to communicate clearly and openly about sexuality. In all these ways, she was indeed impressive.

Mary had worked at Planned Parenthood, but she did not find enough support there for sex education, and so she decided to strike out on her own and found a new organization. At a 1963 Groves Conference, I tried to convince her to stress sex research as much as sex education in her plans for her new organization, but she wanted to give priority to sex education, for she felt it was being neglected. In 1964, she followed through and founded the Sex Information and Education Council of the United States, SIECUS. The acronym sounded like "seek us" and was thus easy to remember. I joined the SIECUS board in 1966 and wrote one of their early pamphlets on sexuality. The organization has been very successful since its founding. In the early 1970s, the journal *SIECUS Report* appeared, and it too has flourished. SIECUS publications are used widely in many public schools, churches, and clinic settings.

Mary's organization brought its knowledge to bear on political discussions concerning sex education. I began to appreciate the fact that by promoting sex education, she was indirectly promoting sex research. One way this can be seen is by looking at the large number of studies that have been conducted on the effectiveness of various sex-education programs. Today, the evidence provided by Douglas Kirby's research has shown the lack of effectiveness of the abstinence-only public school program that the current government supports, and also the relatively more effective outcomes of the consolidated programs that combine abstinence and contraceptive education (Kirby 2001a, 2001b, 2002). But the money from the government keeps coming for abstinence-only education. As I will note many times in this book, in politics, factual evidence often takes a backseat to gaining constituency support.

The three organizations I've discussed above are the ones that I know best, and they are the ones that I was most involved with. I was president of both SSSS and IASR and have been on the board of all three. But these three organizations cover only sex research and sex education, and there was need for an organization for those who do sex therapy. Patricia Schiller, in 1967, founded just such an organization. It was called the American Association for Sex Educators, Counselors, and Therapists (AASECT). It became a place that helped to train and certify sex therapists and counselors. I have been to their meetings, and I know a great many of their members. There is a significant overlap of membership between AASECT and SSSS, IASR, and SIECUS.

There are other organizations, but I will not get into them, for I am giving an account of my experiences in the field rather than an encyclopedic coverage of every aspect of the field. As the title of this book says, I am presenting "an insider's view." For more complete information on any topic I cover, the reader can consult the reference list at the end of this book.

The Value of Sexuality Organizations

I believe that having professional organizations is a major advantage for the work done in any discipline. Organizations first and foremost allow people with similar interests to meet and discuss their work with each other. In addition, these organizations afford a place to present new research and new ideas before they appear in print. Also of great importance is the fact that organizations afford clout. Having thousands of members in organizations gives us political power when we express our views. Keep in mind that studying sexuality acts as a magnet for attracting criticism. When the sexuality organizations were forming, they were all attacked by the likes of the John Birch Society and other far-right political and religious groups. By working together, we can better protect ourselves from these onslaughts when they occur—and you can be sure they will occur.

Organizations also present to the world an identity for any scientific field. They enable future professionals in our colleges and universities to know about the work we do and to realize that they too can choose to work in this field. So, we all owe a debt of gratitude to the people who initiated these organizations, like Albert Ellis, Richard Green, Mary Calderone, and Patricia Schiller. They recruited others to work with them as they built their organizations, and in doing so they helped build the infrastructure of our field. Our organizations will develop and change, but their continued existence remains very important to all of us who work in sexual science.

Hugh Hefner's Party at the Chicago Playboy Mansion

Something else was happening in the 1960s that was relevant to those of us interested in studying sexuality. *Playboy* magazine was now a major enterprise, and the head of it, Hugh Hefner was writing in the philosophy section of his magazine about the need for a more pluralistic approach to sexuality. Believe it or not, many men, in addition to enjoying the photos in *Playboy*, did read the philosophy sections and did discuss them. Playboy Enterprises had an interest in academicians who worked on sexuality. After all, sexuality was the focus of their magazine, and they wanted to keep up with what we knew about sexuality. In August 1965, the American Sociological Association convention was held in Chicago. Playboy's Mansion was then located in

Chicago, and Hugh Hefner invited about twenty sociologists to the mansion. I was one of them. I had never met Hefner, but *Playboy* had commented about my professional publications in several of their issues. The list of invited sociologists included names that some of you might know: Peter Rossi, Sheldon Stryker, Clark Vincent, Al Cohen, Harold Garfinkel, James Coleman, David Caplovitz, Sheldon Messenger, William "Si" Goode, Karl Schuessler, Howie Becker, Edward Borgatta, Peter Blau, James Davis, John McHale, Irwin Smigel, Al Reiss, Alfred Lindensmith, Bill Simon, and John Gagnon. Most of these people did not specialize in writing about sexuality. I would say that myself and three others, Clark Vincent, Bill Simon, and John Gagnon, were the only specialists in the study of sex. But all the others were well-known sociologists, and they either had published an article or two on sexuality or had worked in areas relevant to the study of sexuality, like crime, family, deviance, and the like.

I was eager to see what the Playboy Mansion looked like, and I went over there with Si Goode and a few others. Gagnon and Simon were both there when I arrived. At that time, they were both working at the Kinsey Institute at Indiana University but were still graduate students elsewhere working on their PhDs. I had met them a few years earlier and liked their strong interest in the study of sexuality. I wanted to get them involved in the key organizations, and the three of us became friends. While working at the Kinsey Institute, they had come to know some of the people at Playboy Enterprises, and they had helped Hefner set up this get-together. When we arrived at the mansion, an aide met us at the door and led us up the stairs to a very large room that was dimly lit. There was a bar serving drinks, and at the other end of this huge room, some people were gathered around what seemed like an open trapdoor in the floor. I walked over and saw that the trapdoor was directly above a pool. If you had the courage to do so, you could dive from the living room right down into the pool. There were several women in the pool who worked for Playboy Enterprises in one capacity or another.

Another interesting feature of that massive room was a glassed-in area right across from the bar, where about fifteen or twenty Playboy women were eating supper. I noticed one middle-aged woman there, and I asked her if she worked for Playboy. She responded, "Yes. You might call me a chaperone of the bunnies who live in the mansion. My job is to help organize their day and make sure they have everything they need."

I would add here that the word *bunnies* was used at that time for the women who worked at the Playboy Clubs that were springing up around the country. Today, this word might be taken as a derogatory term, but it wasn't seen that way by many in 1965. The chaperones and the bunnies reminded me of a sorority house with a den mother. One of the sociologists, Jim Coleman, went into the dinning room and began talking to several of the young women there. He later explained to me that he had wanted to get their version of how they felt about posing for the magazine or working in the Playboy Clubs. Did they find it demeaning, and what was their goal in doing it? I was glad to see that a well-known sociologist like Jim Coleman was interested in sexual science. We needed more good people in our area of specialty.

We had been there at least an hour before Hefner made his grand entrance. He came in wearing a shimmering, highly finished brown suit. (The smoking jacket must have come later.) He was of average height and was rather slim. He seemed very intense. As soon as I could, I engaged him in conversation. I wanted to see if he knew of the basic research that had been done by sociologists on sexuality. I was pleasantly surprised. He seemed quite aware of my work and that of others, and even more impressive was his understanding of the distinctive societal approach that sociologists take. In the few places where he wasn't fully informed, one of the two men standing next to him would chime in and respond. He impressed me favorably even though I was a bit turned off by the CEO image that he and his assistants presented. But, after all, that is what he was. He headed the Playboy Enterprises, and he was a multimillionaire.

I hung around a bit more and spoke to some of the women who were living there at the time, and I learned more about their feelings concerning their role in Playboy Enterprises. They seemed certain that being part of Playboy Enterprises in any role would benefit their future careers. They felt it would further their goals in acting, modeling, dancing, movies, or whatever. They indicated that there was no pressure on them to do anything sexual in order to advance themselves. They seemed to be frank and open in what they said to me. After being there a few hours, I said my good-byes, and Si Goode and I headed back to the convention hotel. Goode was a brilliant sociologist who had written about the family and also about love from a cross-cultural perspective (Goode 1963), and I always enjoyed talking with him. We agreed that it had been a remarkable evening. We had been given a glimpse into a sex-related type of enterprise, and it had broadened my understanding of commercial sex in America.

We talked about the very successful Playboy Clubs, where the waitresses wore revealing bunny costumes that we were told were uncomfortably tight. That sort of club seemed very much a part of our ambivalent sexual culture. These clubs offered a look-but-do-not-touch approach, and that was very American. Our culture was still a long way from taking a more relaxed view of sexuality, but at that same time, in 1965, the barriers were beginning to crumble all over America, and at least some of our sexual ambivalence and antihedonism was being dismantled. If you had read *Playboy*'s philosophy writings, you would have seen that they supported sexual change in America. Their philosophy favored increasing the range of sexual behavior that Americans accepted as moral. They wanted homosexuality and a wider range of heterosexuality to be accepted, but even the *Playboy* writers hadn't yet conceptualized how to achieve the sexual pluralism they championed. However, there was no question in my mind that the sexual behavior and attitudes of Americans was at that moment changing dramatically, and I believed that sexual pluralism would be gradually popularized in our society by these changes.

~

CHAPTER FIVE

New Approaches to Sexuality

Getting to Know Masters and Johnson: 1962+

Besides new organizations, journals, and Playboy Enterprises, there were new subfields of sexuality being developed. One of them was sex therapy. Of course, many therapists discussed sexual problems with patients prior to this time. After all, Sigmund Freud stressed the importance of sexuality, and he had a tremendous influence on American psychiatry. But there was no special area of sex therapy within the therapy field. Masters and Johnson gave the field an identity. I had learned some things at SSSS meetings about the research they were doing in St. Louis. I knew they were video-taping couples having sexual relations in order to better understand the physiology of sexual response. We knew more about the physiology of sex-uality in other animals than we did about human sexuality, so this was im-portant research. This type of research would be a shock to many, but un-til their first book appeared in 1966, there was very little awareness in the general public concerning their work.

I met Masters and Johnson in March of 1962. At that time, I was teach-ing at the University of Iowa, and I was invited to participate in a meeting at Washington University in St. Louis sponsored by the National Institute of Mental Health. The title of the conference was "Determinants of Human Sexual Behavior." Seventy-five professionals from a variety of disciplines at-tended. Nine of us were asked to present papers on our research: William Masters, George Winokur, Sheldon Waxenberg, Lucy Ozarin, John Money,

Eli Robins, Franz Kallman, Leo Chall, and myself. The meeting was hosted by Nick Demerath, the director of the Social Science Institute at Washington University. It was also attended by the graduate trainees of that program who wanted to learn more about what they called "community mental health research." I reported on my 1960 NIMH research concerning the societal determinants of trends in sexual standards. This research began at William and Mary, and I discussed it in chapter 2. You'll hear more about it a bit later.

This was an important meeting to me because it was my first meeting with Bill Masters and Virginia "Gini" Johnson. I recall sitting at one of the conference luncheons with Gini Johnson on my right. I asked her why she and Bill Masters hadn't probed more into the societal backgrounds of their subjects and related such social and cultural factors to a person's sexual performance. She wasn't sure if I was curious or if I was being critical of their work, and, according to my journal entry for that year, she said something like the following to me.

"Are you saying that you don't approve of the type of sexual research we are doing?"

She couldn't have been more mistaken and I emphatically responded, "No, not at all. I strongly support your work, and I think it is groundbreaking research. But I am a sociologist, and I feel that society has a major explanatory role even in physiologically centered research. That was the point of my question, not disapproval of your work."

She looked at me, gave me a big smile, and said, "Well, that is great to hear. Let's keep in touch about each of our projects."

Bill Masters was a much more remote and nonresponsive person. His bald head and staring blue eyes were somewhat like looking at a Modigliani painting. It was difficult to feel at ease talking to such a statuesque figure. But I did speak with him, and he did talk to me in his quiet, guarded fashion. He explained to me how he had sought support for his sexuality project from all the social elements in the St. Louis area. He had been able to obtain support even from the representatives of the Catholic Church. He had pointed out to all these people that his research would lead to knowledge that could be used to help those with a variety of sexual problems. I was impressed with his political awareness of what it took to carry on his research. I suppose that knowledge was not gained without some cost over the years since 1956, when his project began. He told me he liked my publications on sexuality and that he shared my high valuation of good scientific research. He said that his emphasis on scientific work had also helped him gain approval for his research.

Masters and Johnson's assumptions posited the physiological naturalness of sexuality. They cited erections in male infants and lubrication in female infants to support this position. They believed that the problem was that so-ciety put up roadblocks against the natural physiological expression of sexu-ality. I had no problem with this view, as far as it went, but I felt it was in-complete, for it didn't deal with the ways that society played a significant role in shaping the way we express our sexuality, both in our behavior and in our attitudes. Kinsey had stressed a physiological view of sexuality, but neverthe-less he had also explored educational, religious, and generational differences in our sexuality and had thereby affirmed that our social background influ-ences us in important ways. I didn't feel that Masters and Johnson were do-ing enough to expand their view of sexuality in that direction. Masters knew Kinsey's work very well and said that he sought to follow in his footsteps. In fact, Masters told me that Kinsey had made movies of people having sex in order to better understand the physiology of sex. It is worth noting that Mas-ters and Johnson's research did have roots in Kinsey's pioneering work.

Let me relate a story about a 1966 convention in order to illustrate the im-pact on the public that Masters and Johnson's first book had. I had been asked to chair the 1966 national meeting of the Groves Conference in Kansas City. I selected the theme of "Sex and Society" for the conference. P. K. Houdek was the chair of local arrangements, and he guaranteed that "everything was up to date in Kansas City." My job was to pick people to or-ganize the panels and also to choose a keynote speaker. I asked John Gagnon to be the keynote speaker. I referred to him in chapter 4 and noted that in the mid-1960s he was a graduate student working at the Kinsey Institute. John was a sociologist, and I valued some of his ideas about sexuality. I knew he had some interesting views on sexuality and children, and he told me he would talk about that as his keynote presentation.

There were two major surprises during the meeting: one by the forces of nature, and the other by the media. First, the forces of nature: We were meet-ing on the top floor of our hotel, in a large room surrounded by windows on three sides. One of the plenary sessions was in process, and most of our mem-bers were there. In the midst of all this, a loud siren began to sound off over and over again. I walked to the entrance of the room and called the hotel per-sonnel. They told me there was a tornado heading straight for downtown Kansas City and that we had a choice of staying there on the top floor or go-ing into the underground levels of the hotel. I consulted with P. K. Houdek, and he suggested that we stay until we got news that sounded more threat-ening. He said that tornadoes were very common in Kansas and noted that it was unlikely that it would come through exactly where we were. I went back into the room, apologized for interrupting the speaker, and notified the audi-ence of the choice and of our decision to continue. I told the people that they could, of course, leave and go to the basement if they wished. Very few people left. I kept looking out the windows for the funnel, and I wondered if we would have time to get a second and more urgent warning. But the tornado never came, and we finished the session with no casualties except our nerves.

The second exciting event involved Masters and Johnson's first book. I had asked Bill to chair one of the panels on medical sexology. I knew he was working on a book with Gini Johnson on their long-term observations of sexual behavior, but I did not know when the book would come out. Paul Gebhard had written to me a few years before this and had told me how much trouble Bill and Gini were having getting financial support for their research, so I expected the book's completion to be delayed. The description in the program of Bill's session did not indicate that he would talk about his book. Then, as the time for all our sessions neared, I noticed television cameras, newspaper reporters, and many other media people flooding the floor where the sessions were to take place. I thought to myself that it looked like the media had heard about our interesting meeting on sexuality and they were coming over to cover it in depth. I soon found out otherwise.

In the hall outside the meeting rooms, the media were all headed to the room where Bill Masters was to give his panel session. Bill saw them and came out of the room, and a mass of media people instantly surrounded him. Cameras flashed, questions were thrown at him, and then he raised up a copy of his book. Much to my surprise, it had just been published that day. The book was *Human Sexual Response*, and it would open up a new era in sex research. Bill was not a person who shared very much, so I wasn't surprised that he hadn't informed me that the first book on his sexuality research was to appear during our meeting. Rather, I was pleased to see the media interest in the work being done in sexuality, whatever their reason might be.

The publication of this book was an important event. A scientific study filming the human sexual response had been conducted, and another way of studying sexuality was added to our research-and-theory agendas. The door was opened wider for further work in this area. His bold venture encouraged others to undertake a wider range of sex research, and that would be of benefit to our knowledge. Kinsey had laid down a new sex-research path, and now alternate routes had been created coming off his pioneering work. Every new carefully done piece of research added to our knowledge of human sexuality and could benefit thousands of people. I thought 1966 was the perfect time for Masters and Johnson's book to appear. The United States was encountering the early stages of a sexual revolution, and Masters and Johnson's work was now one of the lead vehicles pushing our field toward a better understand of human sexuality. I was pleased that the publication event was celebrated at that Groves Conference.

The Sexual Attitudes Reassessment Movement Begins

There was another important development in the field of sexuality besides sex therapy that began at the end of the 1960s. Discussing this will help round out the picture I am portraying of sexual science at that time.

The 1969 American Sociological Association meeting in San Francisco took place just days after I had moved to the Sociology Department at the University of Minnesota to take over the Family Study Center. I was presenting a roundtable on the methodology of sex research at that 1969 sociology meeting. One day, John Gagnon came up to me and said there was something new and very important that I should know about. He mentioned that the Glide Foundation, part of the Methodist Church, was showing some sexually explicit films for a small group of sociologists that night. The films were intended for use in medical schools. John asked me to attend. The films were produced under the leadership of Ted McIlvenna, and they were the result of the excellent filmmaking skills of Laird Sutton. Ted was a former Methodist minister who had begun making sexually explicit films that could be used for the training of medical doctors at universities. The films could also be used by therapists and other professionals trying to help people with sexual problems. But the major goal of the films was to desensitize medical doctors so that they could better deal with the great variety of sexual problems they might confront in their patients.

I went to see the films. They were presented in an auditorium, and there were a good number of people in attendance. The presentation was designed to assault the viewer with sexual stimuli. Several screens were simultaneously showing different sexually explicit movies. This type of film exhibition was later to be known informally as a "fuckarama." Some of the screens were showing male homosexuality, and I noticed that a lot of people had their heads turned away from those screens. At first, I wasn't fully comfortable watching it either, but by the end of a few hours of erotic movies, I had become somewhat more comfortable with watching all of the screens. Most of the screens were showing what I would call standard American erotica. The lesbian screen seemed to get the most attention and the most favorable reactions from the audience. There were not any urophilia or coprophilia sex films. That was probably a wise choice, for that would likely have been the most avoided screen.

After I left, I wondered if watching such films would have an impact on the viewers that would last for more than a day or two. The purpose was to desensitize doctors, so the impact should be more than momentary. Perhaps it would have to be reinforced from time to time. I didn't feel any major impact on myself, but I realized that since I had seen explicit sex films a number of times at stag parties during the years preceding 1969, the impact on me might well be less than on other, more "virginal" viewers. This multiscreen approach to desensitization was called sexual attitude reassessment (SAR), and it was soon to spread to most of the medical schools in the country. I'll explain below just what that entailed.

The New Program in Human Sexuality at Minnesota

Not long after I returned to Minnesota, I learned that our medical school was developing just such a program. The program was being organized in the family practice division of the medical school faculty. It was aimed at medical students. The goal was to broaden their perspective on sexuality so that they would be better able to deal with the wide variety of sexuality-related problems that patients would bring to them. The major tool for producing this increasing competence was SAR. The SAR program was organized to present erotic films, six screens at a time, and to do this for a two-day period. It was a heavy dose in a short span of time, and the aim was to break through the medical doctor's individual biases and resistances and broaden her or his skills in handling a wide variety of sexual problems.

During the SAR, there would be a number of breaks taken. The audience would go into small-group sessions that were led by a person who was instructed to probe the emotional reactions of the viewers. This process of seeing multiple erotic films simultaneously and then discussing one's feelings in small groups was in part aimed at helping the medical students, or any viewer, reassess their own sexual attitudes and hopefully become more able to deal with their own feelings as well as those of others who might practice very different sexual behavior. This was radical stuff for medical schools at that time, but Harold Leif and other MDs had been promoting the need for this in our medical schools since the 1950s (Leif 1981).

I was asked to attend the SAR at our medical school and lead some of the small-group break-out sessions. I agreed, and I became part of an interdisciplinary advisory committee to the new Program in Human Sexuality (PHS) that organized the process. Harriet and I both participated as small-group leaders a number of times during those early years. I did want to help, but I also had some reservations about the effectiveness of the approach. One major concern that I had was the refusal to deal with cognitive factors in the small-group discussions. As group leaders, we were told not to reply to any cognitive questions. For example, if a viewer asked something cognitive like, "Just how common is that behavior?" or "What impact does such sex have on other relationships you might have?" we would tell them that at that time we would discuss only their personal emotional responses to the films.

I found this unfortunate because a great many of the people at the SAR had little knowledge about what we did know about sexuality. The majority of the viewers in my small groups were either uninformed or misinformed, and that might well be a reason for a negative emotional response to the films. I felt that it was counterproductive not to be able to, somewhere in the SAR process, allow for cognitive input that would deal with any lack of knowledge and thereby help people absorb the emotional impact of the films. Emotive and cognitive responses seem to work hand in hand for many people. However, I wasn't able to persuade anyone to change the approach of the break-out sessions. The SAR was in line with a general humanistic movement in psychology and other fields that was gaining popularity at that time. It was also part of an antiscience movement that was coming of age at the time. I didn't like such narrow perspectives. However, I did feel that this expansion of the sexual component of medical school training was a good thing, and I continued to work on the advisory board.

The head of the PHS at the time was Rick Chilgren, a pediatrician. He was a very creative and open person, and he put forth a number of stimulating ideas. For example, in 1971, he suggested that we set up an interdisciplinary division of human sexuality at the university to allow people from medicine and other disciplines to go through the program and be certified when they finished. Relatedly, he also proposed that we establish a new discipline of human sexuality that utilized faculty from many different existing disciplines. At that time, I was focused on establishing a sexuality specialty within sociology, so I wasn't very supportive of the idea. Looking back on it, though, I think it was a great idea, and I regret not supporting it.

The New Sexual Dogma: The SAR in San Francisco

In August of 1972, Rick Chilgren obtained funding from the Playboy Foundation to send twenty-five couples to Ted McIlvenna's eight-day SAR in San Francisco. This was to be an educational experience for the people helping with Rick's SAR program. The University of Minnesota's medical school was one of the first in the country to adopt a SAR program, and the Playboy Foundation heard of us and granted the money so that we could get more training by attending the San Francisco SAR. Harriet and I were one of the couples that went.

This eight-day SAR was the longest SAR Ted McIlvenna had ever offered, and it was also the most diverse in content. As usual, there was a heavy emphasis on emoting, and we heard many personal and at times tearful statements made by the San Francisco SAR staff and some of the attendees. This emoting was treated by the SAR people as therapeutic, but there was something besides the lack of cognitive input that I found even more troublesome at this SAR.

The view presented by many of the staff was supportive of people trying out the full variety of sexual acts that exist (S and M, gay, extramarital, group sex, etc.). The supposed purpose was to allow people to break through their old restrictive sexual attitudes. I had no objection to offering such options. However, as they elaborated, it became clear that this support of broad experimentation was more than just *permission* giving—it was presented more as a *demand* to experiment. There was a negative label applied to those who spoke up and said they didn't want to try a particular type of sexual behavior. This pushy approach of some of the SAR staff did not respect individual choice or take into account individual differences. Instead, it put forth the one "best" way for all of us to "grow" sexually. To me, this was just a new Procrustean bed that demanded that all people fit into what some of the SAR people saw as the ideal way to live sexually. In that sense, it was not really different from the old sexual dogma that said we all should be virginal outside of marriage. Now, instead of no sex, you were expected to try as wide a variety of sex as possible. That was called "liberation."

I favored allowing individual preferences, and I thought the staff seemed unaware of the range of individual differences regarding how people might respond to any specific sexual experimentation. In addition, I felt that a complete picture of sexual choice should include a discussion of the interpersonal nature of sexuality. By examining this interpersonal element, we could see that there are limitations on sexual choice that also must be considered. Rape or forced sexuality, for instance, is something that most of us see as wrong, and the same would be true for an adult having sex with a preadolescent. By examining limits as well as choices, we would become more aware that sexuality is a negotiated act between two people and that the impact on both people needs to be considered. This topic never came up, and in its place we found a pressure to pursue sexual experimentation and to accept it as *the* right way for everyone. This impressed me as a rather narrow approach to sexuality, which made sexuality more of a one-person pleasure choice than an interpersonal act. The social and psychological elements involved in sexuality were just not being carefully examined. This force-feeding approach by many of the SAR leaders was not a sound psychological way to persuade people to be more sexually open.

I voiced my position at one of the sessions and raised the issue of differences in sexual preferences concerning sexual experimentation. Based on my journal notes, I said, "Could not such an emphasis on pleasurable experience with such a wide variety of sexual acts take one's focus away from the other person in the act? What if you want other interests to prevail, such as the emotional quality of the sexual relationship? What if you don't find these other sex acts attractive? Is all this something to overcome? Does the pressure to experiment accept or reject the person who doesn't want to participate?"

The reaction I got from most of the SAR leaders was critical. One of the SAR people said, "Are you hostile to group sex or gay sex, and is that why you are so cautious about trying something new? Are you biased?"

As you might suspect, I didn't take kindly to this comment, and I responded, "To me, to demand a willingness to try a wide range of sexual acts is just as dogmatic as to demand that we refrain from all sexual acts outside of marriage. In both cases, personal choice is severely curtailed. I do not believe that we can, before the fact, judge how good, bad, or neutral some sexuality acts may be for particular people. To me, this try-everything approach sounds like a new sexual dogma and not a liberation philosophy. That is what I object to."

I did get some support, but only from a few of the staff members running the SAR. More clashes were to follow, and they illustrate the attitudes of at least some of the SAR leaders. At one of the sessions, we were all asked by Wilbur and Shirley, the leaders of that session, to sit on large pillows on the floor. I went over to them and explained that just a few weeks before, I had suffered a very painful slipped disk, and it was still difficult for me to sit on the floor. I then pulled over a folding chair and sat in it.

After I sat down, Shirley glared at me and angrily blurted out, "You don't have any back problem! You just want to be higher than everyone else. Isn't that the real reason?"

"No, I really do have a back problem. Why is that so hard for you to believe?"

I took her response to my need to sit in a chair as another sign of the dogmatic attitude that I felt prevailed. Battle lines were being formed. I wasn't the only one who sensed the dogmatism in the SAR leaders' approach, and things came to a head at one of the major sessions. This clash didn't involve me but fourteen of the other participants. One morning, Wilbur and Shirley announced that there would be a nude "sensorium" in the afternoon. We were told that we would all be nude and that we would touch, taste, and smell each other's bodies. They added that everyone "*must*" be nude for that session. A few women in the group said they would prefer to come in bathing suits or underwear. At that point, Lonny Myers, a well-known physician in the field of sexuality, stood up and spoke to the women who raised this issue: "Okay, but first let's have a session to decide why you are so hung up about taking off your clothes." Wilbur and Shirley expressed their agreement with Lonny. That lit the fuse for a number of women.

Harriet, usually a very calm and relaxed person, was offended by Lonny's comment, and she responded, "Fine, but let's also have a session to decide why you are so insistent that we take off all our clothes." Fourteen people objected to having the nude sensorium be obligatory. Finally, the SAR people offered a separate seminude sensorium, so we ended up with one nude sensorium and one seminude sensorium. Harriet and I went to the nude sensorium. We didn't object to being nude; we objected to being ordered to be nude, and also to the denial of the legitimacy of other people's views. We wanted more recognition of individual differences and individual choices. Isn't that what liberation is about?

The prevailing sexual attitude of the SAR leaders was a relativistic one. They noted that all sexual acts should be seen as being of equal moral worth. I felt that surely all sexual acts, short of forced or exploitative sex, were legitimate and ethically acceptable choices. In this sense, I was a strong pluralist in regard to sexual choices. Nevertheless, within that broad category of acceptable sexuality, individuals have the right to rank which acts are, *to them*, of greater or lesser moral worth. For example, I accept someone's right to have coprophiliac sex, in which people are sexually stimulated by defecating on each other, but I would personally rank that act as of less moral worth to me when compared to other sexual acts. In short, all sexual acts that are not forced or exploitative are acceptable moral choices, but the ranking of the vast realm of moral choices is an individual matter and cannot be settled by decree.

The impact of different sexual acts on a person depends in good part on that person's current sexual and other values. The outcome is surely not the same for everyone who performs the same sexual act. Also, the outcome would not be the same at different times in a person's life. An act that seems out of the question at age eighteen may become desirous at age twenty-eight. Our ranking of sexual acts often changes over time. The emphasis on the idea that all sex acts are of equal moral worth avoids assessing your own psyche to see how, at a particular point in your life, you personally evaluate the variety of acceptable sexual acts.

Perhaps the views of many of the SAR people, and of some of the participants, were a reaction to the longstanding criticisms in our society of certain
sexual preferences, such that there developed a desire to end all evaluations
of sexual behavior. Perhaps it was also part of a desire not to allow anyone to
give a low rank, even if just for themselves, to any sexual act that some might
enjoy. But I consider this approach to be one that narrows both our range of
choice and our freedom of thought about sexuality. That was the nub of my
discomfort.

When I returned to Minnesota, I passed along my reactions to the SAR
in a letter to Rick Chilgren. He responded and said that he basically agreed
with my comments, and he asked if he could circulate my letter to the others who had attended the San Francisco SAR. He would then feed this back
to Ted McIlvenna and the San Francisco SAR people. I don't know if Rick
followed through on this, but from what I've learned, very little changed in
the San Francisco SAR program in these regards.

For a few years after this San Francisco SAR, the Program in Human Sexuality at our medical school was flourishing. Many other medical schools
around the nation were introducing similar SARs into their medical cur-
riculum. We had a number of great people working with the PHS. Jim Maddock was one of my favorites, but there were others who took their work very
seriously and did a fine job at it. The SARs here at Minnesota were nowhere
near as dogmatic as the SAR in San Francisco. By 1974, our PHS had opened
up a clinic for people with sexual problems, and it soon became a significant
money producer for the PHS.

In the years right after the San Francisco SAR, many of us connected to
the PHS attended some lecture-and-discussion sessions in San Francisco that
Ted McIlvenna would put on from time to time. Rick's demise as head of the
PHS was related to one of these sessions. At this particular session, a man
and a woman were demonstrating a new machine that was reputed to produce orgasm without contact. It accomplished this by sound waves alone.
The male and female machines differed in shape and sound tone. I was at this
session, and it did seem that the machine worked on these two people, and
they did have orgasms. Rick liked the machines and wanted to purchase
them for the PHS. The cost was $10,000 a piece. I later found out that when
he submitted his request to the medical school, it led to a full investigation
of just how he was running the PHS. Unfortunately, this gave the conservatives in the medical establishment a chance to get rid of Rick, and they did
just that in short order. Despite the loss of Rick, the SARs continued as part
of the PHS. The clinic grew, and the program has continued right up to today. The PHS is currently headed by Eli Coleman, and in 2004, Eli and his

colleagues raised $1,000,000 to endow a permanent chair in sexual health for the PHS. This major accomplishment was due to the exhaustive and very impressive fund-raising efforts of Eli Coleman and his colleagues. The chair will create a permanent place for sexuality in the medical school, and this is of considerable value to the future of our field.

My advisory role in the PHS taught me a good deal about sexuality that I would never have learned by doing regular sociological research and theory. It helped broaden my understanding of our culture, especially of the ideological movements within the field of sexuality. But it also showed me some of the pitfalls that were occurring during our sexual revolution. Let me end this discussion by emphasizing that my criticism of the SAR in San Francisco was only of the way that particular SAR was run, and was not a criticism of all SARs. I believe that the SARs here at Minnesota are a useful addition to our methods of helping people deal with their sexuality.

CHAPTER SIX

~

Building Explanations of Sexuality

The Empirical Basis of the Autonomy Theory

An important event in any new science is the building of a theory. As I noted in the opening of chapter 4, the early studies by Kinsey and others were heavily descriptive and focused on behavior (Kinsey et al. 1948, 1953). They informed us of how many people from one group compared to some other group did a particular behavior, but they accomplished precious little toward explaining the descriptive differences they were reporting. Why did one group do more or less of a particular behavior or have a more or less accepting attitude than another group? This inquiry was left largely unanswered. Of course Kinsey and his associates, Wardell Pomeroy, Clyde Martin, and Paul Gebhard, contributed a great deal by their pioneering studies. They demonstrated that sexuality research could indeed be done and done well. But if our science was to advance, we had to move ahead, and in addition to describing what was happening, we needed to try to develop and test explanations for the sexual behaviors that we found.

In the 1960s, I sought to move the field more toward building explanatory theory in sexual science. Please excuse my immodesty, but since my work has been noted by others as one of the earliest efforts to develop a sociological explanation of sexuality, I feel that I can use this work to illustrate what I mean by scientific explanation (Weis 1998a). I will do this by reference to the two books I published in the 1960s (Reiss 1960a, 1967). In chapters 2 and 4, I talked about some aspects of these books. In them, I predicted that the permissiveness with affection premarital sexual standard would become the dominant premarital sexual standard in America. I spoke of my first test of this prediction in four Virginia schools. My premarital sexual permissiveness scales worked very well on those four schools, and permissiveness with affection was indeed shown to be a sexual standard of both men and women. In 1960, I received the first of three grants from the National Institute of Mental Health to study this further. These grants allowed me to add two more schools and, most importantly, to test my scale and my ideas on a representative national sample. That national survey was carried out in June of 1963.

I should note that my scales worked very well in this representative national sample, just as they had for the student samples. That in itself was a very significant outcome, for it presented to sex researchers the first scientifically devised and nationally tested scale for measuring premarital sexual permissiveness. The scale allowed one to give each person a score ranging from low to high on premarital sexual permissiveness (Guttman 1947). Many other sexual scientists in the years since then have used this scale and have also reexamined my theoretical explanations (Reiss 1964a, 1964b, 1965a, 1967, 1998a, 1998b; Reiss and Miller 1979). In my 1967 book, I wanted to develop an explanation for the extensive differences I had found in the levels of acceptance of premarital sexual permissiveness in the student samples and in the national sample. If I could explain what produced the differences both within and among my various samples, then I would be able to build a theory explaining how society shapes changes in premarital sexual permissiveness. A scientific theory is often a network of interrelated propositions, each of which helps explain a specific outcome. In order to make what I mean by theory building clearer, I need to concretize and illustrate this process. I will do this by discussing my research and theory building explaining attitudes toward premarital sexual permissiveness.

My study of premarital sexual permissiveness had to be an exploratory study because there was no developed theory upon which I could build. I designed my questionnaire to cover the five broad areas of social life that I felt might be influencing changes in the acceptable level of premarital sexuality. The five areas I explored were as follows: (1) general background factors like social class, religion, gender, and so on; (2) dating experiences and love concepts of the respondents; (3) sexual experience and guilt reactions; (4) perceived sexual permissiveness of one's parents, peers, and close friends; and (5) family characteristics, such as age of children, being divorced, and so on. There was some descriptive research in sexuality that indicated that these factors might correlate with the level of premarital sexual permissiveness. First I needed to examine my student and national samples and see which of these variables correlated with my scale of premarital sexual permissiveness. Then I would look for how such correlations held up in various race, gender, class, and other subgroupings. I was searching for patterns of relationships that could tie together several of the variables mentioned above. All this would help me build an inclusive explanation of how and why specific societal factors influence the acceptable level of premarital sexual permissiveness.

For three years, I explored the relationships and the complex interrelationships in these data from my student and national samples. I examined many thousands of statistical tables and ended up with seven explanatory propositions concerning how aspects of our society influence our level of acceptable premarital sexual permissiveness. Then I looked for a common thread that might be present in all seven propositions and that could thus become the general explanation for changes in premarital sexual permissiveness. The common thread that tied together all seven propositions was the amount of freedom or autonomy given to young people in our courtship system. Each proposition explained one aspect of how differences in autonomy would lead to differences in the level of acceptable premarital sexual permissiveness in a group or person. In short, all seven propositions were specificities of one basic theory. I called the basic theory the *autonomy theory*. By autonomy, I meant the freedom a group has to do what they want to do. The theory basically contended that differences in people's autonomy were the key to understanding differences in their premarital sexual attitudes and behaviors. Allow me now to try to make this theory-building process less abstract by discussing how I constructed one of my seven propositions and how that proposition tied in with the broader autonomy theory.

Proposition One: Changing Sexual Permissiveness

One of the checks I did was to see if church attendance was related to levels of acceptable premarital sexual permissiveness. Of course, I expected to find less acceptance of premarital sexual permissiveness in a group that frequently attended church than in a group that rarely attended church. Religion formally preached support for abstinence before marriage, so one would expect that sort of correlation. As expected, I found that higher church attendance went with less acceptance of premarital sexual permissiveness for the overall student sample, but I wanted to check further and see if the relationship held up for each of the important subgroups, like males and females or blacks and whites. When I looked at the data on males and females, I found that female permissiveness was more strongly related to church attendance than was male sexual permissiveness. Then I checked the correlation with church attendance for blacks and whites and found that the correlation for whites was much stronger than it was for blacks.

Now, I could have just described the relationship of church attendance to permissiveness within the male, female, black, and white groups and reported the differences and let it go at that. But I wanted to develop an explanation of these differences, so I asked myself, is there a common factor that blacks and males share that makes them display such a weak relationship between church attendance and premarital sexual permissiveness? And, is there also a common factor that whites and females share that could explain their stronger relationship between church attendance and premarital sexual permissiveness? I mulled this over for a while, and then it hit me that there was indeed such a common factor in both cases. Males and blacks have been the traditionally high groups on premarital sexual permissiveness in our society, and females and whites have been the traditionally low groups on premarital sexual permissiveness. So, the traditional level of acceptance of premarital sexual permissiveness was the common factor that could explain both the race and gender findings. I summed up this explanation by putting forth the following proposition: The lower the traditional level of sexual permissiveness in a group, the greater the likelihood that social forces will alter individual levels of sexual permissiveness. By social forces, I was referring to things such as church attendance and other factors that I also tested but won't bother to bring into the discussion here. This generalization became my first proposition. As you can see, proposition one explains why I found more change in female and white groups then in male and black groups.

There was an excellent way to test the validity of proposition one. I could examine trend data concerning premarital sexual permissiveness over the period of rapid change in premarital sexual permissiveness during the 1960s and 1970s. Proposition one would predict that white women would change the most, since they incorporate the low tradition of permissiveness of both the female and the white groups. If the proposition was valid, then white women should have changed the most during the period of the sexual revolution. I carried out this check years later when the data became available and found that during the sexual revolution in our country, white females did very clearly change the most in their level of accepted premarital sexual permissiveness, as well as in their premarital coital behavior. There were a good number of sources of data that verified this (Davis and Smith 2002; Davis et al. 1978; Hofferth et al. 1987; Klassen et al. 1989; Reiss 1967, 2001b; Scott 1998; Singh and Darroch 1999). This kind of extensive real-world check of one's theoretical explanations can provide a real boost of confidence in one's theoretical explanations. It certainly did just that for me.

This first proposition was interesting because it raised important questions such as why a low traditional level of acceptance would be such a good predictor of change. Why isn't it just as easy to lower a traditionally high group's level of sexual permissiveness as it is to raise a traditionally low group's level? One explanation would simply be that sexuality is pleasurable and can also be psychologically rewarding, so once a group or individual accepts a particular level of permissiveness, there will be resistance to giving it up. One way a change in a low-permissive group can come about is if that group interacts frequently with a high-permissive group. An obvious illustration can be seen in dating. In most cases, women were dating men who were more permissive than they were, so many women were under constant pressure to raise their level of permissiveness. I would add here that the role of our biological inheritance is of course a factor worthy of consideration by other sexual scientists, but bear in mind that our biological potential is always shaped by our society. My theory is focused on the societal shaping mechanisms, so I will leave the biological explanation to others.

Proposition one, as well as the other six propositions I developed, are all logically related to the autonomy theory, which asserts that a reduction in the constraints placed on young people's dating by institutions such as religion, politics, or family will increase the premarital sexual permissiveness of young people in that society. So there is an underlying assumption in my theory that there is pressure toward sexual permissiveness that will result in change whenever societal restraints are lifted. This basic theoretical statement is in very brief form the autonomy theory. The first proposition specifies this broad theoretical statement by asserting that the group most likely to change when autonomy increases is a group with a restrictive level of sexual permissiveness. Groups with high levels of acceptable sexual permissiveness will, according to proposition one, be much harder to change. The other six propositions in their own ways are also logically related to this general theory that changes in the autonomy of the courtship institution are key in explaining changes in the level of acceptable permissiveness in a society (Reiss 1967, 167). In our society, there is a sort of checks-and-balances relationship set up—particularly between the family institution and the courtship group. The more autonomy the courtship group has, the more they will be able to follow their own sexual interests. But certainly a person's family background will have some degree of influence on young people's sexual attitudes and behaviors even when there are increases in autonomy (Reiss 1967, chap. 7).

Throughout the twentieth century, our society granted more autonomy to the courtship group. After World War II, this was in good part a result of large increases in the percentage of married women working outside the home. As mentioned in chapter 4, participation in the labor force by women with preschool children rose from about 12 percent in 1950 to about 30 percent in 1970. This percentage would rise to 45 percent in 1980 and go up to over 60 percent in the 1990s (Reiss and Reiss 1997). This trend inevitably led to less parental supervision and to children's growing up with a stronger sense of their own freedom to make choices, or what I am calling autonomy. At the same time, the increased autonomy and economic power of working women made these women feel more justified in further exploring their own sexual interests. So there were multiple forces promoting increased autonomy for many parts of our society.

In sum, the autonomy theory basically asserts that if you want to predict trends in premarital sexual permissiveness, then you should examine sociocultural changes in the society to see if they promote greater autonomy for young people, either directly or indirectly. After my 1967 book appeared, other sexual scientists began to do research to determine if they could find support for the autonomy theory. The results of their studies were generally supportive. If you want, you can check them for yourself (Hopkins 2000; Reiss 1998a, 2001b; Reiss and Miller 1979).

Some Reactions to the Autonomy Theory

The field of sociology responded to my autonomy theory with a good deal of interest. Over a dozen dissertations were written testing some of my theoretical propositions from my 1967 book. My scales became the most-used measures of premarital sexual permissiveness in the field. The term *premarital sexual permissiveness*, which I coined, has become widely used. I hoped that the reception would be strong for a book that not only presented research findings but also explained them. I was elated, for I felt I had taken a major step toward my number-one goal of advancing the scientific respectability of sociological research into human sexuality. Reviews of the book were filled with high praise, and William Kephart, who had reviewed my 1960 book (see chapter 2), had nothing but praise in his review in the March 1968 *Annals of the American Academy of Political and Social Science* (Kephart 1968): "A scholarly work of genuine sociological importance . . . a masterly analysis—undoubtedly the definitive work on premarital sexual attitudes—an invaluable addition to the literature."

But there was also societal resistance to the study of sexuality. The encounter I had with the *Chicago Tribune* illustrates this point. In 1967, C. G. Petersen of the *Chicago Tribune* interviewed me on tape at great length for an article he wanted to do on my book. He wrote his piece on my work, but then he told me that his editors would not allow him to publish it because they considered some of my comments about trends toward more acceptance of premarital sexuality to be "too shocking to be published in the *Chicago Tribune*." It wasn't until 1969 that he wrote to me again to say that his editors had changed their opinion and that they would permit him to publish his piece on my work. I usually date the sexual revolution as making a clear move forward in the late 1960s. This change in attitude of the editors of the *Chicago Tribune* may have resulted from their realization that by 1969 many of their readers had changed their sexual attitudes.

At the same time as the *sexual* revolution was happening, there was a related *gender* revolution. Betty Friedan's 1963 book, *The Feminine Mystique*, became a best seller. It dealt with women's ambiguous feelings about their gender role in our society. The National Organization of Women (NOW) was formed in 1966 and was soon attracting many members. Women in the civil rights movement were fighting to get more equality with the men in that movement. As I mentioned earlier in this chapter, mothers of preschool children were working in unprecedented numbers, and this was a significant change for middle-class mothers. At the heart of the traditional family was a portrait of mothers at home with their preschool children, so the changes for this group of mothers indeed indicated that a very significant change was happening in the female gender role. Earning money has a way of increasing one's sense of power, and this promotes more autonomous behavior. In line with my autonomy theory, this meant that as women became more economically empowered, they would be more willing to challenge restrictions on their sexuality. And, as noted earlier, that is indeed what happened, particularly for white women. Their sexual behavior and attitudes changed more than men's during the sexual revolution, and they became the leaders in the sexual revolution (Reiss and Reiss 1990, 1997).

Why Was Gender Equality and Sexual Pluralism So Strong in Sweden?

All these changes in gender roles and sexuality in America made me want to explore Sweden, for they were the Western world's leader in those gender and sexuality changes. One thing I wanted to do was see if my autonomy theory could explain trends in Swedish sexuality as well as it seemed to for American sexuality. I had wanted to go to Sweden ever since I was in Europe during World War II and had heard about the changes that were happening in Sweden. I asked Jan Trost of Sweden about working at Uppsala University during my 1975–1976 sabbatical. Jan was a friend who had spent some time at the University of Minnesota. He happened to be going on sabbatical himself at that time, and he helped me get appointed to his research position at Uppsala University. The job was a real gift. I only had to teach a total of twenty hours the entire year. I was very happy to get the offer, and on September 1, 1975, I left for Sweden with my wife and three children.

My major goal was to study the move toward gender equality and sexual pluralism in Sweden since the beginning of the twentieth century. I will deal with sexual pluralism in more detail in a later chapter, but for now I am using this term to refer to the range of sexual behaviors a person accepts as legitimate behavior choices for people to make. The Swedes had more sexual pluralism in their country than we did. After I arrived, I talked with many of my colleagues at Uppsala University and to a number of townspeople that I came to know, and I tried to build a qualitative understanding of sexuality and gender ideas in Sweden. I also read all the research that had been done on Sweden and spoke to as many authors of this research as I could find. However, my informal education on Swedish culture began the first day we arrived at our townhouse in Sweden. We unpacked the essential things and then sat down and turned on the TV. A movie was playing on the channel we tuned into. The first scene we saw was of a couple having intercourse. We knew immediately that we were not watching American network TV. I was grateful for that. This movie was an early sign to us of the greater acceptance in Sweden of the naturalness of nudity and sex. It would take more time for us to grasp more deeply the nature of the Swedish view of sexuality, but this initial experience was a quick primer.

One of the most obvious things about Swedish character was their strong feelings of personal privacy and thus their hesitancy to be intrusive. You could stand at a bus stop without much likelihood that anyone would start up a conversation. However, if you asked for directions, many people would respond. It was the same with neighbors. If you asked for something, they were very quick to respond, and they would be quite helpful. But if you didn't open the conversation, you could live for a long time without ever getting to know anyone. We let our neighbors know that we liked to socialize with them, and we soon exchanged visits to sample each other's smorgasbord and aquavit. After a while, I would ask our closest neighbors questions about their sexual attitudes and those of other Swedes they knew. They were very willing to share their perspectives on sexuality.

It didn't take long to learn how common it was in Sweden to raise children with a great deal of freedom. I had visible evidence of it every morning. When I would exercise, I would look out at a preschool children's playground in the area just beyond our backyard. I would often see the young children physically fighting with each other. The women watching them would hardly ever interfere. Once, one of the children started to push sand down the throat of another child, and then I did see the day-care women stop that behavior. But, short of such very dangerous acts, they let the kids do what they wanted. However, by age sixteen when they entered gymnasium (high school), it was expected that the wildness would be set aside and that the more-typical adult reserved personality would be adopted. It was striking to see this transformation, but it did seem to take place, at least on the outside. Perhaps a remnant of the very free Swedish childhood is what is released in young people's drinking parties that are so common in Sweden on the weekends.

So much in Sweden in 1975 and 1976 was a transition from what they called the old to the new, but the old was still very visible. The language usage had changed after the war so that the informal address of "*du*" instead of the formal address of "*ni*" was very widely used. Nevertheless, the social gatherings were still arranged by status, and people clearly knew who was higher up. Even male-female differences were not hard to detect. You could see this publicly, in that only a third of the Stockholm Council was female. Also, only 40 percent of workers were women, and they earned about two-thirds of what men earned. In addition, when you looked at who was wheeling the baby carriages, it was usually mothers. This seemed all too familiar. But, as I will indicate, Sweden was significantly more equalitarian than we were in the United States. Remember that in 1975, our Congress was less than 10 percent female, and our women earned about 60 percent of what men earned.

One of the most obvious differences between the United States and Sweden was in premarital coital attitudes. The Swedes clearly had more of what Hans Zetterberg called "erotic peace" (Zetterberg 1969). They seemed less obsessive and compulsive about premarital sex. Sexuality in general was seen as a natural interest of human beings. Condom machines were on the streets in Stockholm, and huge billboards promoting condom use were on display around the city. As long as people did their sex acts in private, they would be accepted. From what I could tell, teenagers would gradually advance toward a sexual relationship with the person they were dating. What would speed up the process would be a drunken party or spending a holiday together away from town. The view of the naturalness of drinking thus fit with the acceptance of the naturalness of sex. There was quite a TGIF culture in Sweden, and watching young people on a Friday or Saturday night revealed very different behaviors than on a Tuesday night. Of course, we have TGIF here too, but the contrast was much greater in Sweden. I will illustrate this shortly.

There was a high degree of autonomy in people's lives in Sweden. As I've noted, the right to a private life ranked very high there. People could do what they wanted as long as there was no violence or force involved. I believe this privacy right was one of the foundations of the rights that young people had in their sexual lives. Zetterberg's national study of Sweden indicated that all but a very small percentage of the population engaged in premarital sex. The percentage who engaged in premarital sex was only slightly less among the very small group of people who went to church regularly (Zetterberg 1969). Another support for sexual autonomy was the fact that about 20 percent of Swedes never married. Some of these people probably cohabited, but some did not. In Sweden, it was much more obvious that young people were not all on a clear path to marriage, so their sexual behavior was not necessarily "premarital."

The Swedish Culture in Action at Dalarna

Let me describe an experience we had while vacationing in Dalarna that will afford you a qualitative picture of Swedish culture as we experienced it. Harriet and I reserved rooms for ourselves and for our three children (ages ten through sixteen) in a nice resort hotel in Dalarna for the weekend. This is the area where the well-known wooden horses are carved and painted. We bought our share of these to give as presents. Then we checked into the hotel, unpacked, and came down for dinner. As we walked through the lobby, a bus pulled up, and about sixty or seventy very formally dressed people and a number of children got off and came into the hotel. Right off of the lobby was a large room for children that was filled with game machines and toys for kids of all ages. Our children went in there and joined the others to play before supper.

After a while, we brought the kids into the dining room and sat down at a table. Around us were other couples with children, some couples sitting alone, and also some lone individuals. Everyone was very low-keyed during supper, and the noise level was much lower than it would have been in a similarly filled American dining room. After dinner, an announcement was made that in an hour a band would take the stage and dancing would start. During the next hour, we saw that everyone gathered up their children and took them back to their rooms. We did the same and then came back down for the dancing. The dining room had been quickly transformed into a dance hall with tables. Alcoholic drinks of all kinds were available.

The mood now was clearly different. For one thing, people had brought in their own whiskey bottles and had placed them at their tables. Hard liquor was very expensive in Sweden, so bringing in your own bottle was quite popular. The noise level increased by the minute as people seemed to relax and have more to drink. Then the band started to play. For the next several hours, you could see the same group of people who had been so formal and quiet at dinner increasingly loosen up and talk more openly, laughing and interacting much more with each other. By 1 a.m., the band stopped playing, but the people did not want to stop partying. A small group of them acted to save the day. They announced that they had just returned from Finland and that they had an ample supply of vodka that they would share with everyone else. People cheered openly and moved into the large lobby area where there were many couches and chairs. The lights were now dimmed, and the bottles were passed around the lobby freely. We didn't stay to the end, but the party continued until the wee hours of the morning.

Late the next morning, everyone was packing up and getting ready to leave—the weekend was over. The bus that had brought the people pulled up to the front of the hotel. The people were now dressed as they had been when they had arrived just twenty-four hours earlier, and although they looked a bit tired, they were quite polite and sober in appearance. They boarded the bus and started on their journey back to their more-formal weekday culture. All this could happen in the States, but the contrast between normal day-by-day living and vacation living seemed much sharper in Sweden. Perhaps these vacations were one way that the quieter and more-private Swedish personality opened up, and without it, the percent never marrying might have been much higher.

A Swedish Panel Discusses Sexuality

Let me relate another experience that illustrates the different attitudes toward premarital sex in Sweden. Harriet did some work at the Uppsala library, and she thought it would be good to get several university faculty and townspeople to talk about life in America and in Sweden. The junior high students and their parents, as well as others, attended the session. I was on the panel together with several others. One of the topics was premarital sexuality in Sweden and America. After each of the panel members had spoken, Harriet opened up the discussion to the audience. The junior high school students who came were almost all female students who were about thirteen or fourteen years old and had come with their mothers. A few of the female students spoke up and said they wanted to air a gripe they had. They went on to say that they felt they were old enough to start having intercourse by age fourteen, but their parents objected and wanted them to wait until they were sixteen years old. They did not like the parental restraint. In response, a mother said that she was afraid her daughter would get emotionally hurt or even pregnant if she didn't wait until she was 16. The female students responded by saying that they knew how to handle contraception and they weren't just interested in love relations anyhow but also wanted to experience the pleasures of sexuality. A few other students and some mothers joined in the discussion, voicing their opinions. Then the unexpected happened.

There were some undergraduate Uppsala University students there. One of them was a female American student from California. She stood up, looked over to where the mothers were sitting, and said slowly and firmly, "I am very bothered by the casual view toward premarital sexuality that is being expressed here by both the girls and their mothers. I don't care how old a girl is; she should wait until marriage to have sexual intercourse. That is the only decent and moral thing to do."

The room went silent for a few moments. Swedes are not a confrontational people, and the challenge was not taken up immediately. Finally, one of the Swedish mothers stood up and said, "Do you realize that the average age of marriage for women in Sweden is twenty-six? Are you saying that girls should wait until that age?"

The California woman jumped up and blurted out, "Yes, and if they aren't married at twenty-six, they should just continue to wait until they do marry."

The Swedish mother who had asked the question looked stunned. She hesitated while looking at the American student and then softly said, "How quaint." She said this without any tone of malice and sat down, still with a look of amazement on her face.

The difference between Sweden and America was writ large in this brief exchange. In Sweden, and much of Western Europe, sexuality was taken as a natural act that you could only put off for so long. In America, it was much more likely to be taken as a moral act that you could, by an act of will and character, put off for a long time if need be. This traditional American view was considered quite far out to many middle-class Swedes. Of course, there was a sexual revolution going on in America, and things were changing quite a bit, but the traditional restrictive perspective was clearly still alive and well in that American student. Overall in the United States, there seemed to be more couples on both ends of the distribution—very accepting of premarital sex or not at all accepting. The Swedes seemed to be grouped more toward the center of the distribution rather than at the extremes. In short, sex appeared to be less polarized in Sweden than in America.

Harriet's panel discussions were a success. They had revealed some very basic differences between the American and Swedish views of sexuality—not so much by the panel members as by the exchange of audience comments that took place. I should add one more observation here. There was no discussion of what fourteen-year-old male students should do sexually, and there were very few male students or fathers at the discussion. So, even in Sweden the double standard was far from dead.

Historical Factors Promoting Gender Equality in Sweden

I've tried to illustrate by my experiences some of the basic differences in gender and sexuality in Sweden. The entire Western world in the twentieth century has moved toward more gender equality and acceptance of sexuality. But the question I am focused on is why Sweden has been a leader in that common movement. I have tried to illustrate several characteristics of Swedish sexual culture, such as the strong sense of privacy, the perceived naturalness of sexuality, and the TGIF dualism of their lives, but the question still remains: how did this higher level of gender equality and sexual acceptance come about? For my answer, I'll present a very brief summary of changes in Sweden during the twentieth century.

First, there was the very late start of industrialization in Sweden. In England, industrialization began in the late eighteenth century, and in Sweden, it began in the late nineteenth and early twentieth century. By starting late, Sweden could learn from the mistakes of other Western countries and would be able to move into industrialization more quickly and more efficiently. Also relevant here is that by the end of the nineteenth century, over 1 million Swedes had left their country because of economic hardships. There was also the traditionally very low birthrate of Sweden and the very high proportion of people who never married. All this added up to a severe labor shortage when industrialization began. This situation made the Swedish government aware that with industrialization they would have to encourage women to move into the jobs that men alone had previously filled. To encourage this influx of women into the labor force, laws had to be passed to make going to work easier for both married and single women.

The laws enacted particularly from 1915 to 1920 significantly changed the marital institution. In order to increase the labor force, the government wanted to encourage women to marry and have children. They tried to minimize any constraints on childbirth that were due to divorce restrictions or concerns about having a child out of wedlock. Divorce laws were changed to allow for divorce by mutual consent, and the specification of illegitimacy was removed from birth certificates of infants whose parents were not married. The new legislation gave women independent legal rights once they reached the age of twenty-one. All of these changes were far ahead of many other European nations, and the effect of these changes was to significantly broaden women's choices and make working in industry more attractive.

A second important factor was the late arrival of Christianity to Sweden and the weak position of the Lutheran Church there. The twentieth century saw a further weakening of the Lutheran Church in Sweden even though it continues to run the National Statistical Bureau. In Sweden, the traditional way that couples became married was by receiving parental approval of the match. There could be a wedding in church later. But, even in the early twentieth century, one could enter into a civil marriage as an alternative to a religious one. Church attendance declined in the twentieth century, and by the 1970s, less than 10 percent were regular churchgoers, compared to 40 percent in our country. What this weak position of religion meant was that the Swedish culture was freer to change male-female equality and sexual-acceptance norms than if they had had a powerful church that opposed such changes, such as was the case in America (Reiss 1980b).

A third and final factor in Swedish history that I believe promoted general equality and sexual pluralism was the lack of a militaristic power clique in the early twentieth century. At the time of my visit in 1975–1976, Sweden was spending only 4 percent of its national budget on the military. That was a great deal less than was the case here in America. A national emphasis on military power means stronger male power, which means that gender equality is less likely to advance. Sweden has not been involved in a war since 1809. In World Wars I and II, Sweden remained neutral.

Sweden and Autonomy Theory

Comparing America and Sweden on these three social forces—economics, religion, and militarism—you see a notable difference in how we industrialized and in the power of our religious and military institutions. In fact, compared to most European countries, Sweden is quite different on all three factors. Furthermore, if you compare European countries on these three factors, you will find that the countries that are the most similar to Sweden are also the most gender equal. Thus, I would submit that these societal characteristics are a good part of the explanation of Sweden's leadership in gender equality. More equality for women in Sweden means that women feel more empowered to make their own sexual choices and thus do not allow men to dictate how they should behave sexually. Increased autonomy in the workplace, together with low religiosity and low militarism, tends to produce more gender equality and sexual rights for women.

This increase in female autonomy in Sweden has surely not resulted in universal orgiastic sexual behavior. This realization should allay the fears of some in America that such a change in autonomy here would have this outcome. Bear in mind that autonomy, or the power to choose, is not the only force that affects sexual attitudes and behavior. For one thing, there is also a desire by most Westerners to find a partner who will be emotionally supportive rather than just sexually willing, so the value placed on the interpersonal quality of sexuality acts as a brake on any tendencies to go to extremes.

I will round out this portrait of Sweden by indicating that even in Sweden there is some resistance to the trends toward more gender equality and broader sexual choices. Also, it is not easy to move to a new system of gender roles even when you want to, because most occupations reward those who work long hours and give top priority to their careers. How to change this so that both men and women can work without making work the top priority in their lives is something the Swedish government has been wrestling with for decades. Also, the change in gender equality is far from complete. Women in Sweden still take the great majority of all child-care leaves with pay even though men have the right to do the same. Sweden is surely more gender equal and more sexually pluralistic than we are in America, and than most European countries are, but they are still a considerable distance from achieving full equality in gender and sexuality. One key difference between us is that a much larger majority of Swedes compared to Americans want to achieve gender equality. It is in this area of attitudes and goals that Sweden and America differ the most.

The above examination of Sweden leads me to conclude that my autonomy theory is relevant to international comparisons concerning changes in sexuality and gender, just as it is relevant to these trends within our own country. Of course, we need more empirical studies of the autonomy theory and of the specific causes I have postulated as being relevant for explaining Sweden's gender and sexual customs. A number of such checks have been done, but much more is needed (Hopkins 2000; Reiss 1980b; Reiss and Miller 1979; Schwartz and Reiss 1995). Perhaps some of my readers will venture to undertake this exciting task. I encourage you to do so using both quantitative and qualitative research. They both are congenial to the building of explanatory theory. I have tried in this chapter to illustrate the process of building theoretical explanations. Theory building in science is a never-ending task. We must bear in mind that it is always possible that someone else will put forth an explanation that does a better job of accounting for the evidence. I have spent a lot of my career trying to do just that (Reiss 1960a, 1960b, 1965b, 1967, 1970, 1980b, 1981, 1986, 1993, 1999, 2001b, 2004; Reiss, Anderson, and Sponaugle 1980; Reiss, Banwart, and Foreman 1975; Reiss and Miller 1979; Reiss and Reiss 1990, 1997).

~

CHAPTER SEVEN

Some Clashes of Science, Politics, and Values

The sexual revolution of the 1960s and 1970s won adherents to a more pluralistic view of sexuality. The belief that there was only one right way to behave sexually or to think about sexuality was seriously wounded by this revolution. Nevertheless, the conservatives did not fold up their tents and vanish into the night. Despite their wounds, conservatives were clearly and visibly on the counterattack during this entire period. Also, as you might expect, most politicians were not going to take any risks and did not come out in support of sexual pluralism, for they felt doing so could cost them votes. To illustrate, I'll go over some disputes I was involved in. Similar events are clearly present today and are likely to confront anyone in our field.

The Federal Government's Victorian Standards

I knew from my first National Institute of Mental Health grant in 1960 that the government would only let sexuality sit in the back of the government bus, and they might also place it behind a curtain. When I received that NIMH grant, I was told that I should not use the word *sex* in the title of my grant. Grants for sex research were not made visible to the public, so it should have been no surprise when in the late 1970s I found out that this Victorian stance was still clearly visible and I experienced this censorship again.

Jack Wiener worked in Research Programs at NIMH and was one of the people in the government research bureaucracy who was interested in encouraging good scientific research on sexuality. In November of 1977, Jack organized a conference of many of the top people in the country who were researching sexuality. For a year, he and psychiatrist Richard Green carefully planned for this conference. Richard Green was the man whom I pointed out in chapter 4 was the founder of the *Archives of Sexual Behavior* journal and of the International Academy of Sex Research. The major goal Green and his planning committee set was that the conference would produce a publication on sex-research methodology that would promote greater use of sophisticated methodologies in sex research and thereby help sex researchers submit quality grant applications and increase their ability to obtain research grants. Our planning committee decided to invite about twenty other people who were thought to be at the top of the field of sexual science to be part of the conference. Several of us were asked to write up and present papers at the conference. I was asked to write on researching heterosexuality. Most of the nonpresenters were asked to be discussants for one or another of these papers.

The conference was held November 18 and 19, 1977. There was an abundant amount of good discussion and many interesting papers at the meetings. We sat around a huge wooden table and presented our papers, and then the discussion was opened for informal comments by anyone. The discussion was lively and informative. A couple of interesting events stand out in my memory and in my notes. Evelyn Hooker was a discussant of Marcel Saghir's paper on homosexuality (Hooker 1980). She had been in the field for many years and was well known for her early work on homosexuality. She had stated in print that her research evidence and that of others made it clear that homosexuality was a perfectly normal condition. She talked to us about her strong concern that even though the American Psychiatric Association in 1973 had taken homosexuality off its list of disorders, many still viewed it as abnormal. As she spoke, she became increasingly emotional. You could hear her voice quiver. Her face showed the distress and strong emotion she was feeling. Finally, she broke down in tears and cried. Then she spoke about her disappointment at the slow rate of change in public views about homosexuality despite all the scientific evidence she and others had presented. Clearly, this was a very personal issue to her. Of course, in our group, she was preaching to the converted, but we knew how she felt because we each had the same feelings of despair at the rate of social change in the area of our own work. We tried to comfort her by agreeing with her, and we complimented her on her classic work in the area. She soon regained her composure, but it was obviously a very emotional moment for her.

At a later point, I reported Barbara Voorhies and Kay Martin's findings, which had appeared in a recent book of theirs (Voorhies and Martin 1975, chap. 4). They noted that a number of cultures around the world have more than two genders. They presented anthropological data to back up their assertion. The Navajo in our own country were such a culture. The Navajo had a third gender called the "*nadle*," comprising those born with ambiguous genitalia and those who wanted to change their assigned gender. I suggested that one might well expect more than two genders to be rather common in a culture because in every society there are babies born with ambiguous genitalia, and there are also children and adults who are unhappy with the gender role into which society has placed them. I added that the surprise was not that third genders are present in some societies, but that such options for more than two genders are as rare as they are. Western societies are so used to thinking of male and female as the only possible gender categories that the idea of more than two genders seemed very strange even to those at the conference. I find that today, some thirty years after the Voorhies and Martin book, a number of professionals in our field are still unaware of this cross-cultural reality.

I also reported that the biological risks of something going wrong during a pregnancy or birth for a sixteen- or seventeen-year-old were much less severe in countries such as Sweden than here in the United States. I had obtained data on this from professional friends in Sweden. I suggested that such adolescent pregnancies had poorer outcomes in the United States because of the poorer pregnancy and postpartum health care available for adolescents here. In Sweden, where such health care for teenage mothers was quite available, the health risks were much lower than they were here. Jack Wiener in particular was surprised and very pleased by this information because it supported asking Congress to initiate new health programs for pregnant adolescents.

It was a very productive and provocative conference, and reading the papers would have been a rewarding experience for anyone in the field at that time (Green and Wiener 1980). Those of us who had presented papers agreed to write up our papers as chapters for a book that would come out of the conference. The book, like the conference, would promote improvement of the methodological quality of sex-research grant proposals so that our field could advance our knowledge more quickly. I wrote on heterosexual research, and I discussed a broad range of research issues that needed to be addressed in any research proposal (Reiss, Walsh, et al. 1980). The chapter was divided into sections on premarital, marital, and extramarital sexuality. I had plans to soon extend my own research further into the realm of marital and extramarital sexuality (Reiss, Anderson, and Sponaugle 1980). To obtain a broader range of ideas for my book chapter, I asked Bob Walsh, a 1970 PhD of mine, and his colleagues at Illinois State University, Mary Zey-Ferrell,

William Tolone, and Ollie Pocs, to work with me on the chapter. They explored sources and ideas and were very helpful to me in writing the chapter.
Other people were also preparing their chapters at the same time so that they
could be published by the government. Richard Green and Jack Wiener had
a government contract from the Alcohol, Drug Abuse, and Mental Health
Administration (ADAMHA) promising that the book would be published
by the Government Printing Office (GPO). Little did I suspect what was to
happen next. Once more, I was to confront the roadblocks put out by politicians when they encountered sexuality research.

By October of 1979, the final manuscript was at the GPO and was being
readied for printing. At the last moment, a problem developed. We were notified that someone in the printing division had seen that the papers were all
about sexuality research and had suggested to Gerald Klerman, the head of
ADAMHA, that the book was perhaps inappropriate for the GPO. Soon after that, Jack Wiener informed us all that the book had been derailed and
would not be published by the government. This happened despite the
signed contract with ADAMHA, which expressly said that the book would
be published. We had put in a lot of work, and the government had spent
considerable money to put on the conference. We were all very upset and angry at this development, but Jack Wiener told us that he would try from inside his government position to get things moving again. Dick Green contacted Plenum Press, which was publishing his journal, and asked them to
publish our book, but they pointed out that since the government owned the
copyright, the work was in the public domain. This meant that if the book
started to sell well, nothing could stop another publisher from putting their
own copies on the market. This no-profit situation in effect ruled out all
commercial publishers.

Finally, in April 1980, after six months during which nothing had
changed and the book seemed doomed to oblivion, I wrote to Gerald Klerman, the head of ADAMHA, and told him that his agency's decision to
block the publication of our book offended me deeply and that I viewed it as
a form of government censorship. I pointed out that such action defeated the
explicit purpose of his agency, which was to promote improvements in research on social problems. In my letter of April 11, I noted that his action

> caters to the narrowest, most prudish, and restrictive views of sexuality. Fear of
> publishing a book on sexuality is hardly the foundation upon which to build an
> understanding of how sexuality relates to some of our crucial social problems.
> . . . There must have been political or private moral reasons and . . . those . . .
> work to the detriment of the goals of your agency.

I was very angry, and I made it clear in my letter that I was not alone in these strong feelings. I asked him to write to me and explain his actions. In my letter, I implied that if our book wasn't published, the government would be embarrassed, because the authors would publicize its censorship behavior. In fact, I had already given an interview to *Behavior Today*, a professional newsletter, and had told them about the incident, and they had published an account of it in their January 21, 1980, issue. I hoped this would get back to Gerald Klerman and help change his mind.

I told Jack Wiener about my letter, and he told me that he would also write a letter to Klerman complaining about the decision not to publish our manuscript. He worked in the NIMH, and thus his action carried more risk than mine, and I admired him for writing his letter. In the 1960s and 1970s, Jack had always been a good friend to sex researchers, and he was showing that in his action here. Finally, in July of 1980, I received a letter from ADAHMA informing me that a decision had been reached to "make the material available to researchers engaged in this field of inquiry." That was code for saying that it would be published by the GPO. However, they shortened the book and removed the open discussions that had taken place at the meeting sessions. I wanted more than this, but I still felt good that we were able to salvage a good part of our work. But, it was not over. I was soon to learn just how slippery government bureaucrats can be, even when you think they're at least partially cooperating.

The book was finally published, but only five hundred copies were printed, and it was never advertised in their list of GPO books. To add insult to injury, about ten years later, I discovered that in my published chapter, some of my words and their meaning had been distorted. It was Koray Tanfer, a researcher at the Battelle Institute, who brought this to my attention. On page nine of my chapter in the book, I had written that promiscuity "refers to indiscriminate activity." Someone had changed this to read that promiscuity "refers to relationships with more than one partner." This is hardly a change that could be due to just a typo or printer mistake. By changing my definition of promiscuity, they had made me out as professing a much more conservative view than I ever held. There was no opportunity to examine our papers before they were published. We were told we could not change anything, and we never received any proofs. So the GPO was able to distort whatever they wanted, and there was nothing we could do. Who knows what else was distorted in other people's articles in the book? In effect, the work of our 1977 conference had been given a demeaning and distorting political treatment. The primacy of political values over scientific values in our government bureaucracies was devastatingly demonstrated in this entire event.

Unveiling the Feminine Mystique: NOW

I discovered another illustration of the primacy of politics when I attended the 1979 meeting of the National Organization for Women in New York City. I went to this meeting to get an up-close and personal view of the organization. There were very few men in attendance at the meeting, and I felt a bit awkward, but I was proud to be a member and a supporter of the cause of equality for women. I recall that the Swedes in 1976 couldn't believe that we in America had not passed the Equal Rights Amendment—a rather innocuous amendment that simply asserted the equality of women. I supported NOW as a key organization that was fighting for gender equality in many different areas of our society—including sexuality.

At one of the main sessions, Betty Friedan made a presentation. As I noted in chapter 6, her 1963 book, *The Feminine Mystique*, had been a catalyst for the founding of NOW. She was a major force in the organization and was probably at that time one of their best-known leaders. She spoke of the decreased proportion of families with two parents and children in the home. She said that only 7 percent of all families in America had two parents and children in the home. That 7 percent figure was used to indicate that the family and children were no longer the top priority for most women. Women at that time were clearly employed in increasing numbers, and NOW wanted to continue this trend. Employment for women was seen as the key to greater gender equality, and this 7 percent figure was used to indicate that employment was common and that the raising of children was less widespread than one might think.

I had just finished my final draft of the third edition of my family textbook, and I knew that she was misrepresenting reality (Reiss 1980a). The 7 percent figure was the percentage of *households* with two parents and a child, not the percentage of *families* in such a state. Millions of households consisted of the unmarried, the widowed, or the divorced, and the number of such households was on the rise. Of course, including this large group greatly reduced the percentage of households with two parents and a child. But, if you're going to play around with data in this loose fashion, then someone else might present a percentage showing how common it was to have two parents and a child. For example, you could zero in on married couples aged thirty-five to forty-four and note that over 90 percent of them had children under the age of eighteen (Reiss 1980a, 366, figure 13.4). In addition, at that time, over 90 percent of all married couples did *at some time* have children in their marriage. This, too, would give only part of the total picture needed if we were to paint an accurate portrait of the American family.

After her talk, I went up to Betty Friedan and spoke to her. I told her that the U.S. Census Bureau figures, cited above, showed very different outcomes than she had mentioned. I pointed out that her 7 percent figure was not a percentage of families but a percentage of households, and thus her statement was understating the number of families with children.

According to my notes, she said, "How do you know what the figures are?"

I responded, "I am a sociologist, and I have written a family textbook, so I keep up with these figures. If you want, I can send you a copy of the census reports with the figures I am citing."

She replied, "You expect me to believe the census figures? We know how biased the government is against working women. Getting day-care money from the government is all but impossible!"

I looked at her and said, "But the 7 percent figure you cited in your talk is itself a census figure, so you are using census data."

She shot back, "So what? That is my interpretation of the census figures!"

I was getting nowhere, so I replied, "Well, I can see that your interest is more in making the case you want than in knowing what is really happening." She laughed and smiled at me as if I had finally realized that her talk was about politics and that research accuracy was not a central issue.

I knew enough not to trust what any politician had to say about empirical reality, so I should have known that NOW might at times also be in that same category. This incident showed me how my own partiality toward the gender equality values that NOW represented had made me less able to recognize their biases until I had heard them expressed in very specific statistical terms. I still shared the goals of NOW for female equality, but I was now less ready to support any legislation they backed without carefully examining what it said. My experience at the 1979 NOW meeting reinforced my opinion that sexual scientists need to be more aware of how their own deeply held values can bias their perceptions.

The AMA: Even Doctors Want to Know about Sex

Another, different type of exposure I encountered in the late 1970s involved my work for a committee of the American Medical Association (AMA). The AMA felt that it was time for an updated edition of their book on human sexuality for use in medical schools and for general practitioners. Harold Lief, a Philadelphia psychiatrist, was given the responsibility of putting together an editorial board and selecting key people in the area of human sexuality to write the papers for this book. Harold Lief knew of my work, and he asked me to be one of his eight editors and to write one of the chapters. I asked Frank Furstenberg, a sociologist from the University of Pennsylvania whose work I liked, to jointly author the chapter with me so that it would express more than just my perspective.

Writing that chapter on premarital, marital, and extramarital sexuality in America with Frank Furstenberg was a good experience. He was a fine scholar and someone I respected for his insightful historical work on the family in his 1967 dissertation at Columbia under William "Si" Goode, a well-known Columbia University sociologist whom I briefly mentioned in chapter 4. I soon found out that Frank's values were somewhat different than mine. This experience showed me more about how values can unconsciously slip into a person's research-and-theory work. For instance, when Frank didn't personally like a trend in sexuality that I wrote about, he would ask for much more supportive evidence than when I wrote about a trend he did like. I was doing the same thing in my reactions to what he was writing. For example, when Frank wrote about the negative consequences of teenage pregnancy, I asked for more evidence to support his perspective. My positive attitude toward consensual sexuality caused me to want to see very rigorous evidence of any negative outcome of consensual sex. So, we acted as good checks on each other, and we ended up with lots of evidence for whatever we asserted about sexuality in our chapter. If you are the sole author of a piece, you don't get this coauthor feedback benefit, but you can be sure you'll get feedback from other sexual scientists once they read what you've written. This process helps keep us all more honest and fair in our work.

I had one important disagreement with the editorial board concerning the gender references in the book. I mentioned to the board that in all the chapters, doctors were consistently referred to as men. I suggested to the board that in at least some instances we should use phrasing to indicate that women are also doctors. The board was composed of eight men and one woman—Domeena Renshaw, an MD. I was sure that she would support my suggestion. But, to my surprise, she did not rally to my side. Harold Lief, the chair, responded to my suggestion by saying that it was too cumbersome and could confuse the reader, and that since most doctors were men, it was not really a misstatement to refer to them with male pronouns. I pointed out that the number of females in almost all of our medical schools was increasing and indicated that this meant we would soon have a much higher proportion of women doctors, and I didn't want to alienate them. But I didn't carry the day. The book came out in 1981, and doctors were referred to exclusively as male (Lief 1981). The late 1970s was a time when feminists were promoting the use of the word *woman* instead of *girl*, *chair* instead of *chairman*, and so on. I supported such changes, and I was sorry I couldn't persuade others. To be fair to the AMA, I should note here that I believe things are quite different today because the AMA seems to have moved toward a much more pluralistic view of sex and gender.

Fighting an Obscene Antipornography Bill

This last narrative displays a fascinating mixture of politics, science, and advocacy. It deals with the emotionally charged issue of pornography. In the 1970s, there arose an antipornography subgroup of women who identified themselves as feminists (English, Hollinbaugh, and Rubin 1981). They were becoming more and more vocal about their opposition to what they called pornography. Many of them felt that pornography led to rape and violence against women and that it therefore should be banned. In the early 1980s, they found their leaders for this movement in Catherine MacKinnon, from the University of Minnesota law school, and Andrea Dworkin, a New York lawyer and writer. MacKinnon and Dworkin were promoting legislation that would make it criminal to publish anything that "subordinated or degraded" women. They saw pornography as the subordination and degradation of women and thus as a violation of women's civil rights.

The legislation they proposed was quite vague and was clearly a violation of the First Amendment, but that didn't stop them or their supporters. MacKinnon was desperately trying to get the city of Minneapolis to adopt her antiporn legislation. It was apparent to Mayor Fraser that the proposed law violated the First Amendment's right of free speech. Nevertheless, the members of the Minneapolis City Council were politically motivated to support this legislation and thereby show their constituencies that they defended the status of women. Mayor Fraser openly opposed the bill and indicated that if it was passed, he would likely veto it on the grounds that it was unconstitutional, for it violated the right to free speech guaranteed in the First Amendment. MacKinnon and Dworkin indicated that if the mayor vetoed, they would simply reintroduce the bill to the city council. Regardless of Fraser's veto threat, the Minneapolis City Council passed the bill on December 30, 1983.

I saw pornography as a paper tiger that simply *reflected* the gender inequality in our society. I did not see it as a significant *cause* of this inequality. I sat on the sidelines during the city council's first set of hearings in December 1983. Then, just hours after the bill was passed, Sheila Leik called me. She was the wife of Bob Leik, a colleague of mine in the sociology department at the University of Minnesota. She and Bob were friends of ours. She asked me what I was going to do about this second attempt to pass the bad legislation. According to my recollection and notes, when she heard that I had no plans, she said,

> Ira, this is your chance to use your knowledge for the good of our community. Ask the mayor and the council for permission to testify. You're a professor here at the U, and your specialization is in human sexuality, gender, and the family. You're a perfect fit. Don't keep silent and let the bigots win the battle here.

Sheila was right, and I told her that I would do as she suggested. I wanted to break down the artificial wall between scholarship and the application of that scholarship to community problems. I felt it was time for scholars to have a larger role in policy making, for otherwise their positions would be largely ignored or distorted by those in politics. I just needed a little push to break through my inertia, and Sheila provided that push. There wasn't much academic support in science for doing this. It was thought by many that scientists should not get involved in political issues, for fear that it would indicate bias in scholarship. I did not endorse this view, for the presentation of evidence for the effectiveness of one approach to a social problem over another is not bias. The participation of scientific research professionals was particularly important in areas of high emotionality, such as in issues concerning sexuality and gender. It is precisely in such areas as these that strong ideological values can blind many people to what the reality of the situation is and how best to handle it. I had presented some testimony on political issues over the years. Back even in 1966, when I was in Iowa City, I had testified in support of liberalizing Iowa's restrictive abortion law. I was glad now to have this opportunity to show the value of sexual science in dealing with pornography, and I was grateful that Sheila had helped pull me out of my lethargy.

Shortly after calling me, Sheila called Kathy O'Brien, a liberal Minneapolis council member, and encouraged her to talk to me about my views on pornography. O'Brien called me later that day and asked me for my views on Ed Donnerstein's previous testimony in support of MacKinnon and Dworkin's bill. Donnerstein was a psychologist at the University of Wisconsin who had conducted experimental studies on the impact of showing erotic materials to male college students. I told O'Brien that I disagreed with Donnerstein's previous testimony in favor of the legislation, and I told her that I would detail the evidence and reasoning from my own work and from Donnerstein's when I testified to the city council. I decided that I should also write a letter to the mayor encouraging his continued opposition to the legislation. I wrote Mayor Fraser the next day and explained some of my evidence and reasoning and asked him to allow me to testify before the city council.

I knew that Donnerstein would be asked back to testify, and I wanted to be there to argue against him if he again showed support for what some called the proposed "subordination ordinance." Donnerstein's own research showed that it was the display of violence in videos that produced an aggressive response in college subjects and that this response was not increased or decreased by the presence or absence of explicit sexuality. Violence in the videos, not sexual explicitness, was clearly the primary cause of whatever aggressive responses had occurred in Donnerstein's experiments with college students. Donnerstein, himself, had not clarified this important fact in his previous testimony, and I didn't want that to happen again. I also pointed out to the mayor that many of the citizens who supported the proposed legislation were not gender-equal people who were trying to give women more power. Rather, they were conservatives who opposed increasing gender equality. Supporters of this type of legislation had been shown in national surveys to be people whose sexual values opposed explicit sexuality even if it had no harmful consequences. A few days later, on January 5, 1984, Mayor Fraser vetoed the first MacKinnon-Dworkin Bill that the city council had passed. Here are some key parts of the mayor's veto statement:

> The remedy sought through the ordinance as drafted is neither appropriate nor enforceable within our cherished tradition and constitutionally protected right of free speech. The definition of pornography in the ordinance is so broad and so vague as to make it impossible for a bookseller, movie theater operator or museum director to adjust his or her conduct in order to keep from running afoul of its proscriptions. . . . An administrative panel would decide what can be sold, distributed or shown in the City of Minneapolis. When issues of free speech are raised, granting the decision-making power to an administrative panel is troubling to me. Some might call it a Board of Censors. . . . The ordinance . . . seeks to ban material that meets two requirements: it must be a) sexually explicit and b) degrading to women. But sexually explicit material that is not obscene is protected by the First Amendment. Also protected is the expression of abhorrent or detestable ideas such as the claim that women are mere sex objects or otherwise to be thought of in degrading terms. . . . The chilling effect of an overly broad ordinance is well known.

Shortly after the mayor's veto, I received a letter from Charlee Hoyt, a Minneapolis City Council member. My letter to the mayor was now public, and Hoyt was quite critical of what I had said to the mayor. I wrote back to her responding to her criticism. Here is some of that letter wherein I argued, in agreement with the mayor, that the bill compromised the First Amendment:

> I can quickly summarize my personal views on the second issue concerning the relation of First Amendment rights to erotica. I happen to be Jewish and I am aware that there are movies, books, and other publications that say things about Jews that I consider in error and hostile to Jews. Some of these may in some minor ways shape people's views of Jews in a negative direction. Should we then have a law that forbids such presentations because they compromise my civil rights? Should we do the same for Catholics? For Blacks? What amount of free speech would be left if we took the same logic of the pornography ordinance and applied it to all groups? . . . The best antidote to ideas to which we are opposed is not to try to stifle that idea, but to present a better idea concerning how to create the type of society we prefer without restricting our ability to discuss freely. Instead of this, the proposed ordinance tried by legal decree to declare a whole series of sexual presentations as subordinating women and to thereby restrict our rights to our own judgments about what we view.

After this exchange with Charlee Hoyt, Catherine MacKinnon sent me a copy of a letter she had just written to Kathy O'Brien. O'Brien had criticized her for not bringing in a broader array of expert testimony on pornography. MacKinnon's letter to O'Brien criticized her opposition to the legislation on pornography and said that MacKinnon now knew that O'Brien had "solicited the letter from Ira Reiss which the Mayor secretly used as part of the basis for his veto." She went on to say that I had talked in my letter only of egalitarian erotica, and thus what I had said was irrelevant to her legislative proposal. Her comments were incorrect. As I've noted above, it was Sheila Leik who asked me to get involved and write to the mayor. Also, I had made it clear in my letter to the mayor that I was not just talking of egalitarian erotica. In fact, I had explicitly referred to violent, nonviolent, subordinating, and other forms of erotica. I use the terms *erotica* and *pornography* interchangeably, but I prefer the word *erotica* when referring to explicit sexual materials because I feel it is less loaded with negative cultural meaning. Even though two words may refer to the same behavior, I try to use the more neutral terms in all of my writings. Thus, I prefer *premarital sex* to *fornication*, *extramarital sex* to *adultery*, and *erotica* to *pornography*.

I wasn't going to let MacKinnon's misleading letter go without a response, so I wrote back to her in a January 25 letter and sent copies to the city council, the mayor, and others as well. I explained to MacKinnon that I had reported on research that utilized the full range of sexually explicit materials, and surely not just gender-equal sexual materials. I informed her that her key expert witness, Ed Donnerstein, was one of researchers I had discussed, and thus my work was not "irrelevant." I then concluded by saying,

> If your capriciousness in judging what I said in my letter to the Mayor and your dogmatic view of scientific interpretations are taken into consideration, they raise serious questions about the empirical bases of the proposed ordinance. Much of your thinking seems based on your subjective certainty that you are in possession of "the truth" regarding pornography rather than upon any overwhelming scientific data. You are entitled to your private opinions but I do object to your attempting to transform them into a law for all to obey without the careful empirical examination that should be the basis for any such radical change in our First Amendment rights.

I did not hear back from MacKinnon. On March 6, 1984, the city council's task force on the MacKinnon-Dworkin ordinance took up the issue once again, and Donnerstein and I were asked to testify together. Donnerstein was probably the best-known social-science author of research on the impact of explicit sexual materials. I had read his work, and I thought he had not accurately represented his own research when he had testified in December. At that time, MacKinnon and Dworkin had said that his testimony was supportive of their ordinance. I was eager and ready to challenge that interpretation when we walked into the task-force chambers. Donnerstein and I sat down next to each other, and I was asked to testify first.

I first detailed a number of findings from the 1970 National Commission on Pornography and spoke of more-recent work as well, and I pointed out how all this evidence pointed to the absence of a causal impact of pornography on acts of violence or "subordination" of women. I also reported that I had recently examined six different nationally representative samples gathered by the National Opinion Research Center's annual General Social Survey, which found that those men and women who had seen an X-rated movie in the past year were *more* gender equal than those who had not see an X-rated movie (Reiss 1986, 182–84). So there was no evidence of any negative impact of seeing X-rated videos, and in fact those who did *not* see an X-rated movie were clearly *not* champions of gender equality but rather were people who were *less* supportive of gender equality. It would be very difficult to maintain the belief that viewing explicit sexual materials produces negative attitudes toward women after learning of this direct correlation between gender equality and the viewing of erotica that I had found in all six national surveys.

Having set the stage with these data, I then turned to Donnerstein, with whom I had corresponded in the past but had met in person just that day. I said to him that I would proceed to present his relevant research on the impact of sexually explicit films. In his research, he had divided his subjects into four groups: one group was not exposed to any sexual materials, a second group was exposed to sexual materials that were nonviolent, a third group was exposed to sexual materials that were violent, and a fourth group was exposed to nonsexual materials that were violent. Donnerstein's own results showed clearly that violence alone was the most likely to produce angry responses by the males in the experiment. Sexuality without violence did not do so, regardless of how "subordinating" it might be. His own conclusion was that sexuality plus violence did not produce more aggression than did violence by itself.

I looked at Donnerstein, who was sitting next to me, and asked him how he could have allowed his testimony to be interpreted as being in favor of an ordinance that asserted that there was a connection between "subordinating" sexual materials and violence against women. He looked at me with a puzzled expression and paused for a few seconds. Then he said that he had not testified "in favor" of the ordinance. He said that MacKinnon and her supporters may have taken his earlier remarks that way, but he had not explicitly said that he supported their ordinance. Donnerstein added that he agreed with my interpretation of his research. I had not been at the previous hearing, so I could not judge his earlier testimony. However, Donnerstein had never spoken up before then to say that his research did not support the legislation. When the meeting ended, Donnerstein came up to me and suggested that we all have dinner together and talk further. He was clearly severing any ties he may have had to MacKinnon's legislation. In the years after this encounter, Donnerstein was to testify *against* legislation that restricted sexually explicit materials or that blamed such material for rape or other violent acts against women (Donnerstein et al. 1987).

I had given expression to more of my applied interests at the hearing, and I felt good about it. Many research professors discourage any scientist from testifying for or against a particular piece of legislation. However, I feel that if you have data relevant to a proposed law, then you should move to present it. In fact, after this experience, I would go further and say that if you have such data and do not present it, then you are neglecting your scientific duty to your society. It is our society that supports our research, and when we can, we should use our research to benefit our society.

What happened to the "subordination" porn ordinance in Minneapolis? Despite my testimony and that of others, it was passed by the city council, the mayor vetoed it again, and that ended its life in Minneapolis. Political considerations may well have trumped considerations of scientific reasoning for those on the city council. The city council members represented a constituency, and they may have been afraid of losing votes. In addition, they knew the mayor would once again veto what they passed, and thus they may have concluded that their vote wasn't important. MacKinnon didn't give up on her legislation, though. She took her "subordination" ordinance to Indianapolis, Indiana, where it passed in April 1984 and was quickly challenged and sent to a federal court. The American Civil Liberties Union (ACLU) supported the lawsuit against this legislation, and I supplied them with an affidavit containing my opinion concerning the proposed legislation's lack of merit. The MacKinnon-Dworkin legislation was ruled by the federal court as an unconstitutional violation of our First Amendment rights (Strossen 2000).

A number of years later, MacKinnon and Dworkin finally succeeded in getting a Canadian legal decree that favored their approach. My Canadian friends tell me that it has since been used primarily against gay-and-lesbian bookstores in Canada. Interestingly, some of Andrea Dworkin's own books were found to violate the very antipornography law she had authored, and they were banned in Canada. In fact, at one point, she was detained on her way into Canada for trying to bring her "female-degrading" books with her. Perhaps she thought she should be exempt from her law, since she had helped write it. But her own law had come back to hurt her. This result clearly demonstrates the risk of trying to restrict free speech. If you try restricting our First Amendment rights of free speech, you may ultimately end up restricting your own rights.

~

CHAPTER EIGHT

An Insider's View
of a Major Crisis in SSSS

By 1980, the sexuality organizations that had been formed years earlier were suffering from growing pains and other serious organizational problems. Just like people, professional organizations require nurturance and caretaking in order for them to flourish. As organizations or people age, their needs and ability to handle things change markedly. Unless this is recognized and changes are made, serious disorganization, and even dissolution of the organization, can result. Such a crisis situation is exactly what confronted the Society for the Scientific Study of Sexuality, SSSS, in 1980. These crises occur repeatedly in an organization, so it is important for those of us who want to advance sexual science to understand how these crises come about and what is involved in working through them. So, I will try to illustrate this process by relaying the story of what happened when this sort of serious crisis afflicted the SSSS. Giving the reader an inside view of the board meetings and other professional interactions of SSSS affords a window into how professional sexual scientists relate to each other, as well as how they relate to their organizations. I shall reconstruct these events from letters, notes, my journal entries, my memory, and the minutes of key board meetings (SSSS Board Minutes 1980–1981).

Wanted: One Gunslinger as President of SSSS

In January of 1980, I received a phone call from Dick Green, the psychiatrist I mentioned earlier as the founder of the International Academy of Sex

Research. He was also very active in SSSS at the time and had been president from 1976 to 1978. He told me that SSSS was in serious trouble. It was losing members and money and was suffering from disorganization and conflict that threatened the organization's very existence. Dick said they needed someone who would reorganize SSSS in a way that would stop this downward spiral. He asked me to run for president in the election scheduled to take place a few months later and help the organization to survive.

As one of the charter members, I felt a strong obligation to do what I could to help SSSS survive the crisis. I accepted Dick's request that I run for president. I ran against Vern Bullough. Vern was a well-respected historian of sexuality from California who had started a sexuality-education program at Northridge State College in the Los Angeles area. He received the full backing of the western region in his candidacy. The eastern region backed me. I won by just a handful of votes. I was pleased to win, but I didn't yet realize the full extent of the disorganization I would have to deal with.

Baptism of Fire: September 1980

I was scheduled to take office in November of 1980. The president of SSSS in 1979–1980 was Bill Hartman. Bill was a PhD in sociology who had become a sex therapist and was following the Masters and Johnson format in his therapy approach. He had been raised as a Mormon but had rejected his religion as too narrow. He did sex-therapy work together with his partner Marilyn Fithian. They soon developed their own therapeutic ideas and made some bold innovations in the Masters and Johnson protocol. In the summer of 1979, just months before Hartman took office, the board, at the suggestion of then-President Leah Schaeffer, decided to hire Connie "Tina" Wheeler to be a part-time executive director of SSSS. It had become obvious that someone was needed to help run the organization, and Tina Wheeler had been volunteering to help for a few years. As a hired part-time executive director, she could now be paid for her efforts.

In September 1980, I went to my first executive board meeting at the St. Moritz Hotel in New York. The full board meeting was scheduled for the next day. I was aware that I was thought of as the "gunslinger" who would try to clear up the mess in SSSS, but I did not expect the problems of SSSS to be on display at that meeting as obviously and bluntly as they were. I was about an hour late due to flight delays, and the executive board meeting was under way by the time I entered the room. Bill Hartman introduced me as the president elect to the executive committee, which included Leah

Schaeffer (past president), Clive Davis (editor of the *Journal of Sex Research*), Tina Wheeler (part-time executive director), Daniel Herzog (treasurer), Robert Reitman (western region president), Charity Runden (secretary), and John Sumerlin (eastern region president).

After I greeted everyone, Bill resumed what he had been talking about. The first comment I heard was Bill Hartman questioning Tina Wheeler about her membership status in SSSS. Tina had been a member for years, but when she first joined, she had not filled out a membership application. Tina was clearly bothered by Bill's question about her membership status and told him that she obviously was a member but that she had never filled out the application form. Bill responded by raising the issue that Tina might not be qualified for membership. Tina looked a bit shaken and upset. Bill then made the suggestion that the executive board dismiss Tina as part-time executive director. There was some discussion about this by a few people, but no action was taken. Bill then said that at the full board meeting the next day, he would raise a motion that the board dismiss Tina Wheeler as part-time executive director. This blatant clash between Bill and Tina was just one of the problems that surfaced at this meeting.

The meeting then moved on to economic matters. The organization was in a financial crisis, without sufficient funds to pay bills on time. The treasurer, Daniel Herzog, said he did not have the financial books in his possession. I asked him how he could handle money matters without having any of the financial books in his possession. It seems that Frank and Mary Westervelt in Baltimore were the paid executive secretaries, and they kept the financial books. I asked Herzog how he and the Westervelts integrated and shared financial knowledge and how they handled disbursement of funds. The answer revealed a good deal of acknowledged confusion and showed that financial decisions were being made by many different people without consultation or clear authorization.

As the meeting went on, I sat wondering what I had gotten myself into. I had walked into an executive board meeting and had found the president questioning whether the part-time executive director was a member of the organization, and the treasurer did not have the financial books of the organization. I spoke calmly, but my feelings of dismay were growing. Bill Hartman announced that he would ask me to run part of the full board meeting the next day so that he could argue for dismissing Tina. I was really being placed in the middle of a battle between Bill and Tina. I felt that it was very important that I be as impartial as possible at the full board meeting the next morning.

On the next day, the entire board met. As it turned out, there were only twelve people there—twelve out of the thirty-two still-active board members, out of an original board of forty-five. I asked about a quorum and was told that there were no constitutional rules about quorums, so twelve was enough to hold an official board meeting. Since Tina was the main topic, I thought she would appear to defend herself, but she wasn't there. Leah Schaeffer, who had originally asked the board to appoint Tina as part-time executive director, also did not attend. Leah's absence could be a major blow to Tina's cause, because she was her main defender. I didn't know why she wasn't there. The other six executive board members were present, plus six other regular board members. Shortly after starting the meeting, Hartman asked me to preside so that he could make a motion and be able to join in the discussion of Tina Wheeler.

Bill spoke about his problems with Tina in some detail and moved that Tina be dismissed immediately. Bob Reitman seconded the motion. I asked if the board felt bound by the written two-year agreement with her. Hartman said no, and others agreed that it was not very clear that anyone was bound by that agreement. There was some discussion, and then Clive Davis suggested that we discuss the issue but not take action at that time. This didn't get approved. Others suggested that the basis of the conflict between Bill and Tina was the conflict between the eastern and western regions of SSSS. Hartman was the first president from the western region. The board met several times a year but almost always in New York City. This meant that the entire western region, which had been started some time in the late 1960s, was underrepresented at all the board meetings. This kept the power to do things in the East and alienated the West. There was talk in the western region of breaking away from the national organization.

Clive then moved to table the entire matter until the Dallas meetings, but others said they were sick of talking about the issue, and Clive's motion was defeated. Then I suggested that we poll the entire board on Hartman's motion, since only twelve members were present, but I was told that there is no need to do this, since SSSS had no such rules about polling. The board then voted, and the motion to dismiss Tina failed. Then a compromise motion was put forth to immediately make the executive director position voluntary. That is, no more money would be paid, and in time we would reconceptualize the position. This motion passed with six agrees and three disagrees. Three members, including myself, abstained. I was asked to inform Tina of this important change in her position as soon as the meeting ended. The question arose as to who would take over if Tina resigned. Then another motion was made to poll everyone on the board by mail regarding Hartman's original dismissal motion. This suggestion passed, and I was asked to inform Tina of this motion as well.

Right after the meeting, I called Tina and informed her of the two motions concerning her that had passed. She now had time to consider them before the national meeting in November. The many fundamental problems in SSSS were quickly coming to the surface, and I was realizing the full severity of the crisis we were in. SSSS had grown in the twenty-three years since its founding and now had over six hundred members, but it had not changed its way of operating from the beginning, when there were only forty-seven charter members. The finances had been handled for years by Frank and Mary Westervelt in Baltimore. You could certainly trust the Westervelts, but their management style was rather loose and casual, and formal balance sheets were not routinely presented to the board. That is fine for a small society, but it could not work for the much larger organization that SSSS had become.

No one had set up any standards concerning regular financial reports showing balance sheets of incoming and outgoing moneys. Equally bad, there was no clear accountability as to who was authorized to take money out and what were acceptable reasons for making such withdrawals. Again, this wasn't the Westervelts' fault. The organization was not giving them clear guidance. Too many people had their hands in the financial pot, and there was no functioning national organizational structure capable of cleaning up the mess. As noted, we were now heavily in debt and unable to pay our bills. Something had to be done and done very soon.

Starting the Search for an Executive Director

It didn't take Tina Wheeler long to decide what to do about the board's actions. A week after the board meetings, I received a letter from her informing me that she was resigning her position as executive director. The proper channel for that letter was for it to go to Hartman, the current president, but given the state of their interaction at the earlier meeting, I wasn't surprised that she wrote to me instead. I called Hartman and told him of Tina's resignation. He called off the vote of the full board on her dismissal. He told me that we could now proceed with a full search for a new executive director and requested that I head that search and form a committee. I agreed fully with his feelings that we were in desperate need of a professional person to organize our finances and run a central office. Until we found a full-time executive director to oversee the organization's financial and other activities, we would be teetering on the edge of bankruptcy and dissolution. As the incoming president, I was now in charge of a critically ill patient—SSSS—and I knew that if I failed, my patient could well expire. I had helped found this organization, and I was determined not to preside at its funeral.

In October of 1980, I finished my term as president of the National Council of Family Relations (NCFR). That was a very smooth-working organization, and during my term, I learned a great deal about how to run a well-functioning professional organization. The answer in NCFR was to be found in Ruth Jewson, NCFR's long-time executive director. She did a fantastic job of planning, checking on key committees, setting up the national meeting, and making sure the treasurer and others were carrying out their responsibilities. Of course, NCFR had its own partisan politics to keep under control. Ruth worked very well with members from the left and from the right. This experience with NCFR, as well as experiences I had as president of the Midwest Sociological Society, had shown me how smoothly an organization could operate if it had a competent executive director. Presidents come and go, but the executive director usually stays on much longer than any president or board member. The executive director is in this sense probably the most important person in the organization for keeping things on a stable course over the long term. SSSS needed to be very careful in picking its new executive director.

I wanted more authorization for my search committee than just the fact that Hartman had asked me to do it, so I polled the entire board to get approval for the search for a full-time paid executive director. Almost everyone on the board supported my search (twenty-seven to three). I formed a committee with Clive Davis, who seemed like a calm, reasoned person, and Hannah Lehrman from Los Angeles, whom I didn't know but who was recommended as a good person for representing the West. At the annual meeting in Dallas in November, I would officially become president, and the full board would be meeting there. I would at that time report to them on our search committee activities. I was in for a surprise. Despite the strong vote for the search committee by the board, there was opposition to the search for an executive director that would boil over at the annual meeting in Dallas.

Denouement in Dallas

We had two board meetings in Dallas. I will combine them in my description here. I informed the board of the composition of our search committee and of our plans to have a candidate for the position of executive director presented to the board for their approval at the April 9, 1981, meeting of the eastern region. I didn't expect any opposition to the search itself, but then several people spoke up. Bob Reitman, the western region president, led the charge. Vern Bullough joined in, and they both said we didn't need an executive director, that we should just hire an office manager at much lower pay. John Sumerlin, the eastern region president, agreed with them. Leah Schaeffer and one or two others supported this opposition to a search for an executive director. I noted that the poll of the board had shown only three disapprovals of the search committee, and I wondered aloud where all the opposition was at that time. The opposition responded that when polled, they had only been approving an "endorsement of the search committee" and not an endorsement of the actual search. They were obviously playing with words, and I inquired what they had expected a search committee to do once it was endorsed.

I felt that there was something that those in opposition were afraid would happen if we hired an executive director. To some of them, it may have been, as they said, a genuine fear that we couldn't afford an executive director. But to others, it may well have been that they were afraid that they would lose some of their influence if there was a national executive director. The opposition was not a western or eastern move—as I've indicated above, there was opposition from the leaders of both regions. The people who had the most power to lose if we hired a national executive director were the presidents and their closest associates. So it may well have been the fear of losing their power to the executive director that was the common denominator in the opposition. The sudden expression of frugality didn't hold up as a full explanation. This trait had not been evident in SSSS for some time, and that was precisely why we were in such financial trouble. Besides, we were spending more money to pay the Westervelts and Tina than it would have cost to hire an executive director to do the entire job of organizing and running the society, so it was actually cheaper to hire an executive director.

Whatever their reasons, I was surprised by this sudden turnaround, and I responded to their comments in what I thought was a reasonably tactful statement. I was convinced that without an executive director, the society might well dissolve into chaos and bankruptcy. I felt it was time SSSS had a rendezvous with this organizational reality, so I said,

> I hear what you are saying, and I understand the hesitancy to move into such an important change in the way our organization is run. But it is essential that we do this. In fact, I would go so far as to say that if we do not hire a full-time executive director to organize SSSS, then we may not survive. I have gone over the books, such as they are, with the Westervelts, and we are heavily in debt and rapidly going deeper into debt. We have been afloat on a ship without a compass and without any clear destination, and we're taking on water.

We cannot go on as we have in the past. We need to end our relationship with the Westervelts. We must get a clear set of books and plan our income and expenses in a much more careful way. We cannot depend on a volunteer or a part-time person to do all that. In short, we need a professional who is fully dedicated to this job in order for us to survive.

I tried to be persuasive, but the opposition continued to say, "The finances are fine," "The Westervelts do a good enough job," "Volunteers can do it," and on and on. I was exasperated, and so I showed my feelings about the issue more bluntly: "Look, I've made my case. I think SSSS is on its deathbed. If you think I am wrong and you know better, then vote against the search. But I call now for another vote to either stop this search or to continue it and put us on the path to survival."

The opposition delayed the vote and continued to argue that we couldn't afford a full-time executive director. I reiterated that the money we paid to the Westervelts and to Tina Wheeler would be more than enough for such a position. I also said that I was convinced that we could save a good deal of money by having a centralized office for SSSS and an executive director charged with the responsibility to economize and help our organization grow and thrive.

Bob Reitman, the western region president, entered in again and, as quoted in the minutes, said, "If we have an executive director in charge, then you have another American Association of Sex Educators, Counselors, and Therapists on your hands. The uniqueness of SSSS is that its regions built it, and I wouldn't like to see this lost by centralizing a national office."

It seemed to me that we now had a near admission that the loss of regional power was the key issue in the opposition to "centralizing a national office." I told the board that I felt we had circled the issue enough, and I again asked for a vote. This time, we did vote. To my surprise, continuing the search for an executive director received unanimous approval! I couldn't believe that I had convinced all of the fervent opposition my position. I think the opposition had seen that they weren't picking up support from most of the other board members, so they decided they would make a strategic retreat and perhaps resume their full opposition in April, when our search committee would bring its selected candidate to the board. I knew that we weren't out of the woods yet.

There were other matters that I wanted to discuss at that board meeting. One was the size of the board of directors. It originally was forty-five, and then after the September meeting, J. Jones Stewart's constitutional committee had changed the constitution to make the board membership twenty-seven. I wanted a further reduction. I pointed out that at the board meeting in September, only twelve members of the then-forty-five-member board had shown up. It was demoralizing to attend such a meeting and was thus destructive to our organization. I noted that even at the meeting we were attending right then, there were only fifteen members present of the reduced board size of twenty-seven. I suggested that we cut the board from twenty-seven to fourteen, and then we could better ensure that each member would have a stronger sense of personal responsibility to attend board meetings. I further suggested that we reduce the number of board meetings to two—one at the national meeting and a second one alternately at one of the regional meetings. This would make it easier for board members to attend the meetings, and it would further contribute to the sense of felt obligation by board members to participate more fully. A motion was made supporting my suggestions, and it was approved by the board. Since this involved a change in the constitution, it had to be voted upon by the membership. They were later sent this motion, and the membership approved the change.

There was a severe lack of a national organizational presence in SSSS. There was no assurance that there would even be a national meeting each year. Some years there was, and some years there wasn't. I believe this damaged the cohesion in our organization. This lack of predictable national meetings each year weakened the value of the organization to our members and discouraged organizational loyalty. Even the minutes of the board meetings were unpredictable as to when they would be received—it sometimes took months to receive them. It seemed to me that private and regional interests were overriding any attention to the national organization and its future. The regions seemed to me to be focused on themselves, and no one was building a national organization. I can illustrate this by pointing to the cost of printing the *Journal of Sex Research*. I felt that it was exorbitant, and after the meeting, I contacted Clive Davis and told him that NCFR had their journal (the *Journal of Marriage and the Family*) printed at Stoyles Graphics in Iowa at a much less expensive rate than he was paying in New York. I calculated that we could save $8,000 a year by making this change, and that was a lot of money for us. Clive checked this out and agreed to make the change. This was another indicator that no one on the board was taking a broad view of the needs of the organization, financially or otherwise. This further highlighted the need for an executive director, someone whose job it was to stay on top of keeping the organization functioning in a productive fashion. Of course, we needed to find an executive director who was well organized and understood these things. That is precisely what I hoped our search committee would be able to do.

After the Dallas meetings, the next step was to get our search committee in full gear. We needed to advertise for the position, interview top candidates, and choose a person to be presented to the board at its April 9, 1981, meeting. There were fewer than five months to do all this, so we had to start immediately. I consulted with Clive and Hannah and prepared an advertisement to be placed in publications of the American Sociological Association, the National Council of Family Relations, and other organizations. I also sent a job-opening advertisement to a large number of college departments around the country that might have PhDs or MAs who would be interested. Clive, Hannah, and I agreed on a starting salary of $18,000. Further, we agreed to promise the new executive director that we would budget for an assistant and for an expense account that together would amount to $14,000. If you think this is cheap, keep in mind that these are 1980 dollars we're talking about.

We received forty-two applications for the executive director position. The three of us on the search committee went over all of their forms and ranked them. Then, in early March, I called the other two committee members on a conference call, and we went over our rankings and finalized our choice of the top four candidates. I contacted these four people and arranged for each of them to meet with our committee in person. I scheduled the meeting for the weekend of March 13–15 in Indianapolis. The four candidates were all good people, but after the four interviews, we all agreed that one person was clearly superior: Debbie Weinstein. She had done work with journals at the Massachusetts Institute of Technology; she had other relevant experience; and, best of all, she responded to our questions very directly and with indications of her strong organizational abilities. We told Debbie that we had selected her and that we would present her name to the board at the April 9 board meeting in Philadelphia. As it turned out, Philadelphia was where Debbie lived. I promised her that on April 9, right after the meeting, I would call her with the outcome of board's vote. It was just a few weeks away.

April 9, 1981: Decision Day

The April 9 meeting was scheduled for 7 to 11 p.m., and it was very well attended, with twenty-two of the current twenty-seven board members present. We also invited Mary and Frank Westervelt to attend the meeting. They understood that, after seven years of working for SSSS, they would soon retire, and they knew that the meeting was about their replacement. They displayed no desire to continue their work for SSSS. So, the board now had to make a final decision whether to hire Debra Weinstein as our first full-time executive director. The tension was obvious to all of us at the meeting. I felt that the future of SSSS—in fact, whether SSSS had a future—was at stake. This was, in my mind, the most important board meeting ever held by SSSS, and I was hoping to present as good a case as I could for hiring Debbie Weinstein as our first full-time executive director. I prepared some opening comments, hoping to calm things and set the stage in a positive direction for the vote. My presentation notes read,

> We function best as a cohesive board willing to work together and respect the different ideas of each other. We function poorly if we take each issue as a test of Virtue vs. Evil and turn these meetings into an adversarial procedure. We will have many important items on our agenda tonight, and we will disagree. Let's try to express our views with goodwill toward each other.

Then I asked Clive Davis to move our committee recommendation that we hire Debbie as the new executive director, to start June 1. Julius Winer seconded the motion. The members of the opposition group who had spoken up at Dallas were all there, and several of them expressed their opposition to hiring an executive director. Clearly, I hadn't converted them to my position. Both regional presidents, John Sumerlin (eastern) and Bob Reitman (western), spoke out in opposition to having an executive director. Three or four other people joined in that chorus.

After the opposition spoke, several people in favor of the motion shared their supportive views. Hans Lehfeldt and J. Jones Stewart spoke in favor of hiring an executive director and stressed how important it was to have a full-time person responsible for keeping us well organized. Their views carried weight because Hans was one of the founders of SSSS, and J. Jones was the chair of the constitutional committee. The opposition raised their favorite question as to our ability to afford a full-time executive director. Once more, I pointed out that in the past year, we had budgeted over $41,000 for Tina and the Westervelts, while the total budget for the new executive director was only $32,000: $18,000 for her salary, and $14,000 to pay for an assistant and all the expenses of the office. But there was no sign of change in the opposition. The comments went back and forth for another two hours.

Finally, the vote was taken. Many of the board members had not spoken, and so it was difficult to predict how the vote would come out. I had the ballots counted by several people to be certain of accuracy. Much to my great relief, Debbie Weinstein won, with fourteen votes in favor, six in opposition, and one abstention. To me, that vote was one of the most important victories I had experienced in my career. I had confidence that this move would turn SSSS away from the edge of the cliff toward which it had been rolling and steer it onto a much safer path. It had been an exhausting seven months since the September 1980 board meeting in New York, but the positive outcome made me feel that all the work had been well worth the effort and aggravation.

After the vote, I presented to the board for their approval the contract that I had written up for Debbie Weinstein to sign. The lack of a clear contract for Tina had been one source of argument with Bill Hartman, and so it was essential to correct that situation. One key aspect of the contract was that her raises, in addition to her overall job evaluation, would be tied to increased SSSS income from membership and the journal. She would also be responsible for the budget, for working with the treasurer on regulating disbursements of funds, and for routinely reporting all of this to the board. I was trying to set up a structure in the contract that would help ensure that SSSS would function smoothly and profitably. Debbie had asked that the SSSS office be in her home. She had a small child, which made this arrangement better for her, and she said she would not charge us for the space. This was approved by the board, and so were the terms of the contract.

I informed Debbie of the supportive outcome, and she was very happy. Not long after our April 9 meeting, I was very pleased to receive a letter from J. Jones Stewart that spoke about what had been accomplished at that meeting. Stewart wrote, "I totally agree with others that more was accomplished at the board meeting in Philadelphia than at any other time during the history of SSSS."

Just months later, Vern Bullough, who had questioned whether we should hire an executive director, indicated that he was now supportive of the position and of other organizational changes that had been made. He emphasized the value of having strengthened the national organization, and at the next board meeting he said, "There was no national until Reiss took over last year." I was very pleased to have his support. Vern was voted in as the next president, and I felt good because I knew he would continue to build on the foundation we had laid. Later, at another SSSS meeting, Leah Schaeffer confided to me that she had changed her mind and now supported our hiring of an executive director. I took this as a further sign that the old opposition to changes in SSSS was rapidly dissipating.

It was positive feedback like these comments that helped heal any ill feelings that had come out of our earlier board meetings. One reason for this increased support was the fact that, within a year, our budget was balanced, our membership was increasing, and our organization seemed to have moved out of its crisis. A lot of the credit for this quick improvement goes to the very effective actions of Debbie Weinstein, the executive director. But I also credit all the constitutional and other changes we made in the year before hiring her.

I hope this detailed account of how SSSS met its organizational challenges affords the reader some insight into the life changes that happen in an organization. For those who have been on organizational boards, this will be familiar, but for those who have not, this should give you a better understanding of what can happen (Bullough 1989). As I've indicated earlier, this crisis was not a unique experience of SSSS or of sexual-science organizations. It is a fact of organizational existence. In order to prosper, our professional organizations require the same nurturance and care that each of us needs in our personal lives.

CHAPTER NINE

~

Exploring Therapy and HIV/AIDS

Writing my family textbook and putting out a new edition every few years took a good deal of my time in the 1970s (Reiss 1971, 1976, 1980a). However, I put more about sexuality into that textbook than was in any other family textbook. After the success of my textbook, the newer textbooks started to follow suit. So, in that sense, my work on the family had a payoff for sexual science. Also, since families have a great deal of influence on the sexual attitudes and behaviors of their children, there is a direct relevance for those of us who do work in sexual science to get to know more about this influence (Reiss 1967, chaps. 8 and 9).

At about this same time, I was exploring ways that my autonomy theory explanation of changes in premarital sexuality might help explain changes in marital and extramarital sexual attitudes. I published a chapter on this with Brent Miller (Reiss and Miller 1979). Brent was a doctoral student in sociology, and his role in this paper was to check how well my autonomy theory had held up when it was researched by other sexual scientists in the years after it was first published. I did the part of the paper that proposed ways that the autonomy theory might help explain marital and extramarital sexual attitudes, and Brent covered the premarital area.

I followed through on my interest in explaining changes in extramarital sexual attitudes by exploring these attitudes in four national samples carried out by National Opinion Research Center's (NORC's) General Social Survey (GSS). I worked on this research project with Ron Anderson and G. C. Sponaugle. Ron was a colleague in sociology, and G. C. was a doctoral student

in our department at Minnesota. I was looking for what other attitudes or behaviors might explain variations in the degree to which extramarital sexuality was accepted. After carefully testing my causal diagrams on these four national samples, I found that there were three basic factors that most strongly
predicted extramarital sexual attitudes (Reiss, Anderson, and Sponaugle
1980). The three factors were measures of (1) the general acceptance of sexuality, (2) the degree of intellectual flexibility, and (3) the quality of marital
satisfaction. I should mention that, despite popular opinion to the contrary,
the quality of the marriage was the weakest of the three predictors. I was able
to integrate a good deal of my premarital autonomy theory in explaining these
results. I will not go into these findings further here, but those who are interested can check this 1980 article, and if you wish, you can further test the theory by checking it out using some of the more recent GSS data findings from
NORC. That sort of reexamination of existing theories by other researchers
is a vital part of any science. It is this type of work that helps to advance our
explanations and integrate and qualify the existing theories.

Also in the 1970s, I tried to develop a theoretical explanation that could
predict contraceptive usage. I worked on this with Al Banwart and Harry
Foreman (Reiss, Banwart, and Foreman 1975). Al was a graduate student in
sociology, and Harry was a medical doctor in the Population Study Center
here at the University of Minnesota. I used a large sample of college students
to whom Harry Foreman had administered a questionnaire on the use of
birth control. I tried to build a theoretical explanation of how college students make their contraceptive usage decisions. I sought to integrate my
thinking with existing theories in this area, including ideas put forth by
Frank Furstenberg (1971), John Kantner and Melvin Zelnik (1973), and Prudence Rains (1971).

So, in the 1970s, I had been expanding from my earlier publications on
premarital sexuality into other parts of sexual science. Two additional areas
that I explored further in the 1980s were sex therapy and government research on HIV/AIDS. These areas are very important parts of the sexual-
science field today, and so I will elaborate on my experiences with them in
this chapter.

Sex Therapy: The Program in Human Sexuality

By the 1980s, sex therapy had grown immensely from the early work by Masters and Johnson (1966, 1970). I mentioned in chapter 5 that I had some initial contact with the field of sex therapy as part of my connection with the
Program in Human Sexuality (PHS) here at the University of Minnesota.

And of course I always had friends who were therapists and whom I saw at SSSS and other sexuality meetings. But I wanted more experience observing firsthand the type of therapy that sex therapists were doing in the 1980s, and I set out to do just that.

Since the 1970s, Harriet and I had talked of possibly becoming joint sex therapists and using the model recommended by Masters and Johnson. Harriet had a BA degree in child development and family relations, and she had worked in social service and with young adults with epilepsy. She had also worked with me on all of my books. But we had not yet followed through on this possibility of becoming sex therapists. Finally, in 1986, I decided that it was time to check this out and decide once and for all if we wanted to do it. I wanted to spend much of the summer getting to know the day-to-day therapeutic operations of the PHS here at the University of Minnesota. By this time, I knew the people in the program very well. I spoke to Eli Coleman and Sharon Satterfield, the two people running the program, and asked if over a six-week period I could sit in and observe their everyday operations. They agreed and allowed me to sit in on group therapy sessions and private therapy sessions, as well as staff meetings. Of course, the patient or the group members were always asked if it was okay with them that I sit in. I remained silent during the sessions and just observed. It was a great experience for me because I witnessed discussions of sexual behaviors that were not dealt with in the typical survey or in other research formats with which I was familiar. In addition, the discussions of different cases at the staff meetings were very enlightening.

I found one case particularly different from what I was used to dealing with. This case involved a male who wanted to have a transsexual operation so that he could become a female. He had just finished serving time in prison for trying to kill his two brothers. I was present for two of the therapy sessions, each of which lasted two hours. When he talked to the therapist, he spoke about some of his ongoing violent desires. Needless to say, this made me a bit anxious, since I was sitting right next to him, and he had already been convicted of attempted double murder. He went on to express how angry he was about a variety of things, such as his father ignoring him. Of course, this may well be the reason he went after his two brothers, who were not so ignored, and perhaps it was also involved in his transsexual desire. In prison, he had met a man who was in for murder and who would not be released for another eight years. The patient wanted to wait and marry the man when he was released. But, in all his discussions of strong feelings, there was not even a hint of emotion in his voice. This made me wonder if he was really telling the therapist his true feelings or if perhaps he just wasn't very much in touch with his own feelings. I felt that this was a very complex case for the therapist to deal with. However, I only sat in for those two visits, so I don't know how the case worked out.

I also sat in on several different group therapy sessions at PHS for child sex abusers. I soon noted that there was one common reason these child sex abusers gave for their behavior: "I did it because I loved my child." This explanation was used by fathers who were having sex with their preadolescent children. One father who said this was having oral sex with his three-year-old daughter. I supposed that the statement that they loved their children was to them a justification of what they did. Many of these fathers did not start out in therapy with any regrets or any conscious realization that what they were doing could damage their child. I was struck by the revelation by many of these men that they would not relieve their sexual desires by masturbating instead of by having sex with their child. The reason they gave was that masturbation was morally wrong! Many of them had had a very restrictive and narrow sexual upbringing. Despite all that had to be dealt with, I did notice that some of the fathers seemed to be changing their sexual attitudes. The group therapeutic process was complex and difficult, but I found it fascinating to observe, and I was pleased to see at least some positive outcomes with the clients. However, I still preferred the one-on-one cases, for they allowed more depth of exploration with the client.

I also learned a lot about the Minnesota Multiphasic Personality Inventory (MMPI), which was administered to each patient. I saw how the MMPI was used by the clinic's therapists in their staff meetings when they were discussing their cases. However, I never heard discussions of the validity of the MMPI or of what other personality measures might be substituted for it. But I should add that other personality measures were utilized on the therapy clients, and these supplied much additional information. It was also informative to hear the staff's concerns about possible public criticism of the sexual attitude reassessment weekends they offered. There was care taken so that the explicit films used at the SARs would not promote widespread public criticism.

All in all, sitting in on the PHS here at the University of Minnesota was a broadening and intriguing experience for me. I recommend this sort of experience to everyone in sexual science who is not a sex therapist. The experience puts one in touch with a part of human sexuality that is not typically explored in our sexual-science questionnaires or interviews.

Further Exploration: The Masters and Johnson Institute

In June of 1985, Harriet and I had breakfast with Bill Masters and Gini Johnson when they were in Minneapolis for a meeting. We spoke to Bill and

Gini about our interest in sex therapy and told them that we'd like to visit their clinic in St. Louis for a few weeks the following summer in order to better understand how they did their therapy. They said that would be fine, and we set up a time for our visit in August 1986, right after I finished my six weeks at the PHS. I hoped that after the Masters and Johnson Institute visit, Harriet and I would finally be able to decide if we wanted to do this type of joint sex therapy. We both looked forward to the trip. My interest in doing sex therapy had been heightened during the six weeks at the PHS, and I wanted to see if that feeling would be sustained after visiting the Masters and Johnson Institute.

When we arrived, Bill and Gini suggested that we sit with the clinical trainees and listen in with them on the therapy sessions. The trainees were working toward their certification as sex therapists. Each day, we all listened to a case and then discussed it within our group and with the therapists on the case. Unfortunately, we couldn't observe what was happening in the therapy sessions, but we could listen in on the therapy session that Bill Masters or other therapists were conducting with a particular patient. The patient was told that the session was being recorded for the benefit of the therapy trainees. Bill and Gini would at times come in and sit with us for hours to discuss any cases that interested us. We were being given the VIP treatment, and we made it clear that we very much appreciated their generosity with their time and accommodations.

The trainees and we sat around a large table in a room away from where the therapy was being conducted. After we listened to the live recording of the therapy session, the therapist on that case would come in to talk with us and discuss the case in detail. In addition, there were general sessions at the end of the day at which Bill and Gini would discuss some of the more challenging cases. Harriet and I learned a great deal during the two weeks or so that we were at the institute. I viewed the Masters and Johnson therapeutic approach as a well-run, competent method, with seemingly excellent therapeutic results for the patients. I felt that the staff at the institute was very well trained in the dual-therapist model that Masters and Johnson promoted. The therapists seemed to communicate easily with each other and acted quite professional with the other therapists and with their patients. By the time of our visit, Gini had stopped doing therapy and was instead the director of the institute. But she did come in and talk with us from time to time. She was thinking of retiring, but Bill did not ever want to retire.

One aspect of their treatment protocol that I valued highly was the "sensate focus" technique. Gini informed me that she was the originator of the technique. The idea was based on what had worked for her and her patients over the years. Basically, it involved a nondemanding environment in which a couple was to learn what kind of massage, or stroking on what area of the body, was most enjoyable to each of them. They would each take turns at being the subject. They were clearly told that kissing or other sexual acts were not supposed to happen during these sensate focus activities. It seemed to me that this directive was a good way to reduce performance anxiety. I thought of sensate focus as a sort of adult version of "playing doctor." In both cases, you are exploring each other's bodies, but without any necessary goal of having sex with the other person.

The Masters and Johnson therapeutic approach also stressed not blaming the other person and instead taught their clients to use "I" messages, wherein both people state how they personally feel, rather than blaming their partner for their feelings. The therapists informed the patients of the risks of performance anxiety while having sex. They wanted the patient to avoid becoming overly self-conscious so that they could more fully enjoy whatever sexuality they were having. The therapy format they used lasted for only a two-week period, so patients had to work every day on the therapeutic advice they were given and practice implementing it with their partner. There was no time to explore each person's background in great depth during the two-week session, so interpersonal skills were taught to allow the couples to pursue that goal further on their own.

One of the key assumptions of the Masters and Johnson approach that was constantly mentioned was that "sex is a natural function." I did not really like that assumption, because it implied that all you needed to do was get the societal roadblocks out of the way, and then you would be able to have a satisfying sexual life. I didn't believe that sex in humans worked "naturally." I saw it as requiring societal input that structured people's sexual attitudes and behaviors. I thought Harry Harlow's monkey experiments in the 1960s had given strong support to that perspective, even for monkeys (Harlow 1962). Harlow had found that monkeys raised in isolation were unable to function sexually. I saw our biological inheritance as giving us the hardware for sexuality, but hardware by itself will not function in humans or in computers. You need to add software to program sexual behavior, and I saw the software, not just the roadblocks, as coming from society. Of course, if you had a societal roadblock that restricted all marital sexual behavior, it would have to be removed, but the person would then need to find a more compatible societal input concerning sexual attitudes and behaviors. I talked to Bill and Gini about this, and they showed no strong opposition to my perspective. Nevertheless, they did not incorporate this type of thinking into their program.

In point of fact, despite their "natural function" slogan, they were themselves doing much more than just removing roadblocks. For example, they told one woman that if her husband woke her in the middle of the night, she should have sex with him, even if she was not in the mood. That's doing more than removing roadblocks. I would guess that this advice is something that many wives would not easily accept. So, in addition to removing social roadblocks, there was a need to deal with changing the attitudes of their clientele and to do so in ways that would work for both people in the sexual relationship (Kleinplatz 2001, introduction and chap. 6).

One very interesting case that we listened in on and discussed with Bill Masters was that of a married patient who told Bill that he had fantasies that involved having sex with men, and he was worried that he might be a homosexual. Bill asked him, "Have you ever had sex with a man?" The man replied that he had not. Bill then very firmly and loudly said to him, "You are not a homosexual!"

The man replied, "Oh thank you. Thank you very much! Coming from William Masters, that is something that I can truly believe."

I never did figure out the basis for Bill's statement to this man. Of course, you could be a homosexual and never have a sexual relationship with the same gender, just as you could be a heterosexual and never have a sexual relationship with the other gender. Bill seemed to be using his insight and years of experience to support some of his therapeutic statements in ways that I did not fully grasp. There was an unexplored aspect of this case that I felt was significant. The wife had a good deal of premarital sexual experience, but the husband did not. Perhaps this difference was a part of the man's self-doubt about being a heterosexual. In any case, I thought that in this instance and others, Bill was somewhat too authoritative. One of his favorite phrases was "The answer is . . . ." I thought patients would develop more of their own problem-solving abilities if this teacher-student format were reduced.

One night, when the four of us went out to supper, Bill and Gini asked us why we had come to the institute. I told them again that Harriet and I were thinking about becoming sex therapists, and our visit to the institute was a way to learn more about what was involved in doing sex therapy. I also noted that I was thinking of using my expanded awareness of sexual problems to develop my thoughts about ways in which our society contributes to the sexual problems that people present. I was indeed looking to write a book on the ways that societal attitudes produce sexual problems. I had been thinking of focusing my next book as a critique of American values and pointing up the relevance of some of these values to sexual problems, particularly our very high rates of teen pregnancy, rape, AIDS, and child sexual abuse. I wanted to examine the evidence that our shared societal values about sexuality were producing the very problems that we condemned.

At one point, Bill shared with me that years ago, after reading the Kinsey volumes, he had decided that he wanted to work in the area of sexuality. He had found some physiological errors in Kinsey's work about female orgasm, but he said he never publicly criticized Kinsey for them. Bill was a very hard worker. In this sense, he was like Kinsey, who broke all records with his work efforts (Gathorne-Hardy 2000). Bill was always at the institute very early in the morning, including Sundays. He was always ready and willing to discuss whatever topic anyone would bring up. I should add that he would also stay every day until everyone had left.

Overall, despite some misgivings that we had, Harriet and I both gained a sense of admiration for the therapy work that Bill and Gini's institute was do-ing. The therapy did indeed seem to be quite helpful to most of the patients we monitored. However, I felt that the clinic's follow-up, which was used to judge the patients' long-term success or failure outcomes, was not as carefully conducted as it could have been. Nevertheless, Masters and Johnson had in-troduced the entire field of sex therapy to our country in the late 1960s, and they had thereby done a great deal of good for the psychological health of many people. So I had no doubt that they were both valuable pioneers for sex therapy. But let's remember that pioneers build the first roads—they don't build the final roads. There is always more for others to do.

So, what became of Harriet's and my thoughts of possibly doing joint sex therapy? After the extensive investigation during the summer of 1986, I de-cided against doing sex therapy. I found that I would be interested in a case primarily up to the point when I felt that I understood why the person acted the way he or she did. I did not feel that I would have the persistence to then stay with patients over a period of months to help them gain insight and work with them during the extended process of overcoming their problem. I felt that was important to do, for I thought therapy needed to go on for more than the two weeks that Masters and Johnson used in their therapy. Harriet maintained her interest, and I am certain that she would have had the pa-tience to follow through on her analysis. During our time at the Masters and Johnson Institute, she was very good at putting forth explanatory ideas and thinking of new therapy methods. Nevertheless, she didn't want to follow through by herself, so she also decided not to become a sex therapist. But our experiences that summer were very valuable to both of us. Our awareness of sexuality in America had indeed been enhanced by our close look at therapy in the summer of 1986.

Problems with Washington's Disease Fighters

In 1985, I was president of the International Academy of Sex Research, which held its meeting in Seattle that year. At that meeting, Pepper Schwartz, a sociologist from the University of Washington whom I had known for many years, arranged for Harriet and I to meet with King Holmes. Holmes was a very well-known epidemiologist from the University of Washington's medical school. Although I had never met him in person, I had written a chapter on societal factors influencing STD rates for a book of his (Reiss 1984). After we met in person at his home, Harriet and I met with him for dinner, and we spoke at length about the work we each were doing in the area of sexuality. We all got along quite well. I particularly liked his intense interest in his professional work and the depth of his knowledge, especially about sexually transmitted diseases. He moved the conversation into the area of AIDS, and we talked a great deal about that. Then he asked me to come to Washington, D.C., to attend a March 1986 meeting of the National Academy of Sciences' Special Task Force on AIDS. The National Academy of Sciences was the elite science group in the country, and it was working to contain the spread of AIDS. I was very pleased to be invited to this meeting. I should note here that at this time, *AIDS* was the term used, and the *HIV/AIDS* designation was not yet widely used.

As it turned out, I was the token sociologist at this meeting of the Special Task Force on AIDS. The key members were sitting around a large oval table, and the rest of us were a few feet behind them in chairs against the wall. The meeting commenced with a number of presentations by some of the people there. Mathematicians talked about ways to mathematically estimate the spread of AIDS; army generals talked about rates of AIDS in the army; and there were many epidemiologists, like King Holmes, who spoke about their understanding of the transmission of AIDS. It was the epidemiological viewpoint presented by King Holmes and others that piqued my attention. They repeatedly commented on the promiscuity of gays, saying they had to stop having so many partners if AIDS were to be contained. Others chimed in with the same message. One of these was a Dr. Baltimore, a man who had recently won many prestigious awards. He strongly supported the view that gays had to stop having so many sex partners. After listening over and over to this theme about what gays "had to do," I asked to be recognized. I tried to be tactful, but I felt there was an important point concerning the containment of AIDS that had not even been presented. According to my records and recollection, here's what I said:

> Of course the number of partners increases the risk of infection with AIDS. I am not denying that, but I would add to that important point the important role of condoms. Condoms can be a major factor in the reduction of AIDS. And from a pragmatic point of view, I ask you, what would gays more easily do: (a) become more monogamous or (b) use condoms and keep about the same number of partners? I think there is a much higher likelihood of success if we promote condom availability and use in addition to telling gays that they should reduce their number of partners. I know that trying to reduce the number of partners would have stronger political support compared to trying to increase condom usage. However, I see our task here as promoting what would work to contain AIDS rather than what is the most acceptable political strategy.

King Holmes came in at that point: "Ira, I once felt as you do, but I learned that promiscuity is the target that must be primary in the control of disease, because people just won't use condoms."

I persisted and noted, "This disease is killing many of the close friends of gay men, and that situation could produce a much stronger motivation for the usage of condoms by gay men than would be the case with other less deadly diseases. We all know that AIDS isn't herpes. This disease is deadly, and so I expect that it will be increasingly taken very seriously by gays." The only agreement with what I said came from an anthropologist at the meeting. The group moved on to other topics.

I learned from this meeting that the power structure in this important task force had very little social-science input. By far, the dominant groups were epidemiologists and medical doctors. Nevertheless, I was not excommunicated because of my perspective. In fact, I was invited to attend a September 1986 meeting of the National Institute of Allergy and Infectious Disease (NIAID) in Washington, D.C. I presented a paper entitled "What We Know and What We Need to Know about Sex." The audience there was much larger than at the National Academy of Sciences meeting in March. I found some support in this group for promoting condom use, but I also saw that there was little consensus among the various people at the meeting. The Centers for Disease Control (CDC) people played down what was known about sex because they wanted to persuade the government to fund an annual survey of sexual attitudes and behaviors. I favored that type of survey, but I didn't feel we had to deny that we knew anything at that point in order to encourage funding. By that time, there had been a number of national surveys that had included inquiries about sexuality (Reiss 1980a, chaps. 6 and 7). The most powerful element in the NIAID group also seemed to be those who were into medical and epidemiological research on AIDS. The minimal input by social scientists in these government agency meetings meant that social-science perspectives on AIDS would not likely prevail. The result was to keep in power those who were already in power in these organizations. Their viewpoints would prevail.

At the social gatherings at these meetings, I saw the rather obvious display of a much more powerful pecking order than I had ever noticed at any sociology meetings. The autonomy of individual scientists seemed much more limited in these government groups than at a university campus. Supportive of this hierarchy was the reality that those higher in rank had much more power to impact the life and career of those lower in rank. I thanked God that I was not in the federal government service.

I felt very much an outsider at these two AIDS meetings in the D.C. area. But at least they invited me, and I had the satisfaction of having presented my thoughts. As an addendum, I would note that I was right about condom use becoming more and more common among gays, as well as the nation as a whole. There has been a dramatic increase in condom use, especially from the 1980s to the early 2000s (Abma et al. 2004; Mosher, Chandra, and Jones 2005). In 2002, 65 percent of unmarried males reported that they had used a condom the last time they had intercourse (Mosher, Chandra, and Jones 2005, 4). By the end of the 1980s, government agencies were increasingly favoring the promotion of condom use (Reiss and Leik 1989). In 1988, the Institute of Medicine, which had sponsored the meeting I attended in March 1986, came out in favor of condom use in order to control HIV/AIDS (Institute of Medicine 1988, 176–77). So, things do change—even in institutes and government agencies.

CHAPTER TEN

~

Building a Cross-Cultural Explanation of Sexuality

The Linkage Theory

One other major area that I explored in the 1980s was that of cross-cultural research on sexuality. I became very interested in trying to develop a cross-cultural explanation of sexual attitudes and behaviors that would apply to all societies. I knew this was a very ambitious goal, but that was exactly what made it an exciting undertaking. During the previous fifty years, there had been work by anthropologists that had focused on a number of cross-cultural aspects of sexuality (Ford and Beach 1951; Murdock 1949). These studies and others that followed created valuable knowledge, but there was no thorough attempt in any of these works to build a global explanation of how sexuality fits into all human societies (Beach 1965, 1977; Martin and Voorhies 1975; Ortner and Whitehead 1981). In gender equality, there were some broad cross-cultural theories developed in the second half of the twentieth century (Chafetz 1984, 1990; Roos 1985; Schlegel 1972, 1977, 1979; Whyte 1978). This cross-cultural interest in gender was in part a natural outcome of the success of the feminist movement in the Western world. I was certainly interested in this type of research and theory, since it was surely relevant to any theory of sexuality. However, my goal was to do something different—to develop and test an empirically based global theory of sexuality that covered all forms of sexuality in all types of cultures. Because so little theorizing of this sort had been done, I pretty much had free rein to design from scratch a theoretical model of how sexuality fits into all types of human societies. It was a challenge that strongly aroused my interest, and one that I could not resist.

In the 1980s, there was, among many people in social science, a popular assumption that there could be no all-encompassing theory of sexuality or anything else because all societies are different (Simon and Gagnon 1984). I did *not* accept this a priori assumption about human society. Why should anyone accept such an assumption when it had never been carefully examined cross-culturally? Among others in sexual science, there was a focus on building biological explanations of social behavior and attitudes (Symons 1979; Wilson 1975). I saw no way that a shared biological human inheritance could account for the great range of cultural differences I was examining, so I did not focus on biological factors. In chapter 13, I will talk further about these other approaches. For now, though, I will focus on my attempt to build a sociological theory that could explain the universal linkages of sexuality into human society and that could also throw light on the extensive differences in sexual customs in various societies.

I started out by examining all the literature I could find on cross-cultural sexuality research. I also talked to anthropologists and others to obtain their thoughts and any new references they might recommend as being relevant to understanding sexuality cross-culturally. I was searching for carefully conducted ethnographic studies on a broad range of societies, particularly ones that included descriptions and analyses of sexual customs. For help, I turned to the Standard Cross-Cultural Sample (SCCS) of 186 nonindustrial cultures around the world. This sample of cultures from the six culture regions of the world had been carefully selected in 1969 by George Peter Murdock and Douglas White. They chose these particular 186 societies as the best ethnographical studies existing at the time. The literature on these 186 cultures was read and coded to produce a large number of characteristics describing the basic family, religious, political, economic, and educational life in each culture. The results had been coded and placed on computer tape. There were only a few sexuality variables included in this work, but even a little information on these 186 cultures was important for me to have. Fortunately for my interests, by the 1980s, there were five additional professional researchers who had added information on sexuality and other relevant areas concerning these 186 cultures. I obtained the codes for these new data (Broude and Greene 1976; Hupka 1981; Ross 1983; Sanday 1981; Whyte 1978). These additional codes plus the SCCS computer tape became one of the key sources for my theoretical work.

Defining Sexuality

I started out by trying to clarify the way I would define the concept of sexuality (Reiss 1986, chap. 2). I was developing a theory about how society influences our sexuality, so my definition of sexuality should express that societal input. Surely there were also biological and psychological factors that impacted our sexuality in all cultures. However, at this time, I was building a sociological theory, not a multidisciplinary theory. It was enough of a challenge to try to build a sociological cross-cultural theory of sexuality.

I defined sexuality as consisting of what we used to call societal roles, or what, in the more popular jargon, are now called scripts (Gagnon and Simon 1973). The sexual scripts in a society express the shared views of the group about what sexual behaviors should be pursued in order to produce erotic arousal and genital responses. The recommendations in these scripts do change over time. We can see in our own society the greater acceptance in the second half of the twentieth century of oral sex and of gay sex (Newcomer and Udry 1985). So change occurs in sexual customs over time, particularly in modern complex societies. The cross-cultural scripting of sexual practices can be seen even in what is thought of as the "accepted" sequencing of sexual acts in different societies. In Western cultures, the sequence is kissing first and intercourse last. People in our society assume that this sequence is natural and universal, but upon examination, we see that this is not the case. For example, there are nonindustrial societies in which kissing comes only *after* having had coitus (Marshall and Suggs 1971; Suggs 1966). Other differences can be seen. For instance, in some societies, women's breasts are not thought of as erotic, whereas in ours they surely are seen that way. In short, as many of you are probably well aware, the cultural scripts around the world regarding sexuality vary a great deal among different cultures. However, as I've said earlier, there is no logical reason to take this diversity as proof that there are no universal patterns in sexuality. I took this diversity as a challenge and searched for the common elements underlying it. And, as I will report below, eventually I did conceptualize universal elements in the core infrastructure of our cross-cultural sexual customs.

A great many people feel that reproduction is the only common cross-cultural element in sexuality. Of course, reproduction does have an important role in sexuality, but this does not mean that one must assume that it is the only important factor in an explanation of sexual customs. Here are some reasons to question the priority given to reproduction. First, we know there are a good number of nonindustrial societies in which the role of coitus in producing babies is not known, and there are other societies in which coitus is considered a necessary but not a sufficient cause of pregnancy (Goodale 1971; Gorer 1967; Reiss 1986, 27–31; Elwin 1939). So the sexual customs in these societies must have been formed by elements other than reproductive concerns. Further, even in Western societies, we can see that our moral judgments about sexuality are often not based on the reproductive consequences of coitus. Think of sexual acts of adults with prepubertal children. They are surely not accepted in the West, and yet they have almost no risk of reproduction. Also, think of sexual acts performed by postmenopausal women. They are accepted and valued by the participants but such acts also have no reproductive consequences. As well, gay sexuality has no reproductive consequences and yet is highly valued by those who practice it. Also, as I mentioned earlier, changes in sexual customs regarding oral sex occur and are clearly not due to any biological or reproductive factor. So, while reproduction may well be important, it leaves unexplained a great many of our sexual attitudes and behaviors. To fill this gap was my goal. I was trying to find what aspects of human society are universally involved in shaping our sexual attitudes and behaviors.

Social Bonds: Pleasure and Disclosure

My starting theoretical proposition was that the number-one factor that determines how a society judges particular sexual acts is whether or not the society believes that those sexual acts are tied in some way to strong social bonds between people. Let me explain how I conceptualize the relationship between sexuality and social bonds and thereby explain the starting logic of my cross-cultural explanation.

The two most common characteristics of sexuality in any society are *physical pleasure* and *self-disclosure*. Of course, there is no guarantee that these will occur, but no other outcome of sexual behavior occurs as much as these do. Physical pleasure as a common outcome of sexuality is not controversial. And, although there is much more that could be said about physical pleasure, this is not the place for that discussion. But what about self-disclosure? Is it really such a common characteristic of sexuality cross-culturally, or is self-disclosure just a romantic Western notion? I would argue that it is universally connected to sexuality. I would suggest that the very act of expressing physical pleasure and having an orgasm with another person is a self-disclosing action. Ask yourself this: While having sex with another person, doesn't the degree to which you pay attention to doing what pleasures yourself versus what pleasures your partner reveal something private about yourself?

To further see the self-disclosure aspect of sexuality, ask yourself how many people have seen you have an orgasm. Just for fun, and to make a point, I devised what I called an "orgasmic disclosure ratio." This ratio is the proportion of all the people who know you who have seen you have an orgasm. The ratio achieves the value of one if you have had sex with everyone who knows you, including your parents, siblings, other relatives, and all your friends. I expect that anyone with a ratio of one would likely be in jail or under treatment. A person's orgasmic disclosure ratio reveals the proportion of people who know you who have observed your orgasmic behavior. In this sense, the ratio is an indicator of the degree to which you consider having an orgasm to be a private and intimate act. Sexual relations are not usually on public display in any society, and thus they do reveal an intimate part of your self that is not exposed to everyone who knows you. At the very least, a minimal amount of self-disclosure seems to be unavoidably built into any sexual act with another person.

The basic disclosure element of sexuality, together with the pleasurable outcomes that often accompany sexuality, opens the door to further intimate revelations and thus greater bonding with a particular sexual partner. Now, of course one can take steps to short-circuit this process. For instance, one can consciously work to move frequently to a new partner in order to avoid building up intimacy and bonding. But the potential for bonding is clearly there in sexual relationships, and all societies take note of this by encouraging people to promote bonding or to avoid it. In a society with parentally arranged marriages, the sexual norms will promote casual sex only with people who aren't likely to be the parentally chosen future spouse. On the other hand, in a society like ours, with what I would call a "participant-run courtship system," there would not be the same restraint in the sexuality norms. Nevertheless, modern-day Western societies have developed a preference for stable relationships and bonding even while tolerating more casual sexual encounters. But let's be clear; in most societies, Western or otherwise, access to casual sex is granted much more freely to men than it is to women.

Sexual *and* nonsexual bonding is important in every society because of the importance of cooperation and the sharing of tasks, whether those tasks be in politics, warfare, religion, or the family. I would add here that pleasure and disclosure of some type seems also to be a common thread in nonsexual relationships, such as kinship and friendship relationships. In these nonsexual contexts, pleasure and disclosure is expressed as part of a valued close primary relationship, in hugs or nonsexual kisses and in intimate conversations. In sum, the logic I am developing says that since pleasure and disclosure are involved in almost all important social-bonding relationships, the potential for bonding in sexuality is easily recognized in all societies, and sexuality is seen as something important. This would be so regardless of whether the society encouraged or discouraged sexual behavior.

Three Universal Societal Linkages to Sexual Norms

Since sexuality's role in relation to social bonding is accepted in all societies, we can be sure all societies will find ways to regulate sexuality in one way or another. Therefore, I searched for what parts of societies might be universally linked to this regulation of sexuality. I examined the 186 cultures in the SCCS and checked over my notes on the books on other societies I had examined. This exploration took a good deal of time. As I searched for common aspects of society that were utilized to define sexual customs, a pattern of the common ways in which sexual norms are tied into all these very diverse societies gradually came into focus. I found three important parts of all societies that seem to always be linked to the ways that sexual customs are organized.

The first universal societal linkage was to *gender power differences*. I define power in the usual way: the ability to influence others despite their opposition. The second societal linkage was to *societal ideologies of normality*. Ideologies are the emotionally powerful beliefs in a society that are the sources of judging some behaviors as sexually normal and some as sexually abnormal. The third universal societal linkage of sexuality was to *kinship and extramarital-jealousy norms*. These norms define when and by which mate sexual jealousy should be expressed. These three universal societal linkages are the heart of my theory of the universal determinants of our sexual customs. I'll try now to illustrate the meaning of each of these three universal societal linkages.

Gender Power Differences

All societies have some sort of pecking order, some sort of power system, that favors those who do whatever are the highly valued tasks in that society. Let's follow this idea and look cross-culturally at female roles. If we examine the SCCS of 186 nonindustrialized cultures, we find that in all but eight of them, women have the dominant role in the family concerning child rearing. Even in these eight cultures, women have an important role in child rearing, but other roles such as economic work in agriculture take precedence, so others do more of the work involved in child rearing. In many cases, these others are the daughters of the mother or are other female relatives. So women are very heavily tied to the child-rearing role. But how much importance is placed on the role of child rearing in these societies? Does child rearing afford women equal power with men? Let's look at this question in different types of societies.

In hunting-and-gathering societies, which often have only fifty to one hundred people, the child-rearing role is important and is only slightly outranked by what men do in hunting and other areas. But, once we get to agricultural societies, the child-rearing roles of women are afforded much less power than the political, military, and economic roles that men perform. Agricultural societies, especially intensive agricultural societies, are much larger than hunting-and-gathering societies and can include thousands of people, and they are often stratified, with clear distinctions drawn between social classes. In such societies, the agricultural role is mainly performed by men, and this role is clearly at the top of the power hierarchy. So, the important point here is that by tying women to child rearing in such a society, their role is limited in other very important parts of the society, such as economic and political leadership.

This situation does not mean that child rearing is seen as unimportant—it surely is valued in virtually all societies. Those who do child rearing are often given a good deal of prestige, but not a great deal of power. The top power roles are in the economic and political systems, and so, while women may be respected and highly regarded in such societies, they only very rarely have equal power with men. I checked this linkage of child rearing to women's power in the 186 societies of the SCCS. As expected, I found that the more men dominate in the economic and political institutions of a society, the more likely it is that the society will view women as inferior to men. The societies where men dominate in the economic and political institutions are the ones where there are strong pressures for women to focus on child rearing and thereby decrease their chances of gaining equality in the political and economic affairs of that society. This evidence supports the proposition that if you want to increase gender equality, you need to afford women greater opportunities in the institutions where basic societal power resides, such as the economic and political institutions. In a gradual way, this is exactly what has been happening in the Western world during the last several generations, but clearly we are still a good distance away from gender equality.

Power affords the members of a group the highest access to whatever they desire, and this means that where women are seen as inferior to men, their access to sexuality will be restrained more than it is for men. For example, in horticultural societies, in which women, in addition to child rearing, have the dominant role in growing plants and other essential foods, women also have greater sexual rights (Chafetz 1984; Roos 1985; Whyte 1978). In fact, one of the rare cases of a possible gender-equal society is an American Indian horticultural society—the Hopi Indians (Schlegel 1972, 1977, 1979). But bear in mind that even in this and other horticultural societies that trace descent through the female line, it is often a woman's brother who takes more control than she does. Her brother belongs to her descent group, so he is in a position to usurp power, and he very often does just that. I was unable to find even one society in which women had greater power than men had, and, as noted, there were only a very few where power could possibly be said to be relatively equal (Bachofen 1861; Ellis 1938; Reiss 1981; Westermarck 1891).

Societal Ideologies: Defining Sexual Normality

This is my theory's second universal societal linkage to sexual norms. Ideologies are reflective of the most powerful values of a group. Further, the most powerful people in a group have the dominant voice in defining these values. So here, too, there is a connection to power. All of the basic social institutions, such as family, religion, politics, economics, and education, have ideological beliefs that define the "right" and "proper" ways for people to act in those specific institutional settings, and part of the family institution involves teaching sexual beliefs to the new generation. Because there is a great deal of emotion involved in these ideologies, any belief or behavior that challenges the basic ideology concerning proper sexuality for men and women will be labeled as abnormal. For example, in our society, the more orthodox religious groups define homosexuals as abnormal, whereas the more liberal religious groups define homosexuals as normal. Concerning heterosexuality, we see even today the use of ideology in our society to define women as immoral and abnormal if they have many casual premarital sexual partners. This restriction is much less likely to be applied to men. In sum, whether rooted in the family, religion, or other parts of society, there will be an ideological base that is expressed in the society's beliefs about "normal" sexuality for men and for women. The power difference between men and women that was discussed under the first linkage is what supports a society's specific notions of normal sexual behavior for men and women. Linkage one and two are clearly intertwined.

Kinship and Extramarital Sexual Jealousy

This is the third and last universal linkage in my cross-cultural theory. Kinship creates basic ties in all human societies. Marriage connects different kinship groups, and in all societies, there are norms concerning extramarital sexual relationships. Ralph Hupka examined the occurrence of husband and wife extramarital sexual jealousy in half (i.e., 93) of the 186 societies in the SCCS (Hupka 1981). I used his data to check out my expectation that the expression of extramarital sexual jealousy would be influenced by the relative power of each gender. Every society I examined showed clear evidence of extramarital jealousy. This was so even for those societies that allowed extramarital affairs under some conditions (Reiss 1986, chap. 3).

The research on such permissive societies indicates that violence can result if the allowed extramarital sex oversteps the accepted bounds. For example, you can see this in some Eskimo societies that allow a wife to sleep with a visitor. However, if the visitor starts an affair with the wife, the husband may physically attack him (Reiss 1986, 52). I believe that one important source of the universality of extramarital sexual jealousy is the universal importance placed on stable relationships such as marriage. Anything that is intrusive to marriage and thus challenges the priority of this important union in ways that are not socially accepted can evoke jealousy (Reiss 1986, chap. 3).

To further illustrate this linkage to jealousy, I looked at the data in the SCCS and searched for predictors of the expression of extramarital sexual jealousy by husbands and by wives. I found that those societies in which female *premarital* sexuality was greatly restricted were most likely to display husband *extramarital* sexual jealousy and to be more male dominant (Reiss 1986, 66–72). This indicates that the amount of control of female premarital sexuality is a measure of male power in a society. Accordingly, the greater male power is, the more likely it is that men will be expected to express extramarital sexual jealousy.

I found further support for the predictive ability of premarital sexual norms by looking at a wife's expression of jealousy. I found that a wife's jealousy about her husband's extramarital sex was highest when the society accepted female premarital sexuality. A society's acceptance of premarital sexuality in women can be taken as a proxy measure of female power in that society. In more gender-equal societies, women are given greater premarital sexual rights. When women feel that they are more equal to men, they are also more willing to express their angry and hurt feelings when their husbands have extramarital sexual relationships.

So, this examination of the conditions under which husband and wife sexual jealousy is expressed affords further support for the importance of our first linkage, gender power. In male-dominant societies, the common reaction of women to their husbands' affairs is depression. In these societies, women do not usually have the power to express their jealousy and strike back, so they turn their negative feelings on themselves.

I haven't discussed the cross-cultural data on homosexual relationships that I report in my 1986 book (Reiss 1986, chap. 6). There isn't the amount of cross-cultural evidence for homosexuality that there is for heterosexuality, and, in particular, lesbian relationships are rarely reported (Herdt 1981, 1997). Nevertheless, I would expect that any valued homosexual relationship would have its boundaries, and when those accepted boundaries are violated, jealousy is likely to develop. It would be interesting to compare the boundaries in female couples and male couples. I would expect that the freedom to have extrarelationship sex would be greater in male couples than in female couples (McWhirter and Mattison 1984). However, this is not an area that I have explored as thoroughly as I have heterosexuality, so I will leave it to others to see how well my triple linkage theory applies to homosexuality.

Summing Up the Linkage Theory of Sexuality

My cross-cultural theory asserts that the bonding power of sexuality that results from its pleasure and disclosure characteristics is a key reason for the universal importance that all societies place upon sexuality. Societies universally control sexual bonding by three linkage areas that are always involved in the structuring of the sexual customs of a society: (a) gender power differences, (b) societal ideologies, and (c) kinship and extramarital-jealousy customs. If a Martian came to our planet and asked how he could understand sexuality in our societies, I would advise the Martian to check these three universal linkage areas for an explanation of the particular sexual customs of a society.

I have presented only some of the evidence I gathered and only some of the theoretical ideas I developed, but hopefully the overall logic of my theory is clear by now. The interested reader can check my cross-cultural book for a full account of my theory (Reiss 1986). The theory I am proposing is a macro theory—it focuses on the broad societal inputs rather than on the micro interpersonal relationships that other researchers deal with (Bancroft et al. 2004; Collins 2004; Laumann 2004). My autonomy theory is more of a middle-range theory (see chapter 6). However, dealing with universals was not new to me, since I had done that in a good deal of my earlier work, such as that involving universal aspects of love relationships and universal aspects of family institutions (Reiss 1960b, 1965b). I found it very useful in those instances, and others, to specify universal characteristics, because doing so points out where one should start searching for an explanation of current or changing attitudes or behavior in a particular area. The universal aspects tell you what is not likely to change.

However, to be sure, there is a great deal of variability in exactly how these three universal linkages operate in each of the hundreds of societies on our planet. Therefore, we should work to develop explanations of how and why such differences develop in the specific sexual customs related to these three universal linkages. But, above all, I would emphasize here that there is no inherent clash between a search for universal explanations and a search for explanations of variability. In fact, as I've indicated, the search for universals leads to discovering why particular societies have their specific set of sexual customs.

There are social scientists who have developed their own concepts for further understanding sexuality on our planet (Abramson and Pinkerton 1995a, 1995b; Francoeur and Noonan 2004; Hatfield and Rapson 1996; Laumann 2004). A number of social scientists who are interested in cross-cultural explanations of sexuality have examined my linkage theory and have found it useful in their own work (Deven and Meridith 1997; Hyde and DeLamater 2006; Suggs and Miracle 1993). I encourage all of you who are interested in this area to further explore, modify, and qualify my cross-cultural theory of sexuality, or, if you wish, to strike out and build your own theory. As our world shrinks and nations increasingly become more interdependent, there is a clear need for greater theoretical understanding of our cross-cultural similarities as well as our differences.

~

CHAPTER ELEVEN

Can Sexual Science Really
Help with Societal Problems?

Early Reactions to HIV/AIDS

The sexual revolution in America plateaued out by 1980, but more dramatic changes in the sexual scene were about to appear. In a publication by the Centers for Disease Control (CDC) on June 5, 1981, an unusual new disease was reported. It turned out to be what we now call acquired immune deficiency syndrome (AIDS). William Darrow, a sociologist then at CDC, believes this disease first entered the United States during the July 4, 1976, bicentennial celebration of our Declaration of Independence. Thousands of visitors from every continent in the world poured into New York to celebrate this event. If ever there was a setting for spreading whatever diseases were active in the world, this was it. The celebration left us with a deadly hangover that we are still battling.

Despite the fact that this disease made sexuality much more dangerous, President Reagan's response was virtually nonexistent. In 1985, when the movie actor Rock Hudson died from AIDS, the president and the people of the United States paid a bit more attention. In that year, we had just identified the virus, human immunodeficiency virus (HIV), that caused AIDS. The blood supply was not screened before this, despite the fact that we could have easily screened our blood supply by checking it for hepatitis. That would have been an effective preliminary screen, because we knew that 90 percent of patients with AIDS also had hepatitis. But the blood banks didn't spend the money to do this, and the HIV virus spread a great deal during the early years of the epidemic. One reason for this indifference may have been that in these early years, AIDS was thought to be a disease that only homosexuals contracted, and thus it was not seen as a real threat to heterosexuals. So most people were not alarmed enough to do very much.

In addition, the early reaction to AIDS in the United States was moralistic, not pragmatic. AIDS was seen by some on the religious right as punishment by God for homosexual behavior. For example, Jerry Falwell, the Baptist minister who gave the benediction at Reagan's 1984 nomination, said, concerning AIDS, "You cannot shake your fist in God's face and get by with it" (Shilts 1987, 347). This moralistic response was reminiscent of how, generations ago, our country had reacted to syphilis and gonorrhea (Brandt 1987). In the 1930s, CBS Radio wouldn't allow the words *syphilis* or *gonorrhea* to even be mentioned on the radio. Congress, too, was slow in reacting to HIV/AIDS, and even by the late 1980s, it took powerful pressure by Surgeon General Koop to get the television networks to accept public health announcements and to consider accepting condom advertisements. When it came to sexually transmitted diseases, our nation had a destructive habit of catering to the narrow minded rather than protecting people's health.

It was Magic Johnson's public statement in 1991 that he was HIV infected that forced more people to realize that heterosexuals could also get this deadly disease. The denial of heterosexual risk had prevailed despite the fact that years earlier it had been reported that in Africa AIDS was almost exclusively a heterosexual disease. Many people just would not generalize that finding about Africans to themselves. Our handling of this epidemic in the 1980s made it quite clear that the sexual revolution had not discarded our narrow-minded Victorian morality. It was alive and well somewhere in our psyche. A more positive consequence of this epidemic was the increased pressure on the networks and other media to more forthrightly and openly discuss all the sexual acts that were involved in the spread of HIV. What was formally strictly controlled now burst forth in media discussions of HIV/AIDS. It took thousands of deaths in this tragic epidemic to liberalize our public discussions and thereby broaden our understanding of HIV infection and of our sexuality in general. But this was just the beginning of our knowledge concerning how to cope with this disease.

Sexual Therapists React to HIV/AIDS

How did sexual scientists respond to the HIV/AIDS crisis? As more heterosexuals began to be concerned about HIV/AIDS, the pressure to respond grew. The professional advice given by our best-known sex therapists was to focus on "dry sex," or on love, and to not trust condoms. Let me go over some of these statements so that you can judge for yourself just how helpful our sex therapists were in the 1980s HIV/AIDS crisis.

In 1988, Masters and Johnson, together with their colleague Robert Kolodny, put out a book for heterosexual couples called *Crisis*. I read the book and concluded that it presented an alarmist view of the crisis. Here are some of the assertions made in that book: "The AIDS virus is now running rampant in the heterosexual community. . . . The fact is that it is theoretically possible to become infected with the AIDS virus from skin contact with a contaminated toilet seat" (Masters, Johnson, and Kolodny 1988, 7, 93).

They went on to say that we should avoid nonlove sexual relationships. This, of course, was very popular advice to an American audience. The problem with this advice was that it did not present a careful analysis of the risk of picking up the AIDS virus from a loved one, and it did not present an objective account of the protection that condoms afforded. What was the reason for restricting sex to a loved one as opposed to recommending condom use with all partners, loved or not? After all, at that time, the estimated risk of picking up the AIDS virus from a single unprotected act of vaginal intercourse with an infected partner was one in five hundred. Just for comparison, there was a one-in-two chance for a female to become infected with gonorrhea from a single unprotected act with an infected partner. So, compared to other common sexually transmitted diseases, HIV/AIDS was not easy to contract. Of course, one would still want to minimize even a one-in-five-hundred risk, but Masters, Johnson, and Kolodny did not recommend the best method of dramatically lowering that risk—condom use with all partners, whether you were in love with the person or not. After all, realistically, your current loved one might be infected. Also, it seemed apparent to me that it was more difficult to get people to have sex only with those they loved than it was to get them to use condoms. But Masters, Johnson, and Kolodny were focused on getting people to have only love-based relationships, and the effectiveness of condoms was played down. Unfortunately, love doesn't guarantee that you never have to say "I'm infected!"

Another bit of advice came in a book by Helen Singer Kaplan, who was then a nationally known sex therapist and a professor of psychiatry at New York Hospital, Cornell Medical Center. She, too, recommended a restriction on partners, but with a different twist (Kaplan 1987). She wrote her book for heterosexual women and warned them of the risks of "bodily fluids." In my judgment, she was also an alarmist, for she noted that the bodily fluids from which you could become infected with HIV included tears and saliva. There was research evidence for the risks of semen and blood, but there was no good evidence that one could become infected from tears or saliva. The readers of her book could become afraid to kiss anyone, or for that matter to say anything that might make their partner cry! Kaplan suggested practicing "dry sex" for six months with a new partner. Dry sex included rubbing against each other and massaging and masturbating each other. Here are Kaplan's guidelines to women about what to do to protect themselves after masturbating their partner:

> You must wash immediately and disinfect the places where his semen wet you. . . . Only let him ejaculate on the dry parts of your body. . . . Scrub with soap and water in addition to disinfecting the area with undiluted rubbing alcohol or a dilute solution of Lysol. . . . If you do not wash it off it will stay on your hands and if you bite your nails or eat something with your fingers a few hours later, some virus might have survived and you could become infected. (Kaplan 1987, 111–13)

Kaplan calls this "great safe sex." Would you abide by this regimen? After a woman masturbated her partner, she would excuse herself and go into the bathroom to wash with Lysol. But remember the warning that one could pick up the infection from the toilet seat, so she better not sit down on that seat either. Wouldn't all that make for a lovely evening with your partner? But most importantly, Kaplan's precautions were based upon a gross exaggeration of the risks of infection and ignored what scientific evidence was available at the time. Her suggestions sounded to me more like a panic response than helpful advice. Furthermore, not many people were likely to adopt her "great safe sex" regimen.

Both of these books exaggerated the risks of using a condom. This was a further indication of the panic response of the authors. For example, Kaplan advised, "If he tells you that he's going to use a condom, you know that he doesn't know the facts, and you will have to educate him before you go any further" (1987, 134). And Masters, Johnson, and Kolodny advised, "[It is an] illusion that condoms confer an adequate degree of protection against the AIDS virus" (1988, 119).

Allow me to add the advice of another therapist here: Theresa L. Crenshaw, a president of the American Association of Sex Educators, Counselors, and Therapists. Like William Masters and Helen Kaplan, she was a medical doctor. She testified before President Reagan's AIDS commission and said, "For the sake of health, casual sex and multiple partners must be abandoned" (Crenshaw 1987). On other occasions, she pointed out the foolishness she saw in "putting a mere balloon between ourselves and a deadly virus."

The advice of these therapists seems to reflect their own values and anxieties about risk taking rather than a careful and objective analysis of the risks and the choice of methods for lowering them. Their analyses and the advice they gave appear to be examples of personal values trumping science. Their extreme responses would likely encourage anxiety rather than rational thinking. Do we want an emotional response to a life-threatening crisis, or do we want a calm and thoughtful analysis of various ways to minimize the risks?

Just How Risky Are Condoms?

Despite all these disparaging remarks about condoms, if we look at the conclusion reached by a group of scientists at the Centers for Disease Control, we get a rather different perspective. They suggested that condoms were very effective protection, although of course no protection can be perfect (Centers for Disease Control 1988). The failure rate of condoms was reported as 2 percent when consistently and properly used by married couples who did not want more children, and as high as 14 percent for those who did not use condoms consistently or properly. The CDC scientists noted that the great bulk of the condom failure rate was due to improper or inconsistent use of condoms and not to condom breakage or slippage. More recent research supports this conclusion and indicates that the slippage and breakage rate is between 1.6 and 3.6 percent (Centers for Disease Control 1993; Cates 2001; National Institute of Allergy and Infectious Disease 2001). Even in the mid- to late 1980s, the number of reputable researchers supporting the effectiveness of condoms kept adding up before this CDC final report. Somehow our leading therapists did not take notice of any of this.

This lack of reliance on scientific evidence by those giving advice led me in 1988 to get together with Robert Leik, a mathematical statistician in our sociology department at Minnesota, and write an article comparing the probability of infection for people who used condoms with multiple partners versus the probability for people who did not use condoms and were involved only in committed relationships. Clearly, the most effective strategy would be to do both—use condoms and stay with one partner—but people rarely did that. The typical pattern was to use condoms with casual partners and not use condoms with regular partners.

In order to compare these two strategies (condom use versus partner reduction), we built a computer probability model with people having five hundred acts of coitus in a five-year period. We allowed condom failure rates to vary up to 75 percent, and we varied the prevalence of HIV/AIDS (the percentage in the population that was infected) and other factors as well

(Reiss and Leik 1989). In short, we wanted to check out a very wide range of situations to see which method—condom use or being monogamous—was the riskiest under these different scenarios. Surely the multiple-partner risk was real. It is true that the more partners you pick, the higher are the chances of picking an infected partner. But the question to be answered was whether using condoms with multiple partners led to a higher risk of HIV infection than for those who did not use condoms but had only one or two partners over the five-year period.

Our findings were very clear: The risk of HIV infection was highest for those who restricted themselves to one or two partners and did not use condoms. Those who used condoms and had twenty partners over the five-year period had a significantly lower risk of infection. This result held up even when we assumed a condom failure rate of 10 to 25 percent! This result may seem counterintuitive to many of you, but the reasons for this outcome can be easily explained. Monogamous sex has a number of risks that must be taken into account. For example, if by chance, when you begin your five-year monogamous relationship, your one partner is infected with HIV and you have five hundred unprotected acts of coitus with this partner, your chances of picking up HIV are quite high. Also, keep in mind that extrarelationship affairs do occur, and intravenous (IV) drug use does occur, so even if your committed partner was not infected when you met, your partner may become infected over the five-year period due to an affair or IV drug use. The lack of condom use and the repetition of hundreds of sex acts with one person means that any infection is likely to be passed on.

On the other hand, those who use condoms with multiple partners have powerful protection against picking up HIV. Even if some of the partners are infected, and the condom failure rate is 10 to 25 percent, the use of condoms will block 75 to 90 percent of the possible exposures to the virus. Add to this that you are only having a fraction of your five hundred sexual acts with any one partner, and that too greatly lowers your risk. The advantages of not having many acts with one partner become clearer if you consider that HIV even without any condom use has only a one-in-five-hundred risk of infecting you, and with condom use, you are blocking out the majority of even that low one-in-five-hundred risk. In addition, if you use condoms carefully every time, you can reduce your risk to well below the 10 percent minimum risk that we were assuming in our study. What all this means is that the reduction in risk afforded by using condoms is far greater than the reduction in risk afforded by staying with one partner and not using condoms. Of course, as I have noted, the safest path to take would be to have one partner and use condoms with that partner, but that's not a common choice.

The validity of this analysis is brought home when you read the CDC reports on HIV infection among women. These reports state that the majority of women with HIV were infected while in a monogamous relationship. Unfortunately for them, their partners often were either not monogamous or were IV drug users. In 1988, the Institute of Medicine of the National Academy of Sciences, a highly regarded institute that I spoke of in chapter 9, came out in favor of making condoms more available and promoting consistent use of them to avoid HIV (Institute of Medicine 1988, 176–77). Throughout the 1980s, others were also joining the call to promote condom use for the prevention of HIV infection (Hearst and Hulley 1988). The 1995 National Survey of Family Growth reported that condom use tripled between the 1970s and the 1990s (Abma et al. 1997). So finally more people in America were learning to protect themselves (Darroch et al. 2001).

Is Abstinence the Safest Strategy?

In the 1980s, there was a widespread view among many Americans that promoting abstinence was the most effective way to control HIV infections among our youth. The failure rates of condoms under the worst conditions were stressed and were then compared to what was seen as the 100 percent foolproof method of abstinence. No one publicly challenged this risk comparison, but there was a major flaw in this logic to which our traditional values were blinding many of us. As I briefly noted in chapter 3, when comparing two strategies in a fair and impartial fashion, you cannot estimate the risk of failure for only one strategy and assume 100 percent success for the other. What if we reversed our value bias and suggested that condoms were 100 percent effective? People would be up in arms and see through it right away. But when we assume that abstinence strategies have a zero failure rate, nobody seems to even notice how ridiculous this assumption is. Do we really believe that all those who vow that they will remain abstinent succeed in their vow? This cognitive blindness is caused by the value placed on abstinence by many conservative people and others who have never cleared their minds of the Victorian bias that favors abstinence. Bias has a way of distorting our view of reality.

How about a real estimate of the failure rate for the strategy of abstinence? We know that at age seventeen, about 50 percent of females have had intercourse; by age twenty, the percentage is 70 percent; and before age twenty-five, it is above 90 percent (Abma et al. 2004; Mosher et al. 2004, 2005; Zelnik and Kantner 1980). With the average age at marriage being in the mid- to late twenties, the percentage of females who have experienced sexual intercourse before marriage would likely be over 90 percent. Recent research indicates that vowing abstinence may delay having intercourse by about eighteen months, but 88 percent of those who make the abstinence vow have premarital intercourse (Bruckner and Bearman 2005). So, it does not seem that vows of abstinence prevent sexual intercourse for most young people. No estimate of condom failure rate is anywhere near that high. Accordingly, I believe it would be safe to assume that "*vows of abstinence break far more easily than do condoms*" (Reiss and Reiss 1990, 125).

In addition, if those who vow abstinence do have premarital coitus, they face another risk that many others avoid. Research indicates that the abstinent group has often received negative information about condom use, and so, when they break their vows, they are less likely to trust condoms and thus fail to protect themselves from STDs and pregnancy (Bearman and Bruckner 2001; Brewster et al. 1998; Bruckner and Bearman 2005; Cooksey et al. 1996; Kirby 2002; Studor and Thornton 1987). Since almost all young people will have coitus in their teens or twenties, whether they at one time vowed otherwise or not, it seems that the most protective path would be to accept the reality of sexual choice and work to make sexuality safer for those who choose to become sexually active. If we are really concerned about our young people avoiding disease and pregnancy, then we need to educate them that if they become sexually active, they should use condoms. National polls indicate that sex education that includes contraceptive information is indeed what most parents want for their children (SIECUS Fact Sheet, 2004). Abstinence-only education programs in our schools are promoted by only a minority of parents. Some of the research cited earlier indicates that such programs do not work as well as comprehensive sex-education programs do. Despite this, our federal government gives millions of dollars each year to promote abstinence-only programs (Kirby 2001a, 2001b, 2002). This may get more votes for the Republicans, but it is a clear example of politics trumping science.

Sexual Pluralism: The Way to Reduce Our Sexual Problems

At the same time as the national debate about HIV, condoms, and sexuality was raging in this country, I was trying to decide what type of book I should do next. I have been critical in this chapter of the responses from sex therapists, but the responses from sex researchers in the 1980s were very often not even heard. I wanted to do something that could prove useful for both therapists and researchers. My interests were moving in a multidisciplinary direction and toward research that was more centered on social problems. I still highly valued analyzing good data and carefully developing theoretical explanations of whatever I studied. I was never going to become a full-time advocate or activist for a specific social cause. Nevertheless, my experiences with the McKinnon-Dworkin legislation (see chapter 7), with the Program in Human Sexuality in our medical school (see chapter 9), and with the program at the Masters and Johnson Institute (see chapter 9) were all moving me toward my next book.

It was a presentation by Letty Cottin Pogrebin at the 1986 meeting of the National Council on Family Relations that helped me focus in on my next book. She talked about family politics. She was a strong supporter of feminism and was one of the founders of Ms. magazine. She was clearly an activist, but I wanted to hear what she was proposing as solutions to our family problems, so I listened carefully to her talk about family politics. One simple statement she made hit me as a revelation of what general path to follow for my next book. As my records indicate, she said, "We've focused a great deal in our work on the family on 'what is.' But what we need now is a focus on 'what could be.' We need to search for solutions that will make our lives better."

I knew that I wanted to have my say regarding how to best deal with HIV and other sexual problems, and her statement legitimated and supported that path. I was very interested in finding ways to make our sexual lives safer and better. I wanted to do more than just describe why a sexual problem existed and what the trends were likely to be. Pogrebin's stress on "what could be" was just the extra push I needed. I had the winter quarter of 1987 off, and Harriet and I went to San Francisco to escape the frozen tundra of Minnesota. I intended to start working on my new book during our stay in the Bay Area. I decided that I would zero in on specifically those sexual problems that virtually all Americans wanted to contain. So I chose to deal with rape, HIV/AIDS, teen pregnancy, and child sexual abuse. My goal was to find societal causes and societal solutions for these four major sexual problems. It was not a small order, but it was one that excited my interest.

I felt there were too many people in our country who were saying that the reason for our sexual problems was the increase in sexual behavior by young people. The conservatives were suggesting that we go back to the 1950s type of sex and gender morality. I saw the 1950s as a bigoted and sexist period in American sexual and gender relationships, and not too many women would want to once more be "trapped housewives" or return to that level of male dominance in all our major institutions. I felt it was important for me to write a book that would present a far more workable solution. I planned to write this book for the educated public, not just for sexual scientists. I wanted to reach a broad audience, not just a professional audience.

Being in San Francisco was a blessing for my project. No city in America has more experts on sexual problems. I made up a list of people in the Bay Area who were nationally known for their work on any of the four sexual problems I was dealing with. I spoke for several hours with therapists Lonnie Barbach, Paul Walker, Eve Gendel, and Charles Moser; with activists Diana Russell and Merv Silverman; and with researchers E. J. Bonner and Bob Staples. I also visited for shorter periods of time with many others. Harriet helped me by interviewing several people connected with sex education in the schools and with Planned Parenthood in the Bay Area and by meeting with and talking informally with others. We both taped our interviews so we wouldn't have to write notes while talking to the people. I felt that I was off and running on my next book.

I had never tried to write for a broad public audience, and my early chapter drafts were too heavy on evidence and trends. By late 1987, I realized I needed some advice on what to do to make my book more appealing to a wider audience. I received just what I needed from a literary agent named Heide Lange. I had obtained Heide Lange's name from Beverly Whipple, a member of SSSS and a key person in the 1980s popularization of the G-spot orgasm (Ladas, Whipple, and Perry 1982). She had written that book for the general public and had found her literary agent, Heide Lange, to be very helpful. I visited with Heide and was impressed by her serious literary approach to publication. She asked me to send her a few chapters, which I did, and then I called her for her suggestions.

She told me that my chapters were well written and informative, but they were not *prescriptive* enough. She advised me that what people want in a book written by an expert is more than just information. They want advice concerning ways to help them deal with their sexual problems. I had been too focused on explaining the problems and not focused enough on suggesting what I saw as the ways to best contain them. She said I should write as if I were talking to a friend. I found her advice very helpful. She pointed me where I needed to go in order to write in a style that would attract a broader audience than just professionals in the field. In my past publications, I had not done much with prescribing solutions—the field of sociology focused more on analysis and explanation. But I realized that my old approach was too cerebral, too academic, for a general audience. I needed to move away from my traditional role of explaining and go beyond it to prescribe solutions for our sexual problems. To do this, I had to learn to write in a less technical and more general-reader-friendly fashion.

It had taken two nonsociologists to give me the impetus and the guidance to become more prescriptive: Letty Cottin Pogrebin, a feminist writer, and Heide Lange, a literary agent. There just wasn't anyone in sociology that I knew well who was into this prescriptive direction, so I needed the outside encouragement. I worked to develop a new, more prescriptive style. Harriet read the original and revised chapters and gave me her suggestions. We discussed at length a great deal of the specific sexual problems in the book, and she shared her views about the solutions I was proposing. By no means were we in agreement on everything, but we did agree on more than I had thought we would. I told Harriet that I wanted to list her as a coauthor. She had read all of my chapters and had discussed them all with me. Her editing was very helpful, for she is excellent at grammar and punctuation. She was a major help to me in writing the book, and I valued her assistance a great deal. Nevertheless, in her usual overly modest way, she said she did not want to be listed as a coauthor, but I could list her on the cover as having worked with me.

I also called my nephew Spence Porter, who is a playwright in New York, and asked him for advice on making my writing style more attractive to a wider audience. He helped me a great deal by going over each of my chapters and talking to me in detail about my style. In addition, I read a few books on how to write for a broader audience. I did not expect to reach a mass audience, but I did hope to reach the educated public—that is, all those who had been to college and any others who were interested in a thoughtful analysis of our sexual problems. Ideologists and dogmatists were not part of my intended audience.

The new writing style exhilarated me and gave me a sense of freedom to express a broader portion of my own thoughts and feelings on sexual issues. I was no longer just a mainline professor analyzing social problems; I was an expert on sexual science who was suggesting to the public solutions to these problems. Of course, I still followed my scientific guidelines of fairness in analyzing evidence, developing evidence-based solutions, and avoiding bias. Most sociologists had given over the prescriptive role to the local, state, or federal politicians. But politicians, as we all know, have their own special interests, and they are not trained in careful data analysis and interpretation. Also, why should they be the only voice heard by the public? I knew a great deal more than the politicians did about how to resolve our sexual problems. Why shouldn't I share this knowledge? Politicians focused on what solutions would get approved by the legislature or would help get them reelected. For me, the days of just describing and explaining a social problem and leaving the solutions to politicians had ended.

By 1989, I had finished a full draft of the revised manuscript. It was written in the most popular and most prescriptive style I had ever penned. Now I was anxious to get my book out so it could enter into the intense dialogue that was taking place in America concerning how to handle HIV/AIDS and other sexual problems. I wanted a publisher that would put the book out in no more than six months. I contacted Vern Bullough, who was the editor for books on sexuality by Prometheus Books, and I asked him to read over my manuscript. He read it and told me that he thought it was great, and he said he would strongly recommend it to Prometheus Books for publication. Shortly after that, I received an offer from Prometheus and a promise that they would have it out in less than six months. I knew that Prometheus could not promote the book nationally anywhere near as well as larger publishers could, but I had gone with a very large publisher, Prentice-Hall, for my 1986 book, and they had done very little to advertise the book or promote its sales in other ways. So there was no guarantee that size was better, and it would take longer for the book to come out with a larger publisher. I therefore went with Prometheus on the two editions of the book (Reiss and Reiss 1990, 1997).

Sexual Pluralism Theory

Let me briefly tell you about my explanation of our high rate of sexual problems and my proposal for bringing this rate down. I started by asking how sexual problems that are universally condemned by people in our society could still be so widespread. The American public must unknowingly be doing something that promotes these problems. The million-dollar question was what were Americans doing that promoted these sexual problems? I noted earlier that the way we Americans have handled all our sexual problems has involved a restrictive, narrow, and fearful approach. This style discouraged open and honest discussions of choices and substituted a Victorian one-size-fits-all morality. The evidence I examined supported the view that it was precisely this Victorian approach to sexual problems that was keeping us from gaining control over our many sexual problems.

This was a bit of a shock to those who read the book because many people thought a conservative sexual approach was the safest tactic to follow. I rejected this idea and argued that in a society such as ours, with its high degree of autonomy among young people and its increasing gender equality, promoting a restrictive approach to sexual problems was not only unworkable but also dangerous. Earlier in this chapter, I criticized how sex therapists had dealt with AIDS in this traditional, narrow fashion. So I knew that the restrictive Victorian approach to sexuality was alive somewhere in the American psyche, and it had to be replaced. That narrow and fearful strategy would only exacerbate our sexual problems. Our nation had then, and still has, the Western world's highest rates of rape, HIV/AIDS, teen pregnancy and child sexual abuse, so it was obvious that our traditional approach to such problems needed to be changed (Reiss and Reiss 1990, 1997). I knew that to change our Victorian approach would take the substitution of a new approach that would be better integrated into the type of postindustrial, knowledge-based society in which we lived. The solution I proposed for gaining control of our sexual problems was to adopt a new sexual ethic that would replace the remnants of our Victorian heritage.

The sexual revolution had rejected much of the traditional abstinence-only approach among our young people. As discussed in chapter 6, a permissiveness with affection standard for premarital sex had grown in popularity and had taken over as the dominant position with our youth. But that was just one premarital standard. To overturn a Victorian view of sexuality required a statement of a new sexual ethic that applied to all sexuality. So I proposed the minimalist ethic that was working so well in Scandinavia and other parts of Western Europe. That ethic was *sexual pluralism*. By pluralism, I did not at all mean that we should accept all sexual acts. My examination of societies around the world in my 1986 book had revealed two universal major restraints on sexual choice: (a) force and (b) exploitation. The clearest illustration of force was rape, and the clearest illustration of exploitation was an adult having sex with a preadolescent child. Societies around the world differed regarding just how much force was unacceptable in sexuality, but they all drew a line that should not be crossed. Societies also differed as to age and other restraints on adult-child sexuality, but they all specified a type of adult-child sexual relationship that was unacceptable (Marshall and Suggs 1971). So, in one way or another, societies around the world placed limits on the use of force or exploitation in sexual relationships. Sexual pluralism also declares force and exploitation as morally unacceptable.

The question that follows is what positive values can our society promote if we want to avoid the negative values of force and exploitation in sexual relationships? My answer to this question was to promote the values of honesty, equality, and responsibility. We can set these values up as the moral bases of an acceptable sexual relationship. If you ensure that a relationship has honesty, equality, and responsibility, you are at the same time guaranteeing that force and exploitation will be very unlikely to occur. You can't use force and exploitation in a sexual relationship and still be in an honest, equal, and responsible relationship.

Let me briefly state what I meant by these three values. An honest sexual relationship would be one in which the people reveal to each other what they expect out of the relationship. People would share with their partner whether they sought a casual relationship or a serious committed relationship, and so forth. By equality, I meant that the wishes of both people would carry equal weight in the decision as to what sexual acts would occur. And by responsibility, I meant that the people involved would strive to avoid negative outcomes, such as pregnancy, disease, and emotional upset for their partner and for themselves. I used the acronym HER (pronounced "h-e-r") for these three values and called the broad sexual ethic that I thought would best bring our sexual problems under control HER *sexual pluralism*. This sexual ethic would promote more open and thoughtful discussions concerning how to contain our sexual problems and would thereby help us cope with these serious problems. It fits today's society far better than the nineteenth-century Victorian sexual ethic.

If you endorsed HER sexual pluralism, then only a sexual relationship that was HER would be accepted as ethical. This ethic would apply to all people capable of being reasonably honest, equal, and responsible. So, an ethical relationship could be between people of the same or of different genders. The requirement of having the ability to be honest, equal, and responsible would surely eliminate those who are preadolescents. Whether a sixteen-year-old was old enough to be honest, equal, and responsible would be the key to acceptance or rejection. Also, age alone would not qualify you. We all know people well over sixteen who are not capable of being in an honest, equal, and responsible sexual relationship. Sexual pluralism challenges the notion that it is simply marriage or love that makes a sexual relationship ethically acceptable. It is all too clear that rape, physical abuse, and deception are all found in marital and love relationships, so HER values are a better guide than marriage or love as to what is an ethical sexual relationship. Love and marriage may help to achieve an HER relationship, but this doesn't make them the *measure* of what is sexually ethical. The pluralism in this standard fits very well with our democratic ethic. Americans are pluralist in religion and in politics. We don't demand that everyone accept one religion or one political party. You may think your choice is better, but you would not outlaw choices of other religions or political viewpoints. Isn't it time we accepted this concept of pluralism in the area of sexual relationships?

Let me be clear that sexual pluralism is not just about what you accept for *yourself*. It is very much about what you accept for *others*. As a pluralist, you could be a believer in abstinence for yourself but still accept many other HER types of sexual relationships for other people. In the late 1980s, this is precisely what our surgeon general, C. Everett Koop, did. He favored abstinence, but he gave other people choice and sought to distribute to every household a brochure on condom use (Koop 1986). It is the acceptance of all HER sexual acts for other people that makes one a pluralist. What any person accepts for him- or herself will usually be much less than the full range of HER sexual acts. Accepting a broad range of choices means that you won't so easily condemn yourself if, or when, you decide to change and choose another HER sexual choice.

You can measure your own degree of sexual pluralism by asking yourself how many of all the HER sexual choices would you accept as ethical choices for other people to make. For example, if two people are sixteen but are mature enough to have an HER relationship, would you accept having such a relationship as ethical for them? Or what if two people are urophiliacs and enjoy urinating on each other as part of their sexual relationship? Is that an acceptable choice for them? What if two people want to act out a dominance-submissiveness sexual script that they enjoy? You can fill in other HER choices and see just how fully you accept HER sexual pluralism. A person who fully accepts HER sexual pluralism accepts all HER sexual acts *for others*, even though they may not accept all of them *for themselves*.

Responses to Sexual Pluralism

Starting in the fall of 1988, I offered a new undergraduate course called "America's Sexual Crisis." I tried out my new ideas and my more prescriptive stance in that class. It was helpful in my writing to do this. The course got a large enrollment—over two hundred students every time it was taught. Discussion in class was very open and honest, and a large number of students participated in the discussions, despite the size of the class. They were very much interested in finding an ethical standard for themselves, and my ideas were hitting a home run with them. It turned out to be one of the most popular courses I had ever offered. I gave it at least once a year from 1988 until I retired in 1996. I also covered a good deal of the same material in my graduate courses, and the interest there was also very strong. It seemed that my more applied problem-solving approach, with its ethic of sexual pluralism, fit very well into their personal and professional agendas, just as it fit into mine.

Responses came in right after my 1990 book appeared. I had aroused interest with my evidence and reasoning, arguing that sexual dogmatism was an important cause of our sexual problems, whereas sexual pluralism was an important solution. Most of the reviews were very favorable (Chernick 1992; Gordon 1991; Libby 1991; Rosenbaum 1991). I found that I was being read by an audience that was also seeking solutions for our sexual problems. They wanted solutions in addition to understanding the problems. For example,

Planned Parenthood of Houston, Texas, together with the Sociology Department of Rice University, invited me to come down and talk about my
ideas. Texas is not known as a bastion of liberalism, and I wondered what the
reaction would be. I had an audience composed of students, faculty, and
townspeople that numbered at least five hundred. Bill Simon was teaching at
the University of Houston at that time, and he and his wife were there. I presented the HER sexual pluralism perspective from my book as the best sexual ethic for controlling our major sexual problems. I explained the reasons
and evidence for my view. At the end of my talk, I received a standing ova-
tion from almost everyone in the audience. It was a great night.

Political and religious conservatives did not like my findings or my proposals, and they circled their wagons and fired back at me. By suggesting that
traditional sexual attitudes were a major cause of our sexual problems, I was
directly threatening their traditional sexual beliefs. I threatened them further
by promoting the broad range of sexual choices that fit with the ethic of HER
sexual pluralism. To me, their strong negative reactions indicated that I had
hit a nerve directly attached to their sense of security and power.

The positive and negative responses were further evidence that publishing
for a broader public audience and proposing solutions could well have an impact on our society. Making such proposals afforded sexual scientists leverage
in determining the direction in which our society might move. I thought that
sexual scientists who studied our sexual problems were in the best position to
understand what solutions would be the most effective in containing those
problems. I suggested that proposing solutions to sexual problems should not
be seen as an exceptional practice for sexual scientists but rather as a routine
part of our professional work. Of course, when suggesting our solutions, we
must work hard to do a fair and careful examination of the evidence and of
the reasoning that we present. In order to do this, we should work to get in
touch with our own personal values and make them explicit so that people
can check to see if we are biasing our conclusions. We need to show clearly
why we think a particular solution is the best one to adopt. Maintaining a
scientific approach affords our proposals a special quality not contained in
most political proposals, and it helps elevate the value of our suggested solutions (Collins 1998).

But we should be aware that when we propose solutions, we enter into political territory, and if we are perceived as a threat, we may be personally attacked (Bancroft 2004; Bullough 1994a, 1994b; Laumann, Michael, and
Gagnon 1994; Rubin 1984). I'm sure many sexual scientists are aware of this
and therefore decline to enter the political realm for fear of being attacked.
But to remain silent is a capitulation of our potential power and a weaken-

ing of any influence our scientific work and ideas may have on our society. Ask yourself this: Are we just writing to talk to our fellow sexual scientists, or do we want to help build a better society and gain more control over our sexual problems?

My HER sexual pluralism fit well with my previously published explanations involving the importance of autonomy (see chapter 6) and with my discussion of the universal linkage of sexuality with gender equality, normality, and jealousy (see chapter 10). It was precisely the changes in autonomy and gender equality in our society during the last few generations that helped create a need for a new sexual ethic. These changes also promoted a receptive public for the new ethic of HER sexual pluralism. So my major explanatory ideas all seemed to fit together and blend with my proposal for HER sexual pluralism. If we really want sexual pluralism, we will need to promote in the family, politics, economics, religion, and education those changes that produce more honesty, equality, and responsibility. This is surely not easy to accomplish, but very few things that are valuable come easily into existence (Reiss and Reiss 1990, 1997).

CHAPTER TWELVE

~

New Projects and a New Life Agenda

The Governor's Committee
on Child and Adolescent Sexual Health

In 1992, I moved further into applied sociology and chaired a committee for the Minnesota Department of Health. Bill Seabloom, formerly a therapist at the university's Program in Human Sexuality, had succeeded in persuading the governor of Minnesota to form a special committee on child and adolescent sexual health. I was one of the fourteen people appointed to that task force. I expected that Bill would chair the task force, but he asked me to be the chair, since he would be out of town for the first two meetings. I then met with a few people from the Department of Health who would oversee the committee, and I told them that I felt it was an important area to deal with and that I therefore agreed to chair the committee. In chapter 9, I mentioned some of my reservations about the federal bureaucracy. I was now venturing into the world of state bureaucracy. I thought that by that time I was realistic in my expectations of government bureaucracies. However, I was soon to learn that my political education was far from complete.

The committee held its first meeting in September of 1992 at the Department of Health building in Minneapolis. Of the fourteen people on the task force, I knew only a few of them. The members covered a wide variety of fields, including religion, delinquency, counseling, and other fields. Only a few of the members were from the university. I was pleased to see that the committee was broad enough in backgrounds to contain a variety of viewpoints on our topic. The Department of Health was represented by two staff people who arranged for taking the minutes of the meeting and said they were available if we needed anything.

I opened the first meeting by asking everyone to tell the other members of the committee something about themselves and why they were willing to be on the committee. The reasons given were both personal and professional and further indicated the breadth of the taskforce. I informed everyone that the charge of the committee was to formulate a view about how to improve child and adolescent sexual health in Minnesota. I added that I saw it as my responsibility to keep the group focused on this goal even though our individual interests were broader than that. I informed them that I had accepted the role as chair because I wanted to share some of my own views about how to promote sexual health of children and adolescents. I concluded by promising that I would run the committee democratically. They would all have a chance to present their own thoughts and feelings on sexual health, and we would vote on all proposals so that each person would have an equal chance to influence what viewpoints we would end up including in our final report.

I laid down these guidelines because I wanted us to produce a sound and workable proposal for the Department of Health. I didn't want to simply monitor an unfocused discussion on the topic and then conclude with no useful proposals. I suggested to the committee that we each think about what we meant by "child sexual well being" and bring in our ideas to the next meeting. I hoped that going over these proposals would allow us to arrive at a consensus regarding what type of sexual health we wanted to promote for the children and adolescents of our state. Then we could work on how to achieve that type of sexual health.

I was to learn over and over during my work with this committee that the Department of Health people had a somewhat different agenda than I did. They seemed to be primarily concerned that we avoid upsetting anyone on the task force. They didn't want any problems that might become public or reflect badly on the Department of Health. The key goal for them seemed to be to not rock the boat. Of course, I was not oblivious to pleasing the members of the task force, but the primary goal I had in mind was to decide how to promote sexual health for children and adolescents in Minnesota. If someone on the task force became upset with our discussions or with the positions we democratically selected, so be it.

Before the second meeting, I received a call from the two Department of Health people, Ruth Carlson and Pati Maier, who were monitoring the committee. They wanted to meet with me. I set up a meeting in a room at the Sociology Department. They made it clear that they were bothered because at the first meeting I had indicated that some of the members' interests were not directly relevant to our committee's charge, and so we wouldn't be able to follow up on them. The Department of Health people were worried that some of the committee members might have been upset by that and might not stay on the committee. I explained to them that if we were going to accomplish the goal set for our committee, my top priority had to be to focus on what was relevant to that goal.

They emphasized that they were responsible for the "smooth" functioning of the task force and that they were concerned that perhaps I was running the committee too tightly. They added that they thought it would be best if they took over running the committee, and in that way, I would be freer to express my views as a member of the committee. This suggestion was not acceptable to me. I told them that they were not appointed by the governor to be on the committee and that they were there simply to record our discussions and give advice. I stressed that the committee belonged to the members on it who were appointed by the governor, not to the Department of Health. I assured them that I had run scores of committees of peers and that I had not encountered any serious problems. I reminded them that the committee would vote on all proposals, and so the members should be satisfied with the outcome of our discussions and with the final report that we would submit to the commissioner of health.

I also mentioned that I had worked in sexual science for decades and that I had developed my own ideas of what would work best in terms of sexual health, but if the task force decided to move in a very different direction, I would certainly accept it and submit the conclusions to the Department of Health as the majority report. However, I noted that if I thought it would be useful, I might exercise my right to submit a minority report containing my own ideas to the commissioner of health. I felt that the commissioner of health should be fully informed about possible solutions. Obviously, minority reports were not a typical outcome of Department of Health committees. Pati Maier, in particular, seemed visibly upset by my even suggesting this possibility. She asked me whether I was threatening them and trying to create trouble. I informed them that I would only add a minority report if I felt that something important and relevant to our charge had been left out of the majority report. I felt it was the right thing for the chair of the committee to do, and I asked, "Don't you want the commissioner to be as fully informed as possible?" Clearly the reason we were bumping heads was because their goal of not rocking the boat was not my primary goal. I very much wanted to formulate a workable plan for the protection of child and adolescent sexual health in Minnesota. I tried to reassure them that they were needlessly concerned about the task force and about the outcome. I don't think I succeeded in doing that.

Before the Department of Health people left, they told me that they would distribute the minutes of all task-force meetings to the committee. I knew that the minutes of a meeting could distort what had happened and present things in a biased way, and I told them that, as chair of the task force, I wanted to go over the minutes before they were finalized and distributed so I could be sure that nothing was misrepresented. They said this was unusual for a committee chair. I insisted and said that, as the chair, I was responsible for the accuracy of the minutes. Apparently the purpose of this little get-together at the university was to take control of the task force in a number of ways. I was not going to give them that control—not of the meetings and not even of the minutes of those meetings. I don't believe they were too happy when they left.

We had very good attendance at the second meeting, and everyone brought their statement on the meaning of sexual health that they wanted to share with the task force in order to help us reach a consensus on this concept. I wanted to zero in on the ingredients that make for good sexual health, but I wasn't at all convinced that we could achieve consensus in one meeting with such a diverse group. However, I was very pleasantly surprised. After hearing all the members' comments, I was truly amazed. There was a great deal of agreement on the meaning of sexual health in all the views expressed by that diverse group of people! The perspective shared stated that sexual health included basic elements such as general knowledge about sexuality, contraceptive knowledge, notions of gender equality, and guidelines for making informed decisions about sexual choices. I said nothing about my views until all of the members had presented their own views. Then I told them that I agreed strongly with the views presented but that I would like to add one more element.

I suggested that one way to help achieve the shared conception of sexual health was to promote an ethic of HER sexual pluralism (see chapter 11). I tried to point out how this sexual ethic would help achieve the committee members' aims regarding knowledge of choices, contraception, gender equality, and guidelines for informed decisions. In these ways, HER sexual pluralism would further all aspects of the sexual health we all desired. I asked for their reactions to my suggestion, and they seemed to strongly support the ethic of HER sexual pluralism as a very useful addition to our concept of sexual health.

So, to my surprise, our committee had unanimously arrived at a consensus viewpoint on sexual health in just one meeting. I was very pleased, and I noticed that the Department of Health people looked more relaxed. The agenda for the next few meetings was to discuss strategies for promoting our conception of sexual health for children and adolescents in Minnesota. We planned to examine what community supports we needed to build upon and what community obstacles needed to be removed. This remaining agenda took up several meetings and a great deal of discussion and sharing of sug- gestions. Almost all committee members joined in our discussions. We also had a number of guests who were very informative and helpful.

Four months later, in January 1993, our committee felt that we had clearly delineated ways of obtaining community supports and preventing commu- nity blockages to our program in sexual health. Together, we wrote up a final draft and then discussed and voted on each part of the draft until we had achieved a fully approved report. Despite the fears of the Department of Health people, the task force had worked together exceptionally smoothly and had produced a significant document for the Department of Health. In fact, both the Department of Health and the Governor's Office gave our task force a special certificate of award for our "exceptional" work.

Even after our work was done, most of the members wanted to privately continue pursuing our goals. They wanted us to seek state funding for the com- mittee's future operations. I was willing to serve as a member on the continu- ing task force, but I asked Bill Seabloom to take over as chair of this con- tinuing enterprise. Bill fully supported our efforts, and he took over running the group. With help from a few key legislators, we were able to get legislative money. Our funds came from part of the Omnibus Crime Bill. Our funding was placed at the back of the Omnibus Crime Bill, and I believe that very few leg- islators read the bill carefully enough to even know that we were dealing with the explosive issue of child and adolescent sexual health. By July of 1993, we incorporated the committee into a nonprofit organization. The organization received additional funds for two more years from the state legislature before finally disbanding in 1995. I believe we started things in motion that would continue to improve child and adolescent sexual health in Minnesota.

I met once more with the Department of Health people who were on our committee. They agreed that our task force had ended well. I thought I would close by giving them a little dig about the restraints of their bureau- cracy. I mentioned to them that the University of Minnesota didn't have the bureaucratic restraints that their Department of Health had, and so people at the university were freer to state their views and act upon them. At that time, there was a scandal at the medical school, and so the Department of Health people countered by saying, "But look at the price you have to pay as shown in the current medical school scandal."

I responded, "To me, the value of freedom easily trumps the cost of any scandal." So neither of us were making converts. This experience with the Department of Health deepened my awareness of how multifaceted and complex political encounters can be. It also added to the value I place on the university's support of academic freedom and its encouragement for critically examining our society's shared beliefs. I felt pleased with what we had accomplished, and I believed that we had changed some minds of legislators and others as our taskforce carried out its work and made its views on sexual health known.

Retirement: But Not from Sexual Science

Retirement from the University of Minnesota was one of the very hardest decisions of my life. The thought of full retirement never occurred to me before the 1990s. I loved teaching and other aspects of being at the university. I had thought that I would go half time when I reached age seventy. During the early 1990s, as I approached seventy, I thought more and more about writing a book about my life and about the lives of the key people in our family. This would not be for publication but was to help ensure that our grandchildren and their children would know something about our family members that lived then. There were thousands of letters and photos and many journal entries that would have to be examined to write such a book. I really didn't have time to do such a major project, and that was gnawing away at me.

Also, by the 1993–1994 academic year, after having taught for forty years, my teaching experience began to more and more lose its rewards for me. I had always loved to teach. I felt that it was my chance to pass on my knowledge of the field of sexual science to the next generation, and I loved having the chance to try out my latest ideas on my classes and see how they responded. Teaching had been at the top of my priorities, together with writing. I received most of my rewards as a professor from these two endeavors. When teaching began to become less satisfying, I started thinking more seriously of full retirement. I had about six graduate students, and in 1993, three of them completed their PhDs. I began to ask myself how long I wanted to continue advising graduates. When I added the decline in teaching satisfaction to my desire to write a lengthy family autobiography, I felt more and more favorable about retirement. If I retired fully in June of 1996 after I had turned seventy, I would have the time to do whatever my top priorities were. I gave up on the idea to go half time in part because the university made it impossible to go half time and still obtain the perks that went with the job.

Surely some of the administrators wanted us old-timers to leave so that they could hire new people at much lower salaries.

In the early 1990s, I was still being evaluated as among the top people in the department in teaching and in research by both students and faculty, but the psychic rewards from these evaluations had diminished. I increasingly had my own agenda to tend to, and by June of 1994, I felt convinced that I would fully retire. However, this was such an important decision that I decided I would think it over during my 1994–1995 sabbatical. The moment the sabbatical began, I felt very relieved to be free from university demands for a full year. Of course, that emotion clearly sent me the message that I needed to pull out of teaching, advising, and running committees and retire from the university. By the end of my sabbatical, I had thought of doing another book in addition to the family autobiography. In fact, I wrote in my 1995 journal that the title for that book would be *An Insider's View of Sexual Science*. By now that title should sound familiar to all of you reading this book.

After my other sabbaticals, I had been eager to get back to teaching, but this time, that wasn't the case at all. I decided I would give teaching one more try and revise all my courses to try to make them more rewarding to both myself and the students. This would be one more check to see if I could reignite my joy of teaching. It didn't work. If you've never been in love with your work, then there would be less to lose. But once you've been in love and it disappears, you can't help but feel the immense loss. Even with the revised courses, the feeling of loss was still very palpable. By early 1996, I knew that even though I came from a family that lived well into their eighties and nineties, if I was going to have time to do what I wanted, I had no other choice but to retire now. At that time, I wrote in my journal, "It's as if a curtain has fallen on my career and I have just become fully aware of it. All I have to do now is take a bow and walk off the stage." The two years it took for me to close the tiny gap from 99 percent certainty to 100 percent certainty illustrates how difficult this decision was for me. Breaking my tie to the University of Minnesota was symbolic of a major change.

Right after announcing that I was retiring, I felt a powerful wave of relief sweep over me. Shortly afterward, I publicly "took my bow," had my farewell parties, and started on my retirement years. I want to stress that I retired only from my work at the university. I did not retire from my field of sociology or from my work in sexual science. I did write a two-volume, twelve-hundred-page family biography, complete with letters, photos, and other memorabilia. Also, about six months after retirement, Prometheus Books, the publisher of my 1990 sexual pluralism book, wrote and asked me to update the book for a paperback edition. I agreed and did just that in the spring of 1997. I changed the title because I never liked the publisher's title of *An End to Shame*, and I suggested the title *Solving America's Sexual Crises*. This revision came out in the fall of 1997.

When I retired, I was teaching three courses in the sociology of sexuality: (1) an undergraduate course that focused on the sexual crises in our country that I had written about in my 1990 book, (2) an upper-level course that took a cross-cultural look at sexuality as I had done in my 1986 book, and (3) a graduate course that focused on the major sexual research-and-theory projects in the United States. Did any faculty take up these classes after my retirement? No. It took nine years, until the spring of 2005, before any of my courses were offered again. At that time, two new faculty jointly taught my undergraduate course in sexuality. I hope this is a harbinger of more to come. The faculty respected me, but they didn't give a high priority to the sociology of sexuality. I'm sure this is precisely the situation at many other universities. So, how is our field to prosper and grow if our place in most of the established disciplines is close to the bottom of the academic totem pole? I have a good answer to that question, and I'll detail it in chapter 14.

Al Ellis and Rational Emotive Behavior Therapy

Al Ellis and I have a fifty-year colleagueship and friendship. I spoke of Al in chapter 4 as the key founder of SSSS. He is now a very well-known therapist, and my contact with him over the years has helped keep me in touch with what's happening with the cognitive therapy approach. Al began publishing his innovative cognitive approach to therapy in the late 1950s. He called his approach rational therapy, and in my mind, that new form of therapy was a major contribution to the field of therapy. Instead of Freud's lengthy and complex therapeutic approach, Al dealt less with the client's distant past and more with techniques for replacing a person's self-defeating emotional responses with what he called more rational responses (Freud 1905). In time, this innovative cognitive notion became the basis for the now very popular cognitive therapy movement in our country. In the decade between the mid-1950s and the mid-1960s, Al and I exchanged many letters and argued over some of his rational-therapy ideas. As part of my research for my autobiography, I went through all my old files, and in one folder I found sixty-five letters that we had exchanged in that decade. I contacted Al and suggested to him that we publish these letters and add new chapters indicating how our views had or had not changed over the decades since then. We did all this, and our book was published under the title *At the Dawn of the Sexual Revolution* (Reiss and Ellis 2002).

Among other things, that book reveals the influence of our different professional fields. Al, as a psychologist, stressed the importance of individual differences, and I, as a sociologist, stressed the importance of groups. I promoted the need to build relationships with others, and Al pushed more the need for individuals to do their own thing. In addition, Al stressed people's biological backgrounds—he saw biology as more influential in our sexual lives than I did. I stressed more the cultural influences on our sexuality. Our differences were apparent, but we really weren't very far apart. I surely support a strong individualism, but I also have a concern for how the overall group will survive. Our basic similarities were that we were both strong sexual pluralists, and we both gave top priority to a scientific, evidence-based approach to testing one's beliefs. Our letter exchanges did move each of us a bit closer to each other, and that outcome supports the value of multidisciplinary contacts. But, despite all our interactions, we still had clearly visible differences.

The work we did on our 2002 book restored our old debating habits, and between July of 2002 and April of 2003, we wrote ten letters to each other concerning some issues I raised about Al's current views on rational emotional behavior therapy (REBT) (Reiss 2005). This exchange began after I read Al's 2001 book on the philosophical assumptions of REBT (Ellis 2001). Reading that book led me to raise some issues with the position Ellis put forth in the book. I agreed with his fundamental view that we should not, as he puts it, "catastrophize" or "awfulize" life events. He saw this tendency to emotionalize responses to events as a powerful universal human characteristic. His solution was to "*unconditionally accept yourself and others.*" In this way, he believes people would avoid catastrophizing and awfulizing what others do or what they themselves do. He argued that we might feel sad and frustrated by events, but the unconditional-acceptance approach would allow us to avoid emotionalizing and would thereby enable us to go on with our lives.

I liked his basic thinking about accepting oneself and others, because this promotes tolerance for diversity and helps people to avoid overemotionalizing events in their lives. Sometimes other people's differences in taste and manners make us reject them, and that surely needs to be modified by broadening our mutual acceptance of differences. Still, I thought he went too far in his unconditional-acceptance view. I wanted to qualify this by proposing that we not unconditionally accept all people regardless of what they have done. I suggested that perhaps there is a small percentage, maybe 5 percent, of people whose behavior frequently consists of actions that are exceptionally brave and helpful to others. Don't these people deserve a higher level of acceptance? I felt that it was important to give special praise to these exceptionally helpful people in order to encourage others to behave that way. On the other side of the ledger, I suggested that there are also perhaps 5 percent of human beings who behave repeatedly in ways that are very destructive of other people's lives. Should we not assign these people a lower level of acceptance?

Underlying my position was my belief that societies require some minimal degree of praise and blame in order to promote the key values that encourage very helpful acts, like those that save lives, and discourage very harmful acts, like those that destroy lives. In short, I was stating that no society can unconditionally accept all actions and all people and still maintain even a minimal hierarchy of values that bind its members together. Now, let me stress here that we surely can unconditionally accept the vast majority of human actions by increasing our tolerance and acceptance for diversity. Nevertheless, no society that I know of would equate the people who regularly act to save the lives of others in their community with the people who regularly act to take the lives of others in their community.

As examples of the top and bottom 5 percent, I referred to the events of September 11, 2001. I argued that what the terrorists had done on that day was exceptionally harmful, and thus I could not unconditionally accept people who would do this. At the other end of the ethical curve, I cited the bravery of the firemen and police who went into the towers to help people. They went far beyond everyday behavior and were exceptional in the risks they took to help others. I felt that they should be singled out as special people in this regard.

Al felt that to have these special categories would get people to view others as "totally bad" or "totally good" and would lead to more prejudice. I certainly would not assert that the September 11 terrorists were "totally bad" people because of what they did, or that the firemen and police were "totally good" people because of what they did. I see people as coming in mixed "packages," and so surely no single act in one part of their life defines their entire worth. Nevertheless, I would assert that actions like those that happened on September 11 are exceptional in the harm or the good that they do, and therefore the people who perform them should be singled out in either a positive or a negative way. I believe that if we do not do this, we weaken support for the basic values of our society.

I took a similar type of position in chapter 11 when I discussed HER sexual pluralism. This ethic accepts all forms of sexuality *except* those that involve force or exploitation, as in rape or child-adult sexuality. I stressed the need to learn to tolerate choices that we would not make for ourselves, like practicing urophilia or coprophilia. But I also pointed out that there is a limit to what we ethically accept, and in sex the use of force and exploitation defines those limits. This is the same type of qualified perspective that I took in my letters with Al. I brought in September 11 as illustrating the minimalist ethical principles involved there. Some minimal set of ethics, such as that in HER sexual pluralism, is needed to afford one the feeling of belonging to a social group. I think this is missing in the *total* unconditional acceptance of people in Al's REBT philosophy.

I didn't convince Al. He continued to feel that if you accept even this minor modification of unconditional acceptance of self and others, then people would move back into catastrophizing and awfulizing many more actions and would judge people as totally bad or totally good, and prejudice would increase. Therefore, he wanted a total ban on judging people as worse or better in any way. He felt that you could praise or condemn actions, but you could not praise or condemn a person, even if you qualified that judgment by saying that it was not a total-person evaluation. One illustration of our differences can be seen in a letter that Al sent me shortly after September 11. In that letter, he said that the actions by the terrorists on September 11 made him feel "sad and frustrated." He saw the act as "evil" but would not judge the people who perpetrated it. I felt that he was promoting a totally relativistic and individualistic view of ethics, and it was hard to see how any society could survive long with that sort of public philosophy.

In part, our differences were due to the professional fields to which we belonged. Al was responding as a therapist, and I was responding as a sociologist. He was stressing the individual's rights, and I was promoting the group's needs. Al and I also have somewhat different personalities, and that too, no doubt, contributed to our different positions. In my last letter to him on this topic, I tried to make my suggestions relevant to therapeutic outcomes by suggesting that I believed that his clients would find it easier to accept my more-nuanced and qualified view of acceptance of others and self. I thought that the total acceptance of all people without any ranking would be very difficult for therapy clients or anyone else to accept. I proposed that he do an empirical check of our differing positions by asking some REBT therapists to use my qualified view of people acceptance and other REBT therapists to continue to use his unconditional views. We could then measure and compare how the clients were affected by these different approaches. He said he would talk to other therapists about this. Unfortunately, shortly after we ended our dialogue, Al had a very serious illness that required colon cancer surgery. This incapacitated him for months, and the matter hasn't been acted on yet. Al is now on to writing more books. Perhaps some of the REBT therapists reading this book will undertake this comparative research.

~

CHAPTER THIRTEEN

Problem Areas in Sexual Science Today

Antiscience: Radical Social Constructionism

There is a threat to the future of sexual science, and it comes from some of our own sexual scientists. It is important that everyone dealing with sexuality is aware of what has been happening (Reiss 1999). Around the 1970s, there was a philosophical movement coming from literature scholars and a number of other humanities disciplines. The movement spread to the social sciences and to sexual science and there took on the name of social constructionism. Some of the proponents of this movement I will call *radical* social constructionists. The beliefs they are promulgating pose a direct threat to all scientific disciplines. The radical social constructionists see science as just another subjective and power-centered institution. Their attack on science could push us back to a pre-science time, when evidence and reasoning were dismissed and the strength of our emotional ideological convictions determined what was called knowledge. You don't have to go back centuries to know what I'm talking about. Just fifty years ago, there was a dominance of another ideological perspective in the published writings on sexuality in our country (see chapter 2).

Radical social constructionists often paint a positivistic caricature of science as a narrow, rigid, and dogmatic approach to knowledge. As I sought to make clear in chapter 3, the science that I value and that most sexual scientists value is *not* a narrow, positivistic, and rigid science. Most of the people I know today in sexual science support a much broader, more inclusive view of science that includes qualitative as well as quantitative approaches (Reiss 1993). I also fully accept that science is but one way to view the world. There are other nonscientific approaches to the world. For example, there are valuable literary, religious, and philosophical perspectives that can also afford insight into our world. However, science offers us a unique institution, one that relies heavily on reasoning and evidence, encourages skepticism, and supports theoretical creativity and a willingness to change. Surely there are today many faults that we all can find in the way sexual science and other sciences operate. Humans never create perfect institutions. However, science, more than any other institution, affords us an indispensable source of knowledge that can be used for checking our beliefs and improving our world. Any weakening of the support for science would strengthen the power of unexamined prejudices that abound in our and every society. So I see science as essential to the growth of our knowledge and as a safeguard of democracy. An informed electorate requires widespread knowledge, and science is the main source of this knowledge, whether it be about health, sexuality, or the exercise of power.

Let me be clear about *radical* social constructionism. In a broad sense, all those trained in the social sciences are social constructionists of a *moderate* sort. After all, we do acknowledge the powerful role that society plays in shaping our lives in a myriad of ways. Nevertheless, the *radical* social constructionists have hijacked this concept and have shaped it into a much more extreme position than that held by most social scientists. The radical adherents assert that all reality is socially constructed. Note that this is quite different from saying society *influences* our views and behaviors. Radical social constructionism asserts that society *determines* our total view of reality. Philosophers would call this an epistemological presumption, a philosophical view of how we gain knowledge. This radical position gives total power to social influences and asserts that science cannot get beyond this subjective view of the world that society imposes on us all, because science itself is simply another subjective view that is no better than any other subjective view of the world. It is this extreme version of social constructionism—what some call the "strong" version—that I believe is a threat to all scientific enterprises.

The radical social constructionists are walking far out on an antiscience epistemological gangplank that contends that reality is only seen from the perspective of our place in our society. Things like our gender, our class, and our race do not just *influence* but *determine* how we see the world. The important point here is that they assert that we have no ability to get beyond our individual differences in viewpoint. We cannot test our viewpoints empirically because our viewpoints themselves are seen as the only path to knowledge. There is no "outsider" view of knowledge, only an "insider" view

(Reiss 2004). Clearly, this means that the viewpoint of any group or person cannot be meaningfully compared to that of any other group or person. The name for such a philosophical position is *relativism*, and relativism of knowledge is incompatible with the practice of science.

Science is founded on the assumption that one very important way that we can know the world is through reason and evidence, and thus we do have the ability to get beyond particular views that individual people or groups hold. So in science there is a belief in an outsider view as well as a belief that there are many insider views that we need to examine. For example, if a group of people believes that condoms have failure rates averaging 50 percent, that is their insider view. But science states that we can also get an outsider view of condom failure rates by empirically studying the failure rate of condoms. As discussed in chapter 11, we can show the falsity of this insider belief about condoms. Of course, many people do just accept as fact whatever view of the world is promoted in their group. That is precisely why we need science. Without science, different groups would be reduced to a collection of unique subjective viewpoints that could not be compared. Radical social constructionism rejects the possibility of an outsider view and asserts that there thus can be no objective reality—no view that is more accurate than any other. There are only different insider views. This radical philosophy is a recipe for disaster (Merton 1976; Proctor 1991).

The diversity of people and of societies does not prevent social scientists from carefully comparing the diversity of behaviors and attitudes. We do this all the time when we conduct surveys on attitudes toward abortion, premarital sex, homosexuality, or whatever. But this diversity does not lead science to see each of us as so unique that none of us can be put into the same category as others. We can group people who are not identical in general but who are very similar on one or more particular characteristics into the same category. For instance, we can take those who say that abortion is allowable under conditions of rape, incest, and health risks to the mother and place them into one category and compare them to people who reject this position. We can then go on and check further to see if those who are more accepting are also more likely to be liberal on other issues and if those who are more opposed are also more likely to be conservative on other issues. Social science cannot operate without studying different groups, deriving generalizations, and positing explanations for what differences and similarities are found. Comparisons and generalizations are essential to science. Radical social constructionists deny this possibility and portray science as just another subjective perspective of the world. Accordingly, their approach presents a major attack on all forms of science.

Some of you might wonder who in sexual science would assert these radical views. We don't have to look far. Two of the best-known sociologists in our field, John Gagnon and Bill Simon, are advocates of such a position. Unfortunately, Bill Simon passed away in 2000, but his ideas are well known. Allow me to say up front that both of these scientists have made valuable contributions to sexual science, and I have praised these aspects of their work. Also, John and Bill are people that I consider long-time friends. But, on social constructionism, they have taken a radical position.

Here's John Gagnon: "There are no similarities in the meaning of the conduct by individuals or collectivities in different cultures or eras. . . . Sexual conduct of all kinds . . . has to be understood as local phenomena" (1990, 3, 4). This quote is pretty clear—"no similarities" makes the philosophical position of the radical-constructionist group transparent.

Let's now look at a quote from Bill Simon: "[My] posture does imply an abandonment of the ideals of science; for me, more than being a set of procedures, science is essentially an ethical position" (1999, 132). Note that here too we have an affirmation that it is futile to seek scientific answers to our confusions or differences. Bill was a supporter of the postmodern view of society that sees our behaviors as individualized and as explained by the social context in which they occur. In short, the postmodern view is a close relative of the radical social constructionists' perspective (Simon 1996). Both philosophies assert that science cannot offer any comparisons or generalizations that would apply to the wide variety of individualized behaviors in Western societies today.

But the question remains: Why would Gagnon and Simon, or anyone else, support such an extreme approach? I believe that part of their opposition to science is a result of their strong attraction to literary explanations of reality and an affinity for creating ideas that will not be constrained by the demands for evidence and reason that science imposes. Both Gagnon and Simon pretty much affirm this interpretation in their writings (Gagnon 1999; Simon 1999). Actually, there is a built-in contradiction in the radical approach to reality. Radicals put forth their relativistic perspective but affirm it as an absolute truth. But if you affirm a relativistic view of reality, then how can you assert an absolute truth? If all is relative, then so is the theory that all is relative, and there is no basis to affirm that theory as a universal truth. Radical social constructionism would be just another insider perspective, no better than any other.

Nevertheless, what are the reasons that some sexual researchers are attracted to radical social constructionism? I believe that in part this hostility to science grew from the fact that science put forth views that some saw as threatening. For example, the radical critics note that until 1973, the scientific judgment by the American Psychiatric Association was that homosexuality was an abnormality. Further, the early scientific approach to AIDS was to label it as a gay disease, and in fact, for a short time some called it GAIDS. But keep in mind that scientific approaches insist upon self-examination, and the scientific position has changed on homosexuality and on AIDS. Science has built into it the norm that if evidence and reason do not support a particular view, then that view needs to be altered. Surely change hasn't happened as quickly and easily as this norm decrees, but nevertheless science changes more easily than other major social institutions such as religion or politics. Also, despite its flaws, there is not a better approach available to deal with our narrow and mistaken beliefs in the emotional area of human sexuality. A great many more beliefs hostile to homosexuality are held by millions of people in our society, and these people rarely have a norm of examining evidence and of willingness to change. Accordingly, I have little doubt that weakening science would provide a fertile soil for the prejudices in our society to grow and prosper. So, if you want to change such prejudices, the radical social constructionist position is counterproductive.

I believe that another major reason for the rise of radical social constructionism is the belief that if you make reality subjective and noncomparable, then you can't invidiously compare behaviors. Therefore, the radicals believe this would mean that people could no longer condemn sexual behaviors that are now widely criticized. But is that really so? If you were able to convince people to do away with all comparisons, then what would prevent a dictator from killing off all those who do not support his regime? If people can't compare the validity of beliefs and behaviors, then it is correct that nothing can be said to be *better* than anything else, but it is equally true that nothing can be said to be *worse* than anything else. This relativistic philosophy can blow up in your face and lead to disastrous results for you and the social groups that you support. Relativism opens up a very dangerous pathway that can lead to raw power, to emotion taking control, and to the role of science being grossly weakened. I don't think many of us would want to live in that kind of society. There are faults enough in the society we live in now. Let's not add to them.

In the past, the scientific approach has helped our country reduce prejudice in race relations. Consider the 1954 Supreme Court decision on racial integration in the schools, which decision was based on scientific studies by social scientists indicating that public schools that were separated by race could not be equal. Further, in 1973, it was in good measure the increasing amount of scientific evidence and reasoning that convinced the American Psychiatric Association members to vote to take homosexuality off their list of illnesses.

It is also scientific evidence that has supported the effectiveness of condoms to prevent disease and pregnancy. All these actions would be far less likely to have taken place without public support for scientific work. A relativistic antiscience approach would have lessened the likelihood that scientific findings would be accepted as a basis for changing our views. Science is a friend to those who want to increase our control over our sexual problems and to those who would fight prejudice. Science can encourage people to become more pluralistic by promoting the use of evidence and reasoning to determine reality rather than the strength of their insider prejudices or ideologies.

I am not alone in my criticism of radical social constructionism. John Money has voiced his opposition: "The practitioners of social constructionism attack or deconstruct not only particular scientific explanation (and historical and literary explanations also) but also the entire methodology of science. . . . Social Constructionism is not a scientific movement, but a philosophical and literary one" (1995, 13, 136).

I sent a copy of the paper I wrote criticizing radical social constructionism (Reiss 1999) to Robert K. Merton, a very highly regarded sociologist from Columbia University. He wrote me back and commented on the radical social-constructionist position, saying, "Those self-proclaimed sociologists of science have taken a longstanding sociological idea and driven it into self-contradictory and foolish excess" (Reiss 2005).

Radical social constructionism is a Trojan horse brought into the scientific camp. It is not a friend to those who would fight prejudice or promote pluralism. If we follow its path, we will one day wake up and find that public support for the worth of sexual science has all but disappeared. This would indeed be a tragedy for our field as well as for our society.

The Bush Administration's Hostility to Scientific Research in Sexuality

I just went over an antiscience bias that came from people who in many ways are liberals. Now here's an example of antiscience bias that comes from people who in many ways are conservatives—the Bush administration.

Representative Henry Waxman, Democrat from California, heads the Committee on Government Reform Minority Office, and he has in recent years raised very serious concerns about the bias of the Bush administration toward any scientific research that could be used to oppose George W. Bush's ideological positions (Waxman 2004). In fact, the Union of Concerned Scientists (UCS) has accused the Bush administration of distorting and suppressing science to suit its political goals, and 6,300 scientists have signed onto this charge. This list of scientists includes forty-eight Nobel laureates as well as former presidential science advisors dating all the way back to the Eisenhower administration of the 1950s. The Bush administration appears to be opposed to sex research and shows a disregard for scientific values concerning evidence (Leshner 2003; DeLamater 2004; Abraham 2005). Let me relate some of the specific ways this has been happening.

One favorite of the Bush administration is abstinence-only sex education. Such an approach does not deal with contraception but instead teaches students to be abstinent. Millions of dollars are given to organizations that promote such programs, and claims are constantly made by the Bush administration that it is a "proven" method for reducing pregnancy and disease. As I mentioned in chapter 3, the evidence on abstinence-only programs as presented by nationally recognized expert Douglas Kirby clearly contradicts this position (Kirby 2001a, 2001b, 2002). Kirby explicitly states that abstinence-only programs do not work in delaying sex or reducing its frequency. Up until recently, the Centers for Disease Control (CDC) had on its website a list of comprehensive sex-education programs that did seem to work in reducing teen sexual problems. Such comprehensive programs did discuss abstinence, but they also dealt with contraception so as to help those who might become sexually active. The Bush administration recently appointed a prominent advocate of abstinence-only programs, Dr. Joseph McIlhaney, to the Advisory Committee to the Director of CDC. Not long after that, the CDC removed this list of working sex-education programs from its website (Waxman 2003, 2004). This action is hardly helpful to those wanting to reduce pregnancy and disease for teenagers.

Another illustration comes from the condom effectiveness information that was on the CDC website. It was replaced by a new fact sheet that no longer listed instruction on condom use and that had no specific information on the effectiveness of different types of condoms. Instead, there were more statements that stressed condom failure rates and the effectiveness of abstinence-only programs—despite the fact that our best research refutes these assertions. In addition, the site also dropped the scientific evidence that showed that having comprehensive sex education did not lead to increased sexual activity. Again, this new "fact" sheet would hardly be useful to people visiting the site looking for informed guidance.

Breast cancer research has also been impacted by the antiscience bias of the Bush administration. Again, a fact sheet was removed from the website of the National Cancer Institute (NCI). This fact sheet had reported that there is no link between abortions and breast cancer. When scientists criticized the removal of this fact sheet, they were told that there was one older study that reported a link between breast cancer and having had an abortion. However, what was not said was that several more recent and much better designed studies showed no link between abortion and breast cancer.

I'll skip all the other areas that show the same meddling with scientific reports that contradict the administration's policies. These include reports on pollution, lead poisoning, and more. This antiscience policy is clearly allowing politics to literally trample science. Much of the information on these websites would better be described as Bush administration propaganda rather than factual knowledge. Surely, other administrations have made a few moves in the direction of containing scientific reports they didn't like, but those were small inroads compared to this massive invasion of government scientific websites. The general rule seems to be to disregard any scientific evidence or reasoning that does not show support for administration policies. This sort of action is a threat to governmental science organizations, and it is surely not the way a democracy is supposed to be run. It is also a violation of the trust of the American people and shows a disregard for the consequences on public health (Laumann 2001). The only consequence that seems to count is whether the administration's political agenda is being promoted.

The public should be better informed on what is happening, and to date, the media have failed to do this. The more liberal forces in our country are going to have to develop their organizational skills to match those of the conservatives if they hope to make the public more aware of this blockage of sound scientific findings that could be helpful in containing sexual disease and pregnancy. Our sexual-science organizations are going have to respond more than they have and demand that the government keep its hands off of our scientific work. I suggest that we adopt the motto that is carved into stone at the Thomas Jefferson memorial in Washington, D.C.: "Eternal vigilance is the price of liberty." Ask yourself, if we don't defend our own field and our own work, who will? The alternative to speaking out in a way that will be heard by the public is to remain withdrawn from politics and allow Fox News to give the "fair and balanced" truth about sexuality to the American public.

Sexnet Debates: Biology versus Social Science

Sexnet is a Listserv that connects via e-mail about three hundred sexual scientists from the United States and other countries. Issues in sexual science are raised by one person, and anyone on the Listserv who would like to respond can do so. All the messages go to the three hundred or so members of

Sexnet. A great many of today's key sexual scientists are on Sexnet. I have been on it since the spring of 1996. The exchanges that occur on Sexnet help keep the members informed of some of the new research and thinking that exists in sexual science. These exchanges also reveal a good deal about differences of opinion in our field today. Let me discuss some of the key issues concerning biological and social-science research.

There is a turf war between the biological and the social sciences being fought by some members on Sexnet. These two competing sources of research and theory do indeed bump heads at times. For example, in a recent discussion, a person with an evolutionary psychological orientation said, "Careful studies that pit social transmission against genetic transmission for a variety of traits invariably show that genetics is much more powerful." Another biology adherent said, "I do hold my beliefs as religious dogma in that I am a true believer in evolution by natural selection."

Quotes like this are not a good way to build a cooperative spirit between social scientists and biologically oriented scientists. Of course, the bias can come from the social side as well. As I mentioned in the opening section of this chapter, the radical social constructionists might well make dogmatic statements of their own denying any role to biology. However, I haven't heard such views expressed on Sexnet in the nine years that I've been on it. I would hope that the views in the two quotations above and the views of the radical social constructionists are not representative of many of the leaders in biology or social science.

One more-widespread illustration of the competition between the biological and social approaches to sexuality can be found in the response by both groups when the John-Joan case came front and center onto the public and the scientific stages. This case first became widely known to those in sexual science because of the write-up given to it in John Money and Anke Ehrhardt's 1972 book (Money and Ehrhardt 1972, chap. 7). The John-Joan case involved identical twin boys born in Canada in 1966. Due to a tragic circumcision accident, one of the twins lost his penis shortly after birth. About a year and a half later, the parents were advised to raise this twin as a female and in time to do surgery and administer hormones to help in this process. John Money was one of the key supporters of following this regimen. The reasoning was that a penis was much more difficult to artificially produce than was a vagina, and so raising a male infant as a female was likely to be more successful. Money believed that the infant would eventually accept the female gender identity. Over the years, Money helped examine this identical twin and consulted with the parents on raising the twin as a female. In their 1972 book, Money and Ehrhardt indicated that the female gender assigned to this male twin had been adopted successfully by the child.

However, as time went on, there were questions raised by a number of people. One persistent critic of Money's approach in this case was Milton Diamond from the University of Hawaii (Diamond 1982; Diamond and Sigmundson 1997). Diamond's criticism seemed well placed because the twin eventually rejected the female gender identity that had been assigned. He assumed a male gender identity and later married a woman. A few years ago, the John-Joan case became nationally known when it was discussed on the *Oprah Winfrey Show* on television. Tragically, the misassigned twin committed suicide in 2004. What lessons does this case offer to us as sexual scientists?

When Money and Ehrhardt's book appeared in 1972, sociologically and psychologically oriented sexual scientists grabbed onto this case and used it to show the power of learning in determining one's gender identity. All biological factors involved in gender identity were seen as quite flexible and amenable to change. The case became celebrated in the social-science branch of sexual science. I regretfully admit that I used it in my classes to show the power of learning in the formation of gender identity. Then, more recently, when the failure of this case became known on Sexnet, I observed the same strong supportive response from biological scholars. They leaped upon the findings and celebrated them as evidence that biological and not social factors are the key determinants of gender identity. Examining these responses by sexual scientists to this case provides a lesson in making sound scientific decisions.

The basic flaw in both the social and biological scientists' responses to this case is that this is only one case. How in the world can anyone claiming to be a scientist use what happened in one case as a basis for establishing a generalization about the relative power of biological versus social influences in determining gender identity? The responses by scientists to this case indicate the seductiveness of loyalty to one's own discipline. We are all eager to find and accept evidence of the explanatory power of our own disciplinary affiliation. This instance shows the need for us to become more self-aware, or "reflexive" (Bourdieu and Wacquant 1992). The social scientists who endorsed Money and Ehrhardt's view in 1972 now realize their mistake in relying on just one case. The recent eager response of biologists to this same case reveals how loyalty to their discipline's explanatory power can move them away from a careful analysis of evidence. The biological response didn't take long to be challenged. Ken Zucker reported a case in which the results were quite different than those in the John-Joan case (Zucker 2002). Those of us in sexual science should have been more cautious of such scientific partisanship because most of us have been saying that both biological *and* social forces interact with each other. And yet we jumped on our own bandwagon when the opportunity arose. I think the lesson is that we should stay off of bandwagons.

The Interaction of Social and Biological Factors

The more we learn about biological and social influences, the more we see how complex and interrelated are the issues involved in our sexual behavior (Green 1987). Most of the answers are yet to be discovered (LeVay 2003). Michael Rutter in a recent article discussed this issue of "excessive polarizing claims" in a very enlightening fashion (Rutter 2002). He calls this impulsive tendency to leap upon thin evidence to make excessive claims of causal influence "scientific evangelism." I like this term a great deal, for it helps make us all more aware of our own tendencies to favor our field's explanatory power. Rutter stresses that in humans, biological and social factors are always both operating. Neither factor operates in a vacuum. Behavioral outcomes will always depend on both biological and social-psychological factors, and their relative role may well vary from culture to culture (Wallen and Zehr 2004).

To illustrate this, consider the cross-cultural comparison of male rates of murder and other violent crimes in the United States and in Western Europe. In the United States, we have many times the rate of violent crimes, but our males are not significantly different biologically from Western European males. So, clearly the same biology has different outcomes when you vary the cultural settings (Lippa and Tan 2001; Hatfield et al. 2005). The converse of this is also the case, so if you increase the power of the biological input, then the effectiveness of the culture to modify it will be impacted. Let me further specify how this interaction effect works by referring to three recent sexual-science research-and-theory projects.

One example of the interaction of biological and social forces comes from the work of Kim Wallen (1996). Wallen is a primatologist at Emory University and has studied rhesus monkeys since the 1960s. In a most enlightening paper, Wallen compared the differences between male and female rhesus monkeys under a variety of social conditions. By social conditions, Wallen was comparing differences in social-group rearing, such as peer-group rearing, versus mother/peer rearing of infants. He varied the amount of time the monkeys spent in each of these social contexts. One interesting result was that female submissiveness was only found when the infants were raised predominantly in peer-group rearing settings. Another valuable finding was that the very common presenting behavior of female primates (in which the female

displays her rear to the male) was in some social contexts shown more frequently by males than by females! Kim concluded,

> If it is true that nature needs nurture, that a hormonally induced behavioral
> predisposition can only be expressed in a supportive social environment, then
> the complement is also true; nurture requires nature. . . . The fact that a be-
> havioral sexual dimorphism occurs only within a specific social context does
> not eliminate the need to consider an underlying sex difference in predisposi-
> tion to engage in specific behaviors. . . . Social context and biological predis-
> positions are indispensable components in the development of behavior sex
> differences. (Wallen 1996, 377)

This thought is a beautiful summation of the point I have been trying to
make. We surely do need many more studies of the interactions of environmental and biological influences. Of course, you can just research the biological or the sociocultural forces, and that is also a legitimate way to do research. For example, I did just that only a few years ago and examined trends
in premarital, homosexual, and extramarital sexuality over the past few
decades in a large number of cultures around the world (Reiss 2001b). Any
changes in sexuality that occur in a generation or so are far too rapid to have
any significant biological input, and so this type of research doesn't have to
tie in with biology. Even in such studies, we would ultimately want to know
whether there were any biological factors that were known to promote or resist the reported trends. Conversely, if this were a study by a biologist, we
would also at some point expect acknowledgment that sociocultural forces
could be altering the effect of biological predispositions. The reality of human sexuality requires knowledge of multiple disciplines, and we need to further investigate the interactions of our fields in order to paint a more complete picture of our human sexuality and enable us to build more
sophisticated theoretical explanations.

Here's a second study that uses an interactionist view of biological and
social forces. This one proposes an explanation of sexual orientation. Daryl
Bem of Cornell University, a psychologist, has proposed a theory about sexual orientation that combines elements of biology and sociocultural learning in a most intriguing theoretical approach. He calls his view the exotic
becomes erotic (EBE) theory. The fundamental assumption of Bem's theory
is that we become erotically attracted to a class of individuals that we in
childhood felt were different from us. Bem brings in biological factors as
the determinants of temperament differences in such traits as aggressive-
ness and activity level. Our particular temperament is seen as making us fit
best with the gender role that most incorporates our temperament traits.

So, if you are physically aggressive, then you would likely feel more at home in the male gender role (Bem 2000).

Bem contends that as a child, we associate predominantly with others in the gender that best expresses our temperament. People in the other gender role are seen as exotic, and they may be viewed with disapproval, as dangerous, or as difficult to understand. Physiological feelings can be aroused by the other gender's mysteriousness and unknown qualities, and this can in time turn into erotic attraction. A male homosexual orientation would result when a male in childhood felt different from most other males and thus was more comfortable with the female gender (Reiss 1986, chap. 6). This comfort would be reflected in their childhood friendships. In such a case, it would be those in the male gender role that would be seen as different, and thus in time those people would become sexually attractive. That, in very brief form, is the exotic becomes erotic theory.

Bem tests his theory empirically by using the existing Australian Twin Registry of almost five thousand twins from Australia (Bailey et al. 2000). He compares his theory of sexual orientation with an alternate popular view that asserts that sexual orientation is due predominantly to genetic factors. Support for this alternate biological theory is found in the report that identical twins are more likely to both be homosexual than are fraternal twins (Bearman and Bruckner 2002). But Bem claims that his test using the large Australian Twin Registry shows that the relationship between type of twin (identical versus fraternal) and sexual orientation (homosexual versus heterosexual) is really the result of identical twins being more alike in temperament than fraternal twins and that it is this temperament similarity and *not* any "gay genes" that determines the greater similarity in identical-twin sexual orientation. Bem further contends that it is this similarity of temperament that determines the degree of childhood gender nonconformity and that childhood gender nonconformity then leads to a homosexual orientation. In sum, then, Bem found there to be no direct relationship between genetic similarity and sexual orientation in his examination of the Australian Twin Registry.

This is an impressive test result, and it makes Bem's theory one that others will want to further examine. I find his theory quite enticing in that it integrates biological and sociocultural forces in a way that explains both heterosexual and homosexual orientations. However, the relatively minor role it gives to biological forces will encourage biologists to be less receptive to it than I am. The key to the future of his theory is how well it holds up under reexamination by others. But, for now, Bem's theory is an impressive addition to our multidisciplinary theoretical development.

A third and final example of multidisciplinary theory comes from the recent work of Richard Udry, a sociologist at the University of North Carolina (Udry 2000). Udry wanted to test the idea that a female's exposure to male hormones as a fetus will masculinize her behavior as she grows into adulthood. He used a sample of mothers studied in the 1960s on whom there were extensive data concerning their pregnancy and blood tests indicating how much male hormone was transmitted from them to their fetuses during their pregnancies. In 1990 and 1991, he tested 163 of the daughters of these mothers, who were born in the early 1960s. He gave these daughters a written questionnaire that allowed him to measure their femininity-masculinity. He predicted that this score would be based on the level of male hormones present in their mother's during their pregnancy. His theory predicted that the greater the level of the male hormones in the mothers during their pregnancy, the greater the tendency toward masculine behaviors in their daughters.

The results indicated that exposure to prenatal male hormone (androgen) during the second trimester did indeed predict masculine behavior tendencies reported by the daughters in their responses to the femininity-masculinity questions. Prenatal exposure during the first or third trimester had no effect. It was exposure during the second trimester that was crucial. Interestingly, Udry also found that the lower the prenatal exposure to male hormone, the more likely it was that the daughters had responded favorably to their mother's attempts to increase their feminine behavior. So, the mother's socialization attempts had an impact, but more so on those daughters with low androgen exposure in the second trimester. These results indicate there does indeed seem to be in humans an interaction between biological factors (hormones) and social behavior (masculine versus feminine). Udry encouraged other sociologists and biologists to further study this interaction. To me, an important aspect to measure more specifically would be the degree of resistance to sociocultural parental and peer influences that a child exposed to male hormones exhibits. The biological leash seems to be present, but I for one would like to know just how far it can be extended.

Finally, let me note that Edward O. Wilson, the father of sociobiology and today's evolutionary psychology, also recognizes the interaction of sociocultural forces and biological forces in his classic work (Wilson 2000, vi–viii):

No serious scholar would think that human behavior is controlled the way animal instinct is, without the intervention of culture. In the interactionist view held by virtually all who study the subject, genomic biases mental development but cannot abolish culture . . . acceptance of the interaction of biology and culture as the determinant of mental development. . . . We know that cultural evolution is biased substantially by biology, and that biological evolution of the brain, especially the neocortex, has occurred in a social context.

I should also mention that there are other people in sexual science who point out clearly what issues have to be tended to and what concepts need to be defined, and who offer suggestions as to how to pursue these and other multidisciplinary theoretical issues (Chivers 2005; Diamond 2003; Rosen and McKenna 2002). One of these people is Julia Heiman, the current director of the Kinsey Institute. She has worked to clear the underbrush in a number of conceptual areas, among which are two areas that caught my attention. One of these is child sexual abuse, and the other is sexual desire (Heiman 2001; Heiman et al. 2003). These are two very important areas in sexual science, and anyone interested in sexual science would do well to consult her work.

Defining Gender Roles

The last section gave you the good news about interdisciplinary theories. Now here's some not-so-good news about these theories. As I discussed earlier in this chapter, there is a territorial dispute going on between biological and social scientists. For decades, the learned aspects of sexuality have dominated the public mind, but the advent of mapping the human genome by biologists has led in recent years to a major burst of public respect and regard for biologists. So the relative power of these two fields is being rearranged, and some conflict is to be expected. There are innovative ways of bringing biologists and social scientists closer together that are worth reading about, but our clashes continue (Lieberson and Lynn 2002; Massey 2002).

This conflict between disciplines has impeded efforts to derive a common nomenclature of concepts. The concept of gender role is an excellent example of this lack of shared definitions of key concepts in the study of human sexuality. Together with most social scientists, I see *gender roles* as those behaviors and attitudes that a particular society expects of biological males and females. This is a definition that the prestigious Institute of Medicine agrees with (Institute of Medicine 2001). In most human societies, the assignment to a specific *sex* (male or female) is made simply by an inspection of an infant's genitalia. It is important to distinguish the concept of *gender* from the concept of biological *sex*. Whether a person is seen as belonging to the male or female sex is determined by examination of reproductive organs and of the organization of the X and Y chromosomes. Here, also, the Institute of Medicine accepts this definition (Institute of

Medicine 2001). I mention this so that the reader is aware that my definitions are not just coming from a social scientist.

When I talked of my definitions on Sexnet, I found that many biologically orientated people thought that my definition of gender roles excluded any biological input. In fact, some biologists said they personally defined gender roles as only those aspects of being male and female that are *not* biologically determined. Such differences in definition can make communication and joint research quite difficult. Let me say at the outset that I, for one, would *not* restrict gender roles totally to cultural influences, because I believe there is always some sort of interaction of the biological and social in the gender roles assigned by a society. For example, the female-role emphasis on parenthood and the male-role emphasis on casual sex are surely related to biological as well as cultural factors. So, if you focus in on these very common aspects of gender roles, it is easier to become aware that there are some very widely shared biological differences between men and women that predispose them to the culturally assigned aspects of gender roles. Cross-cultural research is very important, for it makes us aware of the full range of gender roles rather than just the narrow choices made in any one society, and it shows that societies vary in the degree to which they differentiate men and women even on common roles such as parenthood and casual sex (Reiss 1986). The interaction of biological and cultural factors is thus revealed by such broad cross-cultural research.

I believe that for the sake of clarity, it would be well if both social and biological scientists would accept the use of gender roles to describe the roles a society assigns to men and women. Then we could search for both sociocultural and biological factors that may be involved in these role assignments and try to understand the ways in which these forces interact (Schwartz and Rutter 1998). For all explanations of differences between men and women, we should require that the biological mechanisms by which the gender roles are influenced be identified and examined, and the same of course would be the case for the sociocultural mechanisms that are believed to be influential. In short, let's demand specific empirical support and not just an assertion that gender roles must be biologically or socioculturally caused (Hyde 2005).

The definitions of gender roles and of sex that I propose keeps the issue of the sources of influence open, and I strongly believe that it is to our advantage to accept this joint approach to these concepts. Let's avoid the extreme theoretical positions that assert that there is no significant role for biological influences or that there is no significant role for sociocultural influences. Let's instead concede that both biological and sociocultural forces are involved in our definition of gender roles and then work together to unravel them and explain their interaction. This approach will help reduce the separation and conflict between our disciplines.

Some of the complexity of the issues concerning the interaction of biological and social influences is shown by this section's brief examination of some of the variation in both the biological and social spheres. The picture gets even more complex when we realize that there are more than just biological males and females who clearly have the genitalia of only one sex. There are also the intersex people who exist in all major societies. These are infants born with genitalia that are not clearly male or female. This is where the assignment of gender to infants becomes difficult. John Money, as noted above, has proposed that we use our surgical and hormonal abilities to produce a solution such as that tried in John-Joan case. There is increasing opposition to this view today (Diamond 1999; Meyer-Bahlburg 2001). In addition to intersex infants, there are also infants who are chromosomally not just XX or XY. Some have extra Xs and/or extra Ys. So there is a good deal of biological variation. Finally, as I mentioned in chapter 7, there are societies with more than two genders (Martin and Voorhies 1975, chap. 4).

The study of human sexuality is a quite complex endeavor, and we would be wise to learn to work together. If a multidisciplinary understanding of human sexuality is to prosper, we need to develop more agreement on the meanings of our basic concepts such as gender and sex. More cross-disciplinary interaction at professional meetings in both the biological and the social-psychological sciences would be one very helpful step toward this cooperative goal.

~

CHAPTER FOURTEEN

Building a PhD in Sexual Science

In 1981, when I gave my presidential address at the SSSS meeting, I spoke of the value of keeping sexual science as a subfield of established disciplines such as sociology, psychology, and biology. I felt that sexual science would benefit in both research and theory skills by being part of these established disciplines as a subfield in which you could specialize. I felt there was no pressing need to try to also develop our own discipline of sexual science. I hadn't yet realized that we could do both—keep our subfields in existing disciplines and also have our own discipline. After all, this is exactly what all the existing disciplines do. For example, you can minor in a wide variety of existing disciplines within sociology, such as psychology, and biology. By the late 1980s, I had realized this. In fact, by that time, I was convinced that sexual science would not prosper without the addition of a sexual science PhD program. This chapter explains what led me to this change of mind.

Some Programs in Sexuality

College courses in sexuality began to multiply in the late 1960s. Before that, the subject of sex was dealt with in other courses. Kinsey dealt with it in his marriage classes, and that was a common place for others as well (Gathorne-Hardy 2000, chap. 7). As I noted in chapter 2, I dealt with sexuality in my course on the family in 1953. But, by the late 1960s, classes focusing on sexuality, and labeled as such, began to be offered. Over the ensuing years, such courses were offered in departments of sociology, psychology, and biology, as well as in public health, health education, education, home economics, family social science, and other departments. These courses were not standardized in any way. Some had therapeutic aims, some attempted value indoctrination, and some focused on applications to specific problems; only a few stressed a scientific research-and-theory perspective. In addition, a few graduate programs, like sociology and psychology, began to consider allowing a minor area in sexuality within their PhD programs.

By the 1970s, there were attempts to establish graduate programs in sexual science and to award degrees. One of them was initiated by Ted McIlvenna, whose sexual attitudes reassessment program was discussed in chapter 5. In 1976, McIlvenna and several of the same people who had been involved in developing the SAR program decided to found the Institute for the Advanced Study of Human Sexuality. Ted was able to entice Wardell Pomeroy, formerly one of Kinsey's close associates, to become the dean of this new institute. The State of California did give initial approval to the institute to grant graduate degrees in human sexuality. But, despite efforts by Wardell Pomeroy, the institute was unable to obtain traditional academic accreditation for the graduate degrees they were awarding. The problem with obtaining the usual accreditation was the untraditional nature of the program at the institute. It included courses in massage as well as courses focused on sexually explicit films, and there was no adequate training in research methodology or theoretical analysis. There were three two-week periods during the calendar year when students could attend the institute. At those times, the institute would invite academic and other speakers to come in and talk about their work. During the rest of the year, students were expected to spend time reading relevant books or writing papers. McIlvenna did not want to change the program to meet broader standards, so the Institute for the Advanced Study of Human Sexuality has never been able to obtain traditional accreditation.

I was interested in the innovativeness of the program, and in June 1978, I accepted an invitation to talk to their graduate students. I located the building they were in on the 1500 block of Franklin Street in San Francisco. It looked like just another private home, and I wondered if I was at the right place. I knocked on the door, and a man with only a white towel around his waist opened the door. I was puzzled and asked, "Is this the institute?"

He smiled and said, "Yes, of course. Come on in. You must be Ira Reiss. I am Lewis Durham, dean of students at the institute. Several of us are in the hot tub right now. Do you want to join us?"

So it was very clear to me from the outset that this was not a traditional educational institute. Ted McIlvenna came out a few minutes later from his massage class and offered me some wine and cheese and took me on a tour of the building. Upstairs, there was an extensive library of books on sexuality. He said it was the largest collection of books on sexuality of any library in the world. Then he showed me his very extensive collection of erotic videos. Some of the films were ones that Laird Sutton had made for the institute's SAR program, but most of them were commercial or private sex films. It looked like a large enough collection to rival that at the Kinsey Institute.

The next day, I talked to the graduate students for three hours. There were about forty or fifty students in attendance. They were a very diverse group. Many held jobs and were seeking a degree to advance themselves in their workplace. Some were seeking knowledge that might help them in their personal problems. Others wanted to be sex therapists and sex educators. I didn't meet any students who primarily wanted to do scientific sex research and develop explanatory theories. In the years since then, I have gone back to the institute four more times, the last time being in 2001. Unfortunately, I did not notice any progress in the research-and-theory training of the students. There was little evidence in any administrators of an interest in familiarizing the students with the methodology and theory construction techniques that existed in the field of sexuality. As a result, the students seemed ill prepared to do any sort of scientific research, and many of them did not even seem to understand what such work involved. Now, it's fine for an innovative academic program to value nonscientific approaches more than scientific approaches, but it's quite a different thing to oppose or ignore scientific knowledge and its perspectives when you are awarding academic degrees.

It seemed that the narrowness I had detected in the San Francisco SAR that Ted McIlvenna had run back in 1972 was still alive and well (see chapter 5). The heir apparent to Ted McIlvenna was Howard Ruppel. In 2003 at the SSSS meeting, Ruppel told me that he personally didn't place much value on the scientific approach to sexuality. He also told me that the institute was now going to focus on professional degrees rather than academic degrees such as the PhD.

Other, more conventional programs for graduate students interested in studying human sexuality were also developing. The PhD program in education at the University of Pennsylvania developed a sexuality minor, but the minor program went out of existence in the late 1990s. Nevertheless, it had produced a number of students with doctoral course work in sexuality from a major university, and that was a step forward for sexual science. However, there never was a degree in sexuality there, just a minor within the education PhD program. Another program that is still in existence is at New York University. They, too, allowed for a specialization in sexuality within the health education PhD program, but here, as well, there was no degree in sexuality, only a specialization within another discipline. Other colleges developed a master's degree program that dealt with sexuality. I won't try to cover all of these programs, but they do show that there was indeed a strong interest in developing such programs. It also indicates that there are many students out there who would like to learn more about sexuality.

In just the last few years, some new programs have developed. Gil Herdt, an anthropologist, took over the sexuality program at San Francisco State University (SFSU). A program in sexuality had been in existence there since 1970, and Herdt worked hard to get an MA degree in human sexuality studies established. The emphasis in this program's content was on courses dealing with issues in society, but I was pleased to see that there was a methods-and-statistics element in the program. Herdt has established organizational extensions of his academic program with people who work on containing sexual problems. The entire undertaking is most ambitious, and there is much more to it than I am describing here. Unfortunately, since SFSU is not one of the nine California universities, they cannot award a doctorate degree. But their multifaceted efforts are worth keeping in touch with.

Another new program is one established a few years ago at Widener University in Pennsylvania. The program involves an emphasis on sexuality education and on counseling and therapy. The director of the program is Dr. William Stayton. The program links with the Center for Sexuality and Religion and the Council for Relationships. These organizations are described as communities of faith. The Council for Relationships was founded back in 1932 as a training center for couple, marital, family, and sex counseling. There is a clear tie to religion, but the program includes a broad training in other fields. You can obtain a graduate degree in education and sexuality. Some of the tracks in the program allow for social-work degrees that are also tied to sexuality.

There is much more to the San Francisco State University and the Widener programs than I have described. Anyone interested can of course contact the universities and get a much more complete portrait of what is being offered. There are also a number of other programs in the country, such as the Center for Sex Research at California State University–Northridge that Vern Bullough founded in the 1970s and that James Elias now runs. I have presented here only those programs that I have had contact with or where the people running them have spoken to me about their programs. As is the case throughout this book, I am not attempting to present a total survey of all areas of our field but rather to discuss those parts of the field with which I have had some contact.

Working toward a PhD in Sexual Science

What turned my thinking around concerning the need for a new discipline of sexual science was my examination of how sexual science was treated in most of our colleges and universities. It is now almost forty years since the first courses in sexuality were developed. It seems that the study of sexuality within existing departments and disciplines is still evaluated as a low-ranking specialization. This surely is true in sociology, and my contacts in other fields verify that it is the same in their departments. Now, given this state of affairs, what sort of future is there for our field? Being low on most departments' totem pole isn't a solid basis for predicting a happy future for our field. Let's face it; the problem in good part is that we are academic orphans—we have no disciplinary home, and so no academic department places us at the top of their hierarchy of specializations. We are wanderers in the lands of other disciplines. If, after so many decades of classes in sexuality, we are still not highly valued in academia, then I would think it is time we made some changes.

Let me ask a question to those of you who do specialize in the area of sexuality. How would you respond if someone asked you what your field is? Most people would answer with the field they received their degree in: sociology, psychology, biology, education, social work, public health, or whatever. Few of us would say our field is sexology or sexual science. Our degree determines our academic affiliation. As of 2005, we have no PhD program that awards a doctorate degree in sexual science at any major American university.

This lack of a PhD program, in which the future leaders of our field would be produced, is important. The influence of any field in our society is in good measure determined by the public support for that field. The public view of sexual science is still skeptical. They ask what our credentials are and what sort of training we give to future members of our field. By the late 1980s, it seemed clear to me that we had no good answers to such inquiries. If we had our own discipline of sexual science in a major university, then those questions could be better answered. The present situation is a poor basis for getting support for our research proposals from the government or from private foundations. Those agencies also want to know about the competence and knowledge training of the grant applicants. The best solution that I saw as capable of turning things around was for us to work to establish a PhD program in sexual science at a major university.

In the early 1990s, I actively sought to get the Society for the Scientific Study of Sexuality (SSSS) to set up a task force that would promote the growth of a degree program in sexual science. I found it very difficult to get the leadership of SSSS to agree to form a task force to work for this goal. By the mid-1990s, one other voice was heard promoting educational opportunities in the study of sexuality. Diane di Mauro had assessed the current state of sexual science in a project sponsored by the Social Science Research Council (SSRC), and she had concluded that we badly needed additional educational opportunities (di Mauro 1995). But she was not directly supporting the formation of an academic department of sexual science. However, she did help establish an SSRC program that supported PhD dissertation work in sexuality that was being conducted in existing disciplines. That surely was an important step in the direction of improving the status of sexual science, but it was only a step. We needed a PhD program in sexual science in order to show the public and the granting agencies that we did indeed represent a valuable approach that would increase our understanding and our ability to deal with the country's sexual problems.

In 1996, several of us in SSSS started a committee to promote the establishment of a PhD in sexual science. Unfortunately, the chair of that committee never set up a meeting and just left the committee dormant. In 1998, I tried once again to form a task force, and this time I sought and received support from the leadership of SSSS and also from the leadership of the American Association of Sex Educators, Counselors, and Therapists. The boards of both organizations endorsed my proposal to set up a task force to work to encourage the development of a degree program in sexual science at one or more of our major universities. I agreed to chair the committee. Finally things were moving. We were on our way to building our own academic home.

Right after the task force was formed, Stephanie Sanders, the associate director of the Kinsey Institute, suggested to me that the Kinsey Institute might be interested in working with us on a PhD in sexual science at Indiana University. The director of the Kinsey Institute, John Bancroft, also displayed interest in hearing more about our proposal. So the task force set up a meeting in May 1999 at the Kinsey Institute. The Kinsey Institute was and still is the flagship of sexual science. It was there that Alfred Kinsey began his groundbreaking research in the scientific study of human sexuality. I was very excited about the possibility that the Kinsey Institute might take on the development of a new PhD in sexual science. I vowed to myself to do all I could to make it a reality.

The Essential Elements of a
PhD in Sexuality: Making the Case

In preparation for our meeting at the Kinsey Institute, our task force needed to develop a broad outline of the type of PhD in sexual science that we wanted to establish. I wrote up my perspective on such a PhD program and sent it to the task-force members for their suggestions and evaluation. They approved it. There were three basic organizing principles in our proposal. First, we wanted to promote a program that emphasized scientific research and theory. Scientific emphasis seemed to be a missing or weak element in many of the courses offered in sexuality. There was instead a heavy emphasis on personal problems, literary and historical factors, ideological influences in sex, and much more. We felt that at least one program should place a scientific emphasis at the top of its priorities.

Our second organizing principle was that the PhD program be multidisciplinary. We did not want to enthrone medicine, biology, sociology, psychology, public health, or any other field. Rather, we wanted to draw upon the research-and-theory knowledge of all these disciplines. Human sexuality is influenced by multiple forces, and so to really understand it would require a multidisciplinary education. Our third major goal in our proposed PhD program was to use the knowledge of sexual science to help contain the myriad of sexual problems that plagued our personal lives and our society.

On May 24, 1999, John DeLamater, Frank Farley, and I met with the key people at the Kinsey Institute: John Bancroft, Stephanie Sanders, Bill Yarber, and Cindy Graham. John Bancroft had also invited a graduate school dean to attend part of the meeting. I presented our three basic principles to the group. There seemed to be general agreement on them. But I knew that I had to do much more. I needed to make the case for why there was a need for such a new PhD program and why it was reasonable to expect it to be a successful venture. I sought to do this by dealing with the key issues that over the years people had raised with me whenever I would propose the establishment of a PhD in sexual science. I focused on four of these issues.

Issue one: "That sounds good, but this just isn't a good time to do it." My response to this was to pose the question, when would it be a good time? Did our sex organizations wait until it was a "good time" before becoming established? Was the conservative 1950s a good time to establish the Society for the Scientific Study of Sexuality? Should we have taken the opposition of the John Birch Society and other organizations in the 1960s and 1970s as a sign that it wasn't a good time to establish our other organizations like the Sex Information and Education Council of the United States; the American Association of Sex Educators, Counselors, and Therapists; and the International Academy of Sex Research? The pressure to do something now comes from the fact that our work in sexuality has not received the regard or the recognition that the study of sexuality deserves. We need something now to turn this situation around. Shall we wait another few decades and see if a "good time" arrives? Or shall we recognize the need and establish our own degree program now?

Issue two: "Why do you think we could succeed in founding a new discipline of sexual science in our universities?" I started my answer by referring to the increased spending by the government in dealing with sexual problems such as HIV/AIDS, rape, teenage pregnancy, and child sexual abuse. If our new discipline could deliver more effective ways of dealing with these problems, there would be strong economic pressure in our favor. Today, there are already large centers of research funded by the federal government to undertake HIV/AIDS research. There is one at Columbia Medical, one at Wisconsin Medical, and one at San Francisco Medical. Although these research enterprises are all at medical schools, the people employed are from many different disciplines. The funding has continued for years, and these research centers are seen as very helpful in the attempt to control HIV/AIDS. So the success of these research centers is evidence that sexual-science research is one valuable way to deal with our sexual problems. Establishing our own discipline of sexual science would afford us more recognition in the granting agencies and increase our success in obtaining research and teaching grants. The public, too, would respond favorably to the presence of a discipline that would train our PhD researchers. A PhD in sexual science would thus be a major help in establishing sexual science's academic credentials. The university that was the first to establish such a department would be rewarded in terms of access to research funds and an increase in talented students interested in the new degree program.

Issue three: "Where will people with a PhD in sexual science get their jobs?" The people who research or teach in the area of sexuality today are trained in a variety of disciplines such as sociology, psychology, biology, social work, public health, and the like. Many are now employed in medical schools, public health institutes, and social-work organizations, as well as in departments like sociology, psychology, and biology. Those with a PhD in sexual science would be able to apply for these same positions. Furthermore, the presence of a PhD program at a major university would enhance the status of those who minored in sexuality within other disciplines, as there would then be a home discipline they could identify with.

There is a much more multidisciplinary approach in our universities today. People realize that reality extends beyond the borders of any single discipline. In addition, there is a demand for people at our colleges who can teach an undergraduate course in sexuality. These classes are very popular, and this means they have high student enrollment. Departments like to have high enrollments, so there would be an interest in hiring people trained in sexual science. Therefore, there should be no problems with finding jobs for those with a PhD in sexual science. In fact, I would expect them to do better than many of those who are trained within the older disciplines.

Issue four: "Are you proposing that we must stop people from teaching about sexuality in other disciplines?" Some people in our field seem to think that if we develop a PhD in sexual science and work to establish a department of sexual science, then we must want people to stop teaching sexuality courses in other departments. That is not at all the case. In fact, we want people to continue to teach sexuality in sociology, psychology, and biology departments because it is precisely the perspectives of these and other departments that will be the building blocks of any new multidisciplinary degree program in sexual science. We could not have a multidisciplinary degree in sexual science without having people in the different disciplines who are studying sexuality, so we need the continued employment of these people within the older departments.

Keep in mind that all existing disciplines allow people in other disciplines to minor in their discipline. For example, sociologists can minor in psychology, public health, and many other fields, and people in each of these fields can minor in other fields. There is no reason to expect it to be different when a department of sexual science is established. In short, a PhD in sexual science would add a discipline for people to belong to; it would not change the ability to be in an older discipline and specialize in sexual science. In addition, the number of new PhDs in sexual science would be few to begin with. As the new discipline of sexual science becomes established, we will gradually see small new departments of sexual science emerge at a few universities.

I finished my presentation, and others on our task force made their comments. I then waited to see what the reaction would be from the dean. He said that he was indeed interested in such a new program, but he had some questions. He asked where all the faculty would come from to teach the courses in such a PhD program in sexual science. He also wanted to know how such additional faculty would be funded. I responded that the faculty would largely come from the existing faculty at Indiana University's campus who were currently teaching sexuality courses in their own departments. I added that there would also need to be some faculty from other universities, since no other single university had sufficient depth in all the different disciplines needed to teach a multidisciplinary program in sexuality.

My plan was to bring in the specialists not on campus for short sessions in the summer. This could be paid for by obtaining summer grants from the government or from private foundations that would be willing to pay for such faculty to come to Indiana University. Grants could also pay for graduate students to attend these summer classes. Another possibility for using faculty from other universities would be to utilize distance education and have students attend video classes given by professors at other universities. These classes would be monitored by discussion leaders from the Indiana faculty. Such video classes are not very expensive. Overall, then, I suggested that a PhD in sexual science would not involve much in the way of new expenses. The Kinsey Institute staff would be responsible for organizing the courses and the other aspects of the new PhD program.

I went on to point out that there is a similar multidisciplinary structure in most of our medical schools. Part of the medical school teaching faculty consists of faculty gathered from various university departments such as biology, physiology, anatomy, psychology, and genetics. Many of the professors in those departments stay in their disciplines but offer courses open to medical school students. The medical school coordinates the work of these faculty members in the training of medical students. Medical school teaching programs thus were a good illustration of the type of program that our task force was proposing for sexual science.

Over time, as the program progressed, a new department of sexual science would be established. It would take a few years to fully develop the program, and it surely would involve a great deal of work, but it would be worth it. Setting up such a PhD program in sexual science would make Indiana University the first university in America to establish a PhD in sexual science. Such a degree would attract students from all over the country. In addition to those wishing to major in sexuality, there would be students who would come to Indiana University to fulfill their minor in sexual-science requirements. Those in other disciplines who wanted to minor in sexual science could do so right away, for there was already a PhD minor in sexual science at Indiana University. It had been languishing in the past few years, but John Bancroft said that he and his staff had plans under way to build up this existing minor. The students from other disciplines who wanted a minor in sexuality would be among the first to take the summer institute courses that grant funds would support. I mentioned one other feature that I thought the dean would like. I noted the large amount of federal grant money available for research on HIV/AIDS. A sexuality project that had HIV/AIDS as one of its key elements would have a good chance to receive such federal funds. Those funds carry large operating expense budgets that go to the university.

The dean and the Kinsey staff listened to my comments and those from others on our task force. From time to time, the dean, Bancroft, and his staff raised questions. I anxiously waited to see what the dean's overall response would be. It would be very helpful to start out such a new program with support from a graduate school dean. Finally, the dean smiled and said he was impressed by the proposal and that he felt it could be supported by the university, and over time it could win approval by the other administrative units that would have to approve any such new program. I was elated at his supportive response. The dean left, and I waited to hear more from the Kinsey Institute staff. I didn't have to wait long. John Bancroft and his colleagues, Stephanie Sanders, Bill Yarber, and Cindy Graham, not only approved our task force's proposals but showed enthusiastic support for it. Cindy Graham, in particular, said she would make the progress toward a PhD in sexual science one of her top priorities. That night, John Bancroft took us all out to dinner. He toasted to the proposed new program, which he said would "go down in the history books as a major step forward for the entire field of sexual science." I don't know how this meeting could have been better!

Right after I returned home from the task-force meeting, I began to work on locating funding sources for the summer institutes. I called people in Washington, D.C., and found out what grants were available for summer institutes from the various government agencies. I also talked to people in private foundations and learned which ones would be most interested. I passed on my findings to John Bancroft, and he applied for and received a grant for summer institutes, to begin in 2001. In the summer of 2001, the Kinsey Institute brought in professors in sexuality from various universities for the first short summer programs. They had twenty-five places for graduate students, and about three times that number applied. The summer institute was off to a running start.

The summer institute was repeated the next few summers as well and continued to have applicants far outnumbering the number of places available for students. Faculty were very willing to come to Indiana University for these short summer sessions. This success helped the staff of the Kinsey Institute make teaching a significant part of the institute's work. That was something they wanted to do, so working to establish a PhD in sexual science fit very well with the desires of the institute staff. Of course, getting final approval for a PhD in sexual science would take time, but the initial groundwork had been put in place at that May 1999 meeting.

More Progress toward a PhD in Sexual Science

I continued to keep up with what was happening at the Kinsey Institute in terms of the PhD program, and I was very pleased with developments. John Bancroft wrote me in 2002 specifying the progress that had been made at that point. The Board of Governors had given strong support to the graduate program that the Kinsey Institute was developing. Further, they said their support would extend into the future, when a new director of the institute would replace John Bancroft. The interdisciplinary PhD minor in sexuality that had been languishing for years was expanded and was attracting more and more students. This PhD minor involved courses from faculty in a number of departments at Indiana University, and thus it helped in the move toward more coordination between these faculty in the buildup toward a PhD in sexual science (di Mauro et al. 2003, chap. 8).

The gender studies program at Indiana University valued the proposed PhD in sexual science. Stephanie Sanders, the Kinsey Institute's assistant director, was a key professor in the gender group. The gender studies group had years earlier proposed a new PhD in their field, and it is expected that sometime in 2005 that PhD program will be fully approved. The students in gender studies are very interested in taking courses in sexual science, and sexual science will likely become the most popular minor area for gender studies students. One intriguing possibility is to set up a joint PhD program of gender and sexual science. That could be a place for sexual science to launch toward its own PhD. In 2004, the new director of the Kinsey Institute, Julia Heiman, took over from John Bancroft, and she has expressed her support for the PhD program in sexual science. So we are moving closer and closer to our goals, and the faculty at Indiana University, particularly at the Kinsey Institute, are continuing their efforts to make the new PhD in sexual science a reality (Graham et al. 2003).

After things had been set in motion toward the new sexual-science program, I asked John DeLamater to become chair of the task force, and John accepted the role. He has worked to establish a three-university program (including the University of Wisconsin, the University of Chicago, and the University of Minnesota) for graduate students who wish to minor in sexuality. This joint program would connect with the University of Minnesota's Program in Human Sexuality headed by Eli Coleman. I should add here that in 2004, Eli Coleman's PHS raised a million dollars to fund a chair in sexual health that will permanently exist here at the University of Minnesota. I believe this is the first such chair in our country. Eli Coleman's PHS includes major research projects, but it also has a large clinical training program involving a number of sex therapists.

I haven't talked about all the specific fields that could be part of a multidisciplinary program in sexual science. I just want to emphasize here that there is a scientific side to all fields that study sexuality, so they should all become part of any multidisciplinary sexual-science PhD. Sex therapy is surely one important part of sexual science. For example, scientific work is being done comparing the relative effectiveness of different therapeutic techniques and examining the validity and reliability of the different scales and measures used in psychological counseling (Coleman et al. 2001; Laumann, Paik, and Rosen 1999; Leiblum 2001; Leiblum and Rosen 2000; Leiblum and Sachs 2002; Miner and Coleman 2002; Weiderman 1998). As in any scientific field, there are critics within the sex-therapy field who declare that therapists are focusing too much on function and dysfunction, and by doing so, they are overlooking the subjective experiences of their patients and are failing to understand what type of person they are dealing with (Kleinplatz 2001). This criticism raises questions about the theoretical base of sex therapy and concerns a significant scientific issue in the field of sex therapy.

Any new sexual-science field has to be certain that the heterosexual emphasis in our society doesn't dominate their work. There are exciting scientific debates concerning the biological and social sources of homosexuality. I discussed some of this in chapter 13. In addition, there are other provocative ideas being put forth by people specializing in this field, and I would recommend Jack Drescher's work in this area. He is one of the psychiatrists who have contributed much to the discussions on Sexnet, and he has written extensively on some of the key issues involved in the study of homosexuality (Drescher 1998; Drescher et al. 2005). There are many journals and organizations involved in the study of homosexuality that I have not discussed, and any interested reader should consult these to keep in touch with this important area of sexual science.

In addition, the Harry Benjamin International Gender Dysphoria Association (HBIGDA), founded in 1977, is dedicated to developing valid methods of dealing with people diagnosed as transsexuals. Members of this organization raised protests when the *Diagnostic and Statistical Manual* (*DSM*) of the American Psychiatric Association classified transsexuality as a mental disorder. This protest resulted in the diagnosis being changed, and transsexuals were instead placed into the broad category of gender identity disorders. So, the issue of careful definitions, empirical evidence, and reasoning that are essential elements of science also enters into the *DSM* debates over transsexualism (Blanchard 2005; Bullough 1994a, 1994b; Green and Keverne 2000; Green and Young 2001; Moser 2001; Zucker 1999).

The field of sex education is also an important part of the field of sexual science. The 2004 guidelines for sex education in grades K through twelve is widely utilized in the public schools (National Guidelines Task Force 2004). These guidelines were developed by the Sex Information and Education

Council of the United States. You can consult the publication *SIECUS Report* for a great deal more information on various sex-education programs and their effectiveness.

In these brief comments, I am simply trying to illustrate the point that all areas of sexual science are involved in scientific work in one way or another, and thus they should be involved in any PhD program in sexual science. Clearly we need to present a broad array of methods and theories in any PhD program that we develop. It is this work done in the various parts of sexual science that will continue to generate our theories and methods (Bancroft 1997, 2000; Weiss 1998a, 1998b; *Journal of Sex Research* 1999).

Overall, I am very gratified by the moves toward a PhD in sexual science at the Kinsey Institute at Indiana University. The track record of that institute is outstanding, and a PhD program organized by them will be a major boost to the visibility, acceptance, and status of our work in sexual science. I believe that in time other universities around the country will follow Indiana University's lead. We will finally be producing our own scholars to join with the specialists of other disciplines that we now have. The value placed on those who work in this field will increase, and our sexual-science work will be more widely recognized and valued by the public, as well as by other professionals. All this will help immeasurably to increase the achievements in sexual science that we will make in the decades to come.

~

CHAPTER FIFTEEN

To the Next Generation of Sexual Scientists

You've traveled with me in this book through many of the key events that I've experienced in the past fifty-some years in our field. You must be asking, is there a message for future sexual scientists from all that is discussed in this book? I'll give you my answer to that question in this chapter.

The Cultural Wars in Sexuality

The ideological battles over issues like abortion, gender equality, erotica, sex education, and much more *cannot* be grasped by examining one issue at a time. If you think of these clashes separately, you will miss the common cultural infrastructure from which all these debates derive. It is our major differences in this cultural infrastructure that fuel all our battles concerning specific sexual issues. The cultural infrastructure of these sexual debates centers on a fundamental difference in basic beliefs concerning the meaning of living a good life. The sexually liberal group in America believes in a pluralistic culture in all areas of life and in the promotion of individual autonomy that affirms people's ability to make most of their own ethical choices. On the other hand, the sexually conservative group in America believes in a narrower vision. The good life is to live in a society that promotes a lifestyle that they see as embodying a narrower, more restrictive set of values that defines what choices people should make. Each side believes that their concept of the good life leads to a happier and healthier life for people. The liberal side believes that their more open, pluralistic approach will reduce our sexual problems and enhance the psychic and physical rewards of sexuality (Reiss and Reiss 1990, 1997). The conservative side believes that its narrower lifestyle would better promote these same outcomes.

These two opposing fundamental conceptions of the nature of the good life and its consequences for us underlie all our debates in sexuality. I am focusing here on conflict in the area of sexuality, but these same differences also underlie the cultural wars in the political, economic, educational, and religious areas of our lives. If we are to understand the cultural wars in the area of sexuality, we had best get to know more about these fundamentally different beliefs concerning the good life.

Implied in the assumptions regarding the nature of the good life is a belief about the nature of people. Aristotle defined the key difference between humans and other animals as due to our greater rational capacity (McKeon 1941). Other animals are superior to us in all our senses and in our athletic abilities. We are the outstanding species only in the ability to analyze the means that will achieve our goals and to plan accordingly for such outcomes. But Aristotle's view did not go unchallenged. Over the centuries, there have been many philosophers, politicians, religious leaders, and others who have defined humans as basically creatures ruled by their emotions. They agreed that humans were better at rational thought, but they added that people did not often act on such rational thoughts. They believed that, particularly in areas that involve strong feelings such as love, hate, lust, greed, or anger, people's rationality will almost always be overpowered by their emotions.

A number of social scientists and biologists have pointed out that we each have what in layman's terms can be called an "emotional brain" and a "rational brain" that interact with each other (Goleman 1995; Massey 2002). So we all realize that we have elements of both the rational and the emotional in our makeup. But people do differ in the degree to which they believe in the power of the rational and are willing to work to promote its dominance in ourselves and in our social systems versus the degree to which they believe in the power of the emotional and are willing to build a more restrictive social system to restrain this emotional nature. In brief, we differ regarding the degree to which we believe that people are capable of managing their emotions.

There is a rather obvious logical connection between people's conception of the dominant element in human behavior and their conception of the good life. If we believe that the good life involves a great deal of pluralism and autonomy and thereby allows people to make a wide range of ethical decisions, then we are likely to endorse the rational view of human beings as creatures capable of making such life choices. On the other hand, if we believe that the good life is living in accord with a much narrower range of ethical choices, then we are likely to believe that people are ruled by their emotions most of the time and therefore require such strict ethical limits. In sum, pluralistic choices go with a rational view of human nature, and narrow choices go with an emotional view of human nature. In chapter 3, I discussed research I did on this, so I will not elaborate more here.

Bear in mind that acceptance of different sexual acts doesn't mean that you want to engage in them yourself. One may have no interest in having sex with a person of the same gender but still feel that it is an acceptable ethical choice for others to make. As I've noted many times, pluralism focuses on what you accept for others, not what you accept for yourself. But if you have a very restrictive view of what is sexually acceptable for all people, then this separation of what is a good sexual choice for you and what is a good sexual choice for others is unlikely to occur.

You can see the relevance of these fundamental beliefs about human beings when you examine the debate about abortion. Most everyone sees aborting a fetus as a negative event. However, people differ in the degree to which they believe having an abortion may be justified if the life of the mother is at risk, if the pregnancy was due to rape or incest, or if the pregnant woman was twelve years old. One might think that since we all agree that it is regrettable when a pregnancy has to be terminated, then it makes sense not to argue about the reasons we accept or don't accept abortion and simply work hard to reduce unwanted pregnancies. This was the thinking of Surgeon General Koop, an advocate of abstinence. In the late 1980s, he publicly said that, in a culture where millions of our teenagers elect to have coitus, the most effective path to lowering abortion rates was to make knowledge and access to contraception easily available to our teenage population. That would reduce unwanted pregnancies and therefore reduce abortion rates.

Dr. Koop encountered strong opposition from his fellow believers in abstinence. Why did they object to this obvious way of reducing the occurrence of abortion? As I discussed in chapter 11, I believe it was because many abortion opponents are also opposed to sexuality outside of marriage (Reiss and Reiss 1990, 1997). In fact, both abortion and premarital coitus are seen as violations of their conception of the good life. These people believe that the only way to reduce abortion is to stop having sex before marriage. They often say they don't trust condoms and that they don't believe young people are capable of making reasonable sexual choices. Clearly, we have here a restrictive view of the good life that blocks the path that could do the most to reduce abortion rates. The opposition to a wider acceptance of sexuality is very often derived from a religious belief that opposes any sexual behavior that is not in line with the restrictive moral perspective that their religion or their cultural group has taught them.

Gender roles are another area that clearly reveals the centrality of our basic assumptions of the good life. Our traditional gender roles assert that women should focus on the home and children and that men should focus on earning a living. The acceptance by women of premarital sex presents a challenge to a traditional conception of segregated gender roles because women now are exercising more power and are showing their interest in more than just the home. Orthodox religion does condemn premarital sex for both women *and* men, but this norm has never been equally enforced in our society, and women have always been subject to greater social criticism. As I discussed at some length in chapter 10, the greater power of men in society is a core root of men's greater sexual freedom. Accordingly, when you increase the power of women in society, it follows that their sexual rights will also increase. As I've noted in the autonomy theory, it was the economic power that women gained by their employment that was a major impetus for the greater sexual rights they also claimed. Such important changes in gender inequality challenge the conservative view of the good life and of the "proper" roles of men and women. It is this challenge to their core beliefs that is sensed by those who have opposed almost all of the increased acceptance of sexual choices of the last half century.

You can make this same analysis of our conceptions of the good life and human nature by going over any area of sexuality. Just think about the debate that is raging today over marital rights for homosexual couples. There, too, we clearly have a restrictive versus a pluralistic view of the good life that is the basis of the dispute. It would be very useful to raise people's awareness as to what they are assuming by their positions on these controversial issues. Then people can ask themselves if they accept the assumptions they are making—do they prefer to live in a restrictive society or in a pluralistic society? If we want to deal with these opposing positions, we need to understand that what is at stake is much greater than what is usually revealed by any single sexual issue. In the most basic sense, what is at stake is the type of society in which we will live. This is the root of our culture wars.

Sexuality Trends around the World

So, which basic cultural infrastructure is winning out in the world today? What are the trends in sexual attitudes and behaviors? In 2001, I was asked to do an article on trends in sexual attitudes and behaviors in various societies around the world for the new edition of the *International Encyclopedia of the Social and Behavioral Sciences* (Reiss 2001b). I used nationally representative surveys from a large number of countries around the world. I compared the trends in the United States with those I found in other countries. Such comparisons can reveal just how common the trends in our country are and what underlying set of assumptions about sexuality is gaining adherents.

Using the 1994 International Social Survey Program (ISSP), we can compare premarital coital attitudes in the United States and five other Western societies (Scott 1998; Davis and Smith 2002). The five other countries are Ireland, Germany, Sweden, Britain, and Poland. Ireland was the only country less permissive in their acceptance of premarital coitus than the United States was. Germany and Sweden were a great deal more accepting, and even Britain and Poland were significantly more accepting than we are. Overall, the examination of these Western European societies shows that they also underwent a sexual revolution in which their acceptance of premarital sexuality increased, although not necessarily in the exact same time period as ours did. The changes in our sexuality since the 1960s were part of an overall Western European change in sexual attitudes toward premarital coitus (Francoeur and Noonan 2004). In the post-World War II world, the economies in these Western European countries increasingly employed married women, and this tends to raise the power and autonomy of women. So, the trends in Europe fit well with the autonomy theory explanation that I have proposed for the American sexual revolution, as discussed in chapter 6.

I also examined cross-national trends in attitudes toward homosexuality. In the United States between 1973 and 1992, the General Social Survey reported that about 20 percent of Americans said homosexuality was "wrong only sometimes" or "not wrong at all," and the other 80 percent thought it was "always wrong" or "almost always wrong" (Davis and Smith 2002). Then, in 1993, the total percentage in the two accepting categories rose to 29 percent, and by 2002 and 2004, it had risen to about 40 percent. The increased acceptance occurred more in female respondents than in males, but it was present in both groups. Bear in mind that the GSS used only one question, and that question did not distinguish between male and female homosexuals. This global-type question is useful, but it also cries out for someone to use tested scales or other more complete measuring instruments to more accurately track these trends regarding attitudes toward homosexuality.

I should add that homosexuality is one of the very few areas in which female acceptance of sexual behavior exceeds male acceptance. I checked Inglehart's World Value Surveys for other national samples to see if this male-female difference in homosexual acceptance was present in all of them. I found that it was present in most Western European societies, but it was not found very often in Eastern European or Asian countries (Inglehart 1997). This gender difference in homosexual acceptance in Western societies is enticing and begs for someone to theorize and test ideas about why this occurs. Is it related to greater gender equality in Western Europe and to males being trained in more rigid roles than females regarding homosexuality? To my knowledge, no one has carefully checked this out.

I also examined acceptance of homosexuality in the same ISSP countries that I had used to compare premarital attitudes between the United States and Europe. I found that Poland and Ireland were less accepting of homosexuality than was the United States, whereas Britain, Germany, and Sweden were more accepting (Scott 1998, 833). I then looked for trends using Inglehart's World Value Surveys. He examined attitudes toward homosexuality in twenty countries, measuring them in both 1981 and 1990 (Inglehart 1997). Inglehart found that between 1981 and 1990, seventeen of these twenty societies increased their acceptance of homosexuality. The three that did not were Ireland, Japan, and South Africa (Inglehart 1997, 297). So, in homosexuality as in premarital sexuality, there has been a significant increase in acceptance in large areas of the world.

There was a very different trend line in attitudes toward extramarital sexuality. I looked at the GSS in the United States and found that between 1973 and 1988, the percentage of Americans who accepted extramarital sexuality as "wrong only sometimes" or "not wrong at all" dropped from about 16 percent to 8 percent and hasn't changed much since then (Davis and Smith 2002). Perhaps the fear of HIV/AIDS played a role in this change. Also, during the 1980s, people were at the peak of the rise in divorce rates, and perhaps that also contributed to this drop in the acceptability of extramarital sex. It is also possible that the 16 percent rate was a temporary rise in the 1970s due to the premarital sexual revolution, and by the late 1980s, we had reverted back to our lower rates. The only nationally representative data measuring extramarital sexual attitudes in the United States before 1973 showed an acceptance rate of 13 percent in 1970 (Klassen et al. 1989, 18).

I again examined Inglehart's World Value Surveys of 1981 and 1990 and found data on extramarital sexual attitudes for twenty of the countries in Inglehart's samples. He reports that the sharpest decreases in acceptance of extramarital sexuality occurred in France, Northern Ireland, Sweden, Argentina, and South Africa. However, there was increased acceptance of extramarital sexuality in Mexico, Italy, Finland, and Hungary. The other eleven countries showed only small changes in both directions. These findings present us with another fascinating puzzle. What explains the differences in trends in extramarital sexual attitudes among these countries? What are the societal and cultural conditions that lead to a rise or a fall in acceptance? The trends in extramarital-sex acceptance do not seem to correlate with the trends for premarital sex or homosexuality. So the factors impacting extramarital acceptance are an excellent area for sexual scientists to investigate (Reiss, Anderson, and Sponaugle 1980).

To further whet your theoretical appetite, let me note that Inglehart asked a question concerning the belief that a child needs two parents in order to be happy. He reported that in almost all of the countries, a majority believed that a child would be happier with two parents, so we cannot say that the countries that increased their acceptance of extramarital sex were those that did not endorse the value of the two-parent family. Could it be that in those countries that experienced a rise in acceptance of extramarital sex, at least the men do not perceive extramarital sex to be a threat to their marriage? I would also speculate that perhaps those countries that experienced an increase in acceptance of gender equality were the same ones that witnessed a decrease in the acceptance of extramarital sexuality. Increased gender equality may bring home to husbands the risks they run if they have an affair.

There are serious limitations in the data we have on extramarital sexuality. We lack information on just what type of affair people had in mind when they answered the extramarital question. There is a variety of ways to have extramarital sex, ranging from having a casual encounter to having an extramarital love relation. I have talked about such differences and have developed a scale to measure four different kinds of extramarital affairs (Reiss 1986, chap. 3; Reiss 1998b; Reiss, Anderson, and Sponaugle 1980). Also, the double standard in sexuality is surely not dead, and so it would be helpful if researchers asked questions separately about the acceptance of extramarital sex for wives and for husbands.

Overall, my examination of trends around the world supports the idea that a pluralist view is winning out in the increased acceptance of premarital sexuality and homosexuality. If the Western world continues to influence economic development around the globe, we will see a continuation of pluralist and rational assumptions about the good life. This should promote increased acceptance of choice in both premarital sex and homosexuality. The data on extramarital sexuality indicates powerful opposition to expanding acceptance of this type of sexuality.

Do Attitudes and Behaviors Correlate?

There are some researchers who think it is futile to ask about sexual attitudes, because they believe that attitudes do not predict behavior very well. Is this a valid conclusion? I examined the evidence concerning this when I was writing my encyclopedia article. One way to check was to see whether the representative national samples showed that sexual behavior had changed during the same time periods as sexual attitudes had changed. Sexual attitudes were measured in national samples in the 1960s, but we had no national surveys measuring sexual behavior in the 1960s. However, there were retrospective data from the 1982 National Survey of Family Growth. The women in that study who had been teenagers in the 1960s were asked about their sexual behavior back in the 1960s. Also, younger women in the study who were teenagers in the 1970s were asked about their sexual behavior at that time. The findings indicate a very steep rise during these decades in the proportion who were nonvirginal during their teenage years (Hofferth et al. 1987; Hopkins 2000). There is also evidence from a 1992 national sample that in the late 1960s there was a sharp rise in sexual behavior (Laumann, Gagnon et al. 1994, 199–201).

In chapter 4, I spoke about the three national surveys of premarital sexual attitudes from 1963 to 1970, and I indicated that these surveys showed a very sharp rise in acceptance of premarital coitus during this time period. So we do have evidence from national samples that indicate a very rapid rise in premarital coital behavior at the same time that there was a very rapid rise in the attitudinal acceptance of premarital coitus. The exact percentage is far less important than the fact that there is a significant correlation between premarital coital attitudes and premarital coital behaviors.

Another check on the relation between attitudes and behaviors concerning premarital sex, homosexuality, and extramarital sex can be made by looking at the GSS data on attitudes and comparing it with their data on behavior. For example, the GSS data reported by Tom Smith indicates that, of those who said premarital sex was "always wrong," 32 percent had engaged in premarital coitus in the last year, whereas if you look at those who said premarital coitus was "not wrong at all," 86 percent had engaged in premarital coitus in the last year (Smith 1994, 89). The comparable figures for homosexuality are 1 percent versus 15 percent, and for extramarital sexuality, 2 percent versus 18 percent. These data display a very significant correlation between attitudes and behaviors regarding premarital, homosexual, and extramarital sexuality. Other studies have reported similar findings showing the correlation between sexual attitudes and behaviors in other countries as well (Reiss 2001b, 13972).

So I feel that it is time to put to rest any bias against the existence of a significant correlation between sexual attitudes and sexual behaviors. Of course the correlation is far from perfect, and we still need to unravel whether attitudes and behaviors are influencing each other or whether there is another factor, like changes in gender equality, that produces a change in both of them. Nevertheless, being aware of this correlation is very useful because it is often far easier to ask attitude questions than to ask behavior questions.

Explaining Trends in Sexuality

There is increasing acceptance of the fact that increased employment of mothers was a major factor in the increased autonomy and power of women in a number of Western countries. This change in women's role encouraged greater tolerance of women's perspectives on sexual and gender issues and thus expanded the diversity that we accepted in our society. The autonomy theory explains how these changes came about. It also ties into the emphasis my cross-cultural linkage theory places on the importance of social power in predicting sexual attitudes and behaviors (see chapter 10). Greater autonomy for a group is an indication of greater power for that group. This is precisely what has happened to women in the Western world. As a result of greater gender equality, there is growing support for the ethic of HER sexual pluralism. This is precisely the type of ethic that one would expect to develop in a society with increasing female autonomy. So, in all these ways, my three major explanatory ideas all interrelate and help explain the trends in sexuality in a large number of societies (see chapters 6, 10, and 11). Of course, each of these theories has its own hypotheses, but together they present a broad explanation of the sexuality trends we have witnessed in our country and elsewhere in the Western world over the past fifty years (Reiss 1967, 1986; Reiss and Reiss 1997). I hope others will develop and examine my theoretical conceptions and further specify and elaborate on this macro explanation of sexuality (Weis 1998a, 1998b).

Inglehart, the World Values Survey author, presents his own explanation of the trends he finds in his surveys (Inglehart 1997). He contends that as capitalist societies have become more affluent and their people feel more secure, there has been a rise in nonmaterialist values that promote well-being and quality of life as more important than the accumulation of economic wealth. This change, he believes, liberates and pluralizes our sexual values in the premarital and homosexual areas. I find this theory compatible with my own theoretical position. Inglehart and I both envision a new type of society that is evolving, and we both see significant changes in terms of autonomy and pluralism. Young people in these Western societies evidence stronger support for pluralism than do older people, and so we can expect that changes will continue on a pluralist path. In addition to Inglehart, there are other social scientists who theorize about cross-cultural trends in sexuality (Abramson and Pinkerton 1995a, 1995b; Collins 2004; Haeberle 2004; Suggs and Miracle 1993).

Future Goals

As I've indicated in this book, the field of sexual science has undergone numerous challenges from many different sources over the past fifty years. We in sexual science need to be unified if we want to be able to deal with today's threats to our scientific research that emanate from the federal government as well as from right-wing religious groups and other ideological organizations. Fortunately, in 2002, a new organization was formed that unites most of our North American sexuality organizations. It is called the North American Federation of Sexuality Organizations (NAFSO), and it is now part of the World Association of Sexology (www.worldsexology.org). One way this new organization can be helpful is by protecting the integrity of our peer-reviewed scientific-grant procedures. I would hope that when the government or any group tries to compromise our research-and-theory rights, we will hear loud and clear protests from NAFSO. As I've said before, if we do not defend our professional rights, we will soon find those rights disappearing.

Each of the individual sexuality organizations also needs to find its own voice. The Bush administration's challenges to our sexuality-research grants and its distortion of our research findings should sound a wake-up call for all of our organizations and for us as individuals. I discussed in chapter 14 how having our own discipline of sexual science in our major universities will enhance our standing in the public and private sectors of our society. I encourage all of you to lend your support to this very important goal of developing our own PhD in sexual science.

Throughout this book, I have stressed the value of a scientific approach to the study of sexuality. I have done this because my experience over the years has shown me the harm that the lack of such an approach can produce. When we deal with controversial sexual areas without a scientific approach, we empower those who prioritize their own personal ideological and dogmatic approaches to sexuality. Bear in mind that these dogmatists and ideologists do not exist only on the right. They also occupy what people call the left. There are left-wing sexual philosophies that stress the "more-is-better" approach to sexuality and that denigrate science. But such a "liberated" ideology is not part of a pluralist philosophy, for their ideology demands that we all seek to have more sexuality. Pluralism allows each of us to define what type of sexual life we want to live. The key element in pluralism is that we should not impose our personal preferences on others. The scientific approach helps us see the harm of both right- and left-wing sexual dogmas. The demand for evidence in science is a powerful barrier to prejudice. We would all benefit by promoting a scientific approach to sexuality as a key way to contain the sexual problems in our society and better understand the rewards that sexuality offers to us all.

This book is my way of passing on what I have learned in the last fifty years. I wish you all a very rewarding voyage into the future world of sexual science. Some of you reading this book will be important in the advance of our field in the next fifty years. Perhaps one of you may someday write your own account of the next fifty years. I encourage all of you to strive to ensure that the story told then will be one about the achievements of sexual science and will note that people in society have arrived at a greater level of erotic peace and psychic satisfaction in the sexual and other aspects of their lives.

References

Abma, Joyce C., A. Chandra, William D. Mosher, William D. Peterson, and L. Piccinino. 1997. Fertility, family planning and women's health: New data from the 1995 National Survey of Family Growth. *Vital and Health Statistics* 23, no. 19: 1–114.

Abma, Joyce C., Gladys M. Martinez, William D. Mosher, and Brittany S. Dawson. 2004. Teenagers in the U.S.: Sexual activity, contraceptive use, & childbearing in 2002. *Vital and Health Statistics* 23, no. 24:1–48.

Abraham, Carolyn. 2005. "No faith in science." *Toronto Globe and Mail*, April 9, F1, F8–9.

Abramson, Paul R., and Steven D. Pinkerton, eds. 1995a. *Sexual nature: Sexual culture*. Chicago: University of Chicago Press.

Abramson, Paul R., and Steven D. Pinkerton. 1995b. *With pleasure: Thoughts on the nature of human sexuality*. New York: Oxford University Press.

Bachofen, J. J. 1861. *Das Mutterrect* [The Mother Right]. Basel, Switzerland: Benno Schwabe, 1948.

Bailey, J. Michael, Michael P. Dunne, and Nicholas G. Martin. 2000. Genetic and environmental influences on sexual orientation and its correlates in an Australian twin sample. *Journal of Personality and Social Psychology* 78:524–36.

Bancroft, John, ed. 1997. *Researching sexual behavior: Methodological issues*. Bloomington: Indiana University Press.

Bancroft, John, ed. 2000. *The role of theory in sex research*. Bloomington: Indiana University Press.

Bancroft, John, Eric Janssen, Lori Carnes, David Goodrich, and David Strong. 2004. Sexual activity and risk taking in young heterosexual men: The relevance of sexual arousability, mood, and sensation seeking. *Journal of Sex Research* 41:181–92.

Bancroft, John. 2004. Alfred C. Kinsey and the politics of sex research. *Annual Review of Sex Research* 15:1–39.

Beach, Frank A., ed. 1965. *Sex and behavior*. New York: John Wiley.

Beach, Frank A., ed. 1977. *Human sexuality in four perspectives*. Baltimore, MD: Johns Hopkins University Press.

Bearman, Peter S., and Hannah Bruckner. 2001. Promising the future: Virginity pledges and first intercourse. *American Journal of Sociology* 106:859–912.

Bearman, Peter S., and Hannah Bruckner. 2002. Opposite-sex twins and adolescent same-sex attraction. *American Journal of Sociology* 107:1179–205.

Bem, Daryl J. 2000. Exotic becomes erotic: Interpreting the biological correlates of sexual orientation. *Archives of Sexual Behavior* 29:531–48.

Blanchard, Ray. 2005. Early history of the concept of autogynephilia. *Archives of Sexual Behavior* 34:439–46.

Bourdieu, Pierre, and Loic J. D. Wacquant. 1992. *An invitation to reflexive sociology*. Chicago: University of Chicago Press.

Brandt, Allan M. 1987. *No magic bullet: A social history of venereal disease in the United States since 1880*. New York: Oxford University Press.

Brecher, Edward M. 1969. *The sex researchers*. Boston: Little, Brown & Co.

Brewster, Karin L., E. C. Cooksey, D. K. Guilkey, and R. R. Rindfuss. 1998. The changing impact of religion on the sexual and contraceptive behavior of adolescent women in the U.S. *Journal of Marriage and the Family* 60:493–504.

Broude, Gwen J., and Sarah J. Greene. 1976. Cross-cultural codes on twenty sexual attitudes and practices. *Ethnology* 15:409–29.

Bruckner, Hannah, and Peter S. Bearman. 2005. After the promise: The STD consequences of adolescent virginity pledges. *Journal of Adolescent Health* 36:271–78.

Bullough, Vern. 1989. *The society for the scientific study of sex: A brief history*. Mt. Vernon, IA: Society for the Scientific Study of Sexuality.

Bullough, Vern, ed. 1994a. *American sexuality: An encyclopedia*. New York: Garland Publishers.

Bullough, Vern. 1994b. *Science in the bedroom: A history of sex research*. New York: Basic Books.

Burgess, Ernest W., and Paul Wallin. 1953. *Engagement and marriage*. New York: J. B. Lippincott.

Capellanus, Andreas. circa 1184. *The art of courtly love*. New York: Frederick Ungar, 1959.

Cates, William, Jr. 2001. The NIH condom report: The glass is 90% full. *Family Planning Perspectives* 33:231–33.

Centers for Disease Control. 1988. Condoms for prevention of sexually transmitted diseases. *Morbidity and Mortality Weekly Report* 37 (March 11): 133–37.

Centers for Disease Control. 1993. Update: Barrier protection against HIV infection and other sexually transmitted diseases. *Morbidity and Mortality Weekly Report* 42 (August 6): 588–91.

Chafetz, Janet. 1984. *Sex and advantage: A comparative, macrostructural theory of sex stratification.* Totowa, NJ: Rowman & Allanheld.

Chafetz, Janet. 1990. *Gender equity: An integrated theory of stability and change.* Thousand Oaks, CA: Sage Publications.

Chernick, Berl A. 1992. Review of Reiss's 1990 book. *Journal of the Canadian Medical Association* 146:965–66.

Chivers, Meredith. 2005. A brief review and discussion of sex differences in the specificity of sexual arousal. *Sexual and Relationship Theory* 20:377–90.

Coleman, Eli, Michael Miner, Fred Ohlerking, and Nancy Raymond. 2001. Compulsive sexual behavior inventory: A preliminary study of reliability and validity. *Journal of Sexual and Marital Therapy* 27:325–32.

Collins, Randall. 1998. The sociological eye and its blinders. *Contemporary Sociology* 27:2–7.

Collins, Randall. 2004. A theory of sexual interaction. In *Interaction Ritual Chains,* 223–57. Princeton, NJ: Princeton University Press.

Cooksey, E. C., R. R. Rindfuss, and D. K. Guilley. 1996. The initiation of adolescent sexual and contraceptive behavior during changing times. *Journal of Health and Social Behavior* 37:59–74.

Coutu, Walter. 1949. *Emergent human nature.* New York: Alfred A. Knopf.

Crenshaw, Theresa L. 1987. Medical news and perspectives. *Journal of the American Medical Association* 257 (May 1): 2263.

Darroch, Jacqueline E., Susheela Singh, Jennifer J. Frost, and the Study Team. 2001. Differences in teenage pregnancy rates among five developed countries: The roles of sexual activity and contraceptive use. *Family Planning Perspectives* 33:244–50.

Davis, James A., and Tom W. Smith. 2002. *General Social Surveys: 1972–2002.* Chicago: National Opinion Research Center.

Davis, James A., and Tom W. Smith. 2004. *General Social Surveys: 1972–2004.* Chicago: National Opinion Research Center.

Davis, James A., Tom W. Smith, and C. Bruce Stephenson. 1978. *General Social Surveys, 1972–1978.* Chicago: National Opinion Research Center.

Davis, Katherine B. 1929. *Factors in the sex life of twenty-two hundred women.* New York: Harper and Brothers.

DeLamater, John D. 2004. Values trump data: The Bush administration and sexual science. Paper presented at the annual meeting of the Society for the Scientific Study of Sex, Orlando, Florida, November 4.

Deven, Fred, and Philip Meredith. 1997. The relevance of a macrosociological perspective on sexuality for an understanding of the risks of HIV infection. In *Sexual Interactions and HIV Risk: New Conceptual Perspectives in European Research,* ed. Luc Van Campenhoudt, Mitchell Cohen, Gustavo Guizzardi, and Dominique Hausser, 142–58. London: Taylor & Francis, 1997.

Diamond, Lisa M. 2003. What does sexual orientation orient? A biobehavioral model distinguishing romantic love and sexual desire. *Psychological Review* 110:173–92.

Diamond, Milton. 1982. Sexual identity, monozygotic twins reared in discordant sex roles and a BBC follow-up. *Archives of Sexual Behavior* 11:181–85.

Diamond, Milton. 1999. Pediatric management of ambiguous and traumatized genitalia. *Journal of Urology* 162:1021–28.

Diamond, Milton, and H. K. Sigmundson. 1997. Sex reassignment at birth: Long-term review and clinical implications. *Archives of Pediatrics and Adolescent Medicine* 151:298–304.

Donnerstein, Edward I., Daniel G. Linz, and Steven Penrod. 1987. *The question of pornography: Research findings and policy implications.* New York: Free Press.

Drescher, Jack. 1998. *Psychoanalytic therapy and the gay man.* Hillsdale, NJ: Analytic Press.

Drescher, Jack, T. S. Stein, and W. Byne. 2005. Homosexuality, gay and lesbian identities, and homosexual behavior. In *Comprehensive Textbook of Psychiatry*, 8th ed., ed. Benjamin J. Kaplan and Virginia A. Sadock, 1936–65. Baltimore, MD: William and Wilkins.

Ehrmann, Winston H. 1959. *Premarital dating behavior.* New York: Holt, Rinehart and Winston.

Einstein, Albert, and Leopold Infeld. 1950. *The evolution of physics: The growth of ideas from early concepts to relativity and quanta.* New York: Simon & Schuster.

Ellis, Albert. 1954. *The American sexual tragedy.* New York: Twayne.

Ellis, Albert. 2001. *Feeling better, getting better, staying better: Profound self-help therapy for your emotions.* Itascadero, CA, Impact Publishers.

Ellis, Albert, and Albert Abarbanel, ed. 1961. *The encyclopedia of sexual behavior.* New York: Hawthorn Books.

Ellis, Havelock. 1938. *Studies in the psychology of sex.* New York: New American Library. Originally published as six volumes between 1897 and 1910.

Elwin, Verrier. 1939. *The Baiga.* London: John Murray.

English, Deirdre, Amber Hollibaugh, and Gayle Rubin. 1981. Talking sex: A conversation on sexuality and feminism. *Socialist Review* 11:50.

Ford, Clellan S., and Frank A. Beach. 1951. *Patterns of sexual behavior.* New York: Harper & Row.

Francoeur, Robert T., and Raymond J. Noonan, ed. 2004. *The international encyclopedia of sexuality.* New York: Continuum Publishing Group.

Freud, Sigmund. 1905. *Three contributions to the theory of sex.* New York: E. P. Dutton, 1962.

Friedan, Betty. 1963. *The feminine mystique.* New York: Dell.

Furstenberg, Frank F., Jr. 1971. Birth control experiences among pregnant adolescents: The process of unplanned parenthood. *Social Problems* 19 (Fall): 192–203.

Gagnon, John H. 1990. The explicit and implicit use of the scripting perspective in sex research. *Annual Review of Sex Research* 1990:1–43.

Gagnon, John H. 1999. Sexual conduct: As today's memory serves. *Sexualities* 2:115–26.

Gagnon, John H., and William Simon. 1973. *Sexual conduct: The social sources of human sexuality.* Chicago: Aldine Publishing.

Gathorne-Hardy, Jonathan. 2000. *Sex, the measure of all things: A life of Alfred C. Kinsey.* Bloomington: Indiana University Press.

Goleman, Daniel. 1995. *Emotional intelligence: Why it can matter more than IQ.* New York: Bantam Books.

Goodale, Jane C. 1971. *Tiwi wives.* Seattle: University of Washington Press.

Goode, William J. 1963. *World revolution and family patterns.* Glencoe, IL: Free Press.

Gordon, Sol. 1991. Review of Reiss's 1990 book. *Family Life Educator,* Winter, 17–18.

Gorer, Geoffrey. 1967. *Himalayan village: An account of the Lepchas of Sikkim.* 2nd ed. New York: Basic Books.

Graham, Cynthia A., John Bancroft, William Yarber, and Stephanie A. Sanders. 2003. The Kinsey Institute as a center for graduate education in human sexuality. In *Handbook of Sexuality Research Training Initiatives,* ed. Diane di Mauro, Gilbert Herdt, and Richard Parker, 100–109. New York: Social Science Research Council.

Green, Richard. 1987. *The "sissy boy syndrome" and the development of homosexuality.* New Haven, CT: Yale University Press.

Green, Richard, and E. B. Keverne. 2000. The disparate maternal aunt-uncle ratio in male transsexuals: An explanation invoking genomic imprinting. *Journal of Theoretical Biology* 202:53–63.

Green, Richard, and Jack Wiener, ed. 1980. *Methodology in sex research: Proceedings of the conference held in Chevy Chase, Maryland, November 17–19, 1977, Washington, D.C.* Rockville, MD: U.S. Department of Health and Human Services Publication ADM-80-766.

Green, Richard, and Robert Young. 2001. Hand preference, sexual preference, and transsexualism. *Archives of Sexual Behavior* 30:565–74.

Guttman, Louis. 1947. The Cornell technique for scale and intensity analysis. *Educational and Psychological Measurement* 7:247–80.

Haeberle, Erwin J. 1978. *The sex atlas: A new illustrated guide.* New York: Seabury Press.

Haeberle, Erwin J. 2004. The global future of sexology. Speech given in Beijing on October 16, 2004. (The text can be found at Haeberle's website in Berlin: www.sexology.cjb.net. My 1960, 1967, and 1986 books are at this website.)

Harlow, Harry F. 1962. The heterosexual affection system in monkeys. *American Psychologist* 17 (January): 1–9.

Hatfield, Elaine, and Richard L. Rapson. 1996. *Love and sex: Cross-cultural perspectives.* Boston: Allyn & Bacon.

Hatfield, Elaine, Richard L. Rapson, and Lise D. Martel. 2006 (in press). Passionate love and sexual desire. In *Handbook of Cultural Psychology,* ed. Shinobu Kitayama and Dov Cohen. New York: Guilford Press.

Hearst, Norman, and Stephen B. Hulley. 1988. Preventing the heterosexual spread of AIDS: Are we giving our patients the best advice? *Journal of the American Medical Association* 259:2428–32.

Heiman, Julia R. 2001. Sexual desire in human relationships. In *Sexual Appetite, Desire and Motivation: Energetics of the Sexual System,* ed. Walter Everaerd, Ellen Laan, and Stephanie Both, 117–34. Amsterdam: Royal Netherlands Academy of Arts and Sciences.

Heiman, Julia R., Johan Verhulst, and Amy R. Heard-Davison. 2003. Childhood sexuality and adult sexual relations: How are they connected by data and by theory? In *Sexual Development in Childhood*, ed. John Bancroft, 404–20. Bloomington: Indiana University Press.

Herdt, Gilbert. 1981. *Guardians of the flutes: Idioms of masculinity*. New York: McGraw-Hill.

Herdt, Gilbert. 1997. *Same sex, different cultures: Explaining gay and lesbian lives*. Boulder, CO: Westview Press.

Hofferth, Sandra L., Joan R. Kahn, and Wendy Baldwin. 1987. Premarital sexual activity among U.S. teenage women over the past three decades. *Family Planning Perspectives* 19:46–53.

Hooker, Evelyn. 1980. Discussion of Marcel Saghir's paper. In *Methodology in Sex Research: Proceedings of the Conference Held in Chevy Chase, Maryland, November 18 and 19, 1977*, ed. Richard Green and Jack Wiener, 292–301. Rockville, MD: U.S. Department of Health and Human Services Publication ADM-80-766.

Hopkins, Kenneth Wu. 2000. Testing Reiss's autonomy theory on changes in nonmarital coital attitudes and behaviors of U.S. teenagers: 1960–1990. *Scandinavian Journal of Sexology* 3:113–25.

Hupka, Ralph B. 1981. Cultural determinants of jealousy. *Alternative Lifestyles* 4:310–56.

Hyde, Janet S. 2005. The gender similarities hypothesis. *American Psychologist* 60: 581–92.

Hyde, Janet S., and John D. DeLamater. 2006. *Understanding human sexuality*. 9th ed. Boston: McGraw-Hill.

Inglehart, Ronald. 1997. *Modernization and postmodernization: Cultural, economic, and political change in 43 societies*. Princeton, NJ: Princeton University Press.

Institute of Medicine, National Academy of Sciences. 1988. *Confronting AIDS: Update 1988*. Washington, DC: National Academy Press.

Institute of Medicine, National Academy of Sciences. 2001. *Health and behavior: The interplay of biological, behavioral and societal influences*. Washington, DC: National Academy Press.

Jones, Elise F., J. D. Forrest, N. Goldman, S. Henshaw, R. Lincoln, J. Rosoff, C. Westoff, and D. Wulf. 1986. *Teenage pregnancy in industrialized countries: A study sponsored by the Alan Guttmacher Institute*. New Haven, CT: Yale University Press.

Jones, James H. 1997. *Alfred C. Kinsey: A public/private life*. New York: W. W. Norton.

Journal of Sex Research. 1999. Special issue on methods of inquiry about sex: New advances 36: 1–120.

Kantner, John, and Melvin Zelnik. 1973. Contraception and pregnancy. *Family Planning Perspectives* 5:11–25.

Kaplan, Esther. 2004. *With God on their side: How Christian fundamentalists trampled science, policy, and democracy in George W. Bush's White House*. New York: New Press.

Kaplan, Helen Singer. 1987. *The real truth about women and AIDS: How to eliminate the risks without giving up love and sex.* New York: Simon & Schuster.

Kephart, William M. 1961. Review of premarital sexual standards in America. *American Sociological Review* 26:294–95.

Kephart, William M. 1968. Review of the social context of premarital sexual permissiveness. *The Annals of the American Academy of Political and Social Science* 376: 201–2.

Kinsey, Alfred, Wardell Pomeroy, and Clyde Martin. 1948. *Sexual behavior in the human male.* Philadelphia: W. B. Saunders.

Kinsey, Alfred, Wardell Pomeroy, Clyde Martin, and Paul Gebhard. 1953. *Sexual behavior in the human female.* Philadelphia: W. B. Saunders.

Kirby, Douglas. 2001a. *Emerging answers: Research findings on programs to reduce teen pregnancy.* Washington, DC: National Campaign to Prevent Teen Pregnancy.

Kirby, Douglas. 2001b. Understanding what works and what doesn't in reducing adolescent sexual risk-taking. *Family Planning Perspectives* 33:276–81.

Kirby, Douglas. 2002. Effective approaches to reducing adolescent unprotected sex, pregnancy and childbearing. 2002. *The Journal of Sex Research* 39:51–57.

Klassen, Albert D., Collin J. Williams, and Eugene E. Levitt. 1989. *Sex and morality in the U.S.* Middletown, CT: Wesleyan University Press.

Kleinplatz, Peggy J., ed. 2001. *New directions in sexual therapy: Innovations and alternatives.* Philadelphia: Brunner-Routledge.

Koop, C. Everett. 1986. *Surgeon general's report on acquired immune deficiency syndrome.* Rockville, MD: U.S. Department of Health and Human Services.

Krich, Aron. 1965. *The sexual revolution—seminal studies into 20th century American sexual behavior.* New York: Dell Publishing.

Kuhn, Thomas. 1962. *The structure of scientific revolutions.* Chicago: University of Chicago Press.

Ladas, Alice K., Beverly Whipple, and John D. Perry. 1982. *The G spot: And other recent discoveries about human sexuality.* New York: Holt, Rinehart and Winston.

Laumann, Edward O. 2001. *Sex, love, and health in America.* Chicago: University of Chicago Press.

Laumann, Edward O. 2004. *The sexual organization of the city.* Chicago: University of Chicago Press.

Laumann, Edward O., John H. Gagnon, Robert T. Michael, and Stuart Michaels. 1994. *The social organization of sexuality.* Chicago: University of Chicago Press.

Laumann, Edward O., Robert Michael, and John H. Gagnon. 1994. A political history of the national sex survey of adults. *Family Planning Perspectives* 26:34–38.

Laumann, Edward O., Anthony Paik, and Raymond C. Rosen. 1999. Sexual dysfunction in the United States: Prevalence and predictors. *Journal of the American Medical Association* 281:537–44.

Leiblum, Sandra R. 2001. Critical overview of the new consensus based definitions and classifications of females' sexual dysfunction. *Journal of Sex and Marital Therapy* 27:159–68.

Leiblum, Sandra R., and Raymond C Rosen. 2000. *Principles and practice and sex therapy*. New York: Guilford Press.

Leiblum, Sandra R., and Judith Sachs. 2002. *Getting the sex you want: A woman's guide to becoming proud, passionate and pleased in bed*. New York: Crown Publishing.

Leshner, Alan I. 2003. Don't let ideology trump science. Editorial. *Science* 302:1479.

LeVay, Simon. 2003. The biology of sexual orientation. http://members.aol.com/slevay/page22.html.

Libby, Roger. 1991. Review of Reiss's 1990 book. *SIECUS Report* 19:16–17.

Lieberson, Stanley, and Freda B. Lynn. 2002. Barking up the wrong branch: Scientific alternatives to the current model of sociological science. *Annual Review of Sociology* 28:1–19.

Lief, Harold. 1981. The physician's role in practice and in the community. In *Sexual Problems in Medical Practice*, ed. Harold Lief, 99–110. Chicago: American Medical Association.

Lippa, Richard A., and Francisco D. Tan. 2001. Does culture moderate the relationship between sexual orientation and gender related personality traits? *Cross-Cultural Research* 35:65–87.

Locke, Harvey J. 1951. *Predicting adjustment in marriage: A comparison of a divorced and a happily married group*. New York: Henry Holt.

Longino, Helen. 1990. *Science as social knowledge: Values and objectivity in scientific inquiry*. Princeton, NJ: Princeton University Press.

Longino, Helen. 2002. *The fate of knowledge*. Princeton, NJ: Princeton University Press.

Malinowski, Bronislaw. 1929. *The sexual life of savages in N.W. Melanesia*. New York: Harvest Books.

Marshall, Donald, and Robert C. Suggs. 1971. *Human sexual behavior*. New York: Basic Books.

Martin, M. Kay, and Barbara Voorhies. 1975. *Female of the species*. New York: Columbia University Press.

Massey, Douglas S. 2002. A brief history of human society: The origin and role of emotion in social life. *American Sociological Review* 67:10–29.

Masters, William H., and Virginia E. Johnson. 1966. *Human Sexual Response*. Boston: Little, Brown.

Masters, William H., and Virginia E. Johnson. 1970. *Human sexual inadequacy*. Boston: Little, Brown.

Masters, William H., Virginia E. Johnson, and Robert C. Kolodny. 1986. *Masters and Johnson on sex and human loving*. Boston: Little, Brown.

Masters, William H., Virginia E. Johnson, and Robert C. Kolodny. 1988. *Crisis: Heterosexual behavior in the age of AIDS*. New York: Grove Press.

de Maupassant, Guy. 1883. *A woman's life*. New York: Lion Books, 1954.

di Mauro, Diane. 1995. *Sexuality research in the United States: An assessment of the social and behavioral Sciences*. New York: Social Science Research Council.

di Mauro, Diane, Gilbert Herdt, and Richard Parker, eds. 2003. *Handbook of sexuality research training initiatives*. New York: Social Science Research Council.

McKeon, Richard, ed. 1941. *The basic works of Aristotle*. New York: Random House.

McWhirter, David P., and Andrew M. Mattison. 1984. *The male couple: How relationships develop*. New York: Prentice Hall.

Merton, Robert K. 1976. *Sociological ambivalence and other essays*. New York: Free Press.

Meyer-Bahlburg, Heino F. L. 2001. Gender and sexuality in classic congenital adrenal hyperplasia. *Endocrinology and Metabolism Clinics of North America* 30:155–71.

Miner, Michael, and Eli Coleman. 2002. Advances in sex offender treatment and challenges for the future. *Journal of Psychology and Human Sexuality* 13:5–24.

Money, John. 1995. *Gender maps: Social constructionism, feminism, and sexosophical history*. New York: Continuum Publishing.

Money, John, and Anka A. Ehrhardt. 1972. *Man and woman, boy and girl*. Baltimore, MD: Johns Hopkins University Press.

Money, John, and Herman Musaph, eds. 1977. *Handbook of sexology*. New York: Excerpta Medica.

Moser, Charles. 2001. Paraphilia: A critique of a confused concept. In *New Directions in Sexual Therapy: Innovations and Alternatives*, ed. Peggy J. Kleinplatz, 91–108. Philadelphia: Brunner-Routledge, 2001.

Mosher, William D., Anjani Chandra, and Jo Jones. 2005. Sexual behavior and selected health measures: Men and women 15–44 years of age, United States 2002. *Vital Health Statistics*. Advanced Data, no. 362. Hyattsville, MD, September 15.

Mosher, William D., Gladys M. Martinez, Anjani Chandra, Joyce C. Abman, and Stephanie J. Wilson. 2004. Use of contraception and use of family planning services in the U.S.: 1982–2002. *Vital and Health Statistics*, advanced data, no. 350. Hyattsville, MD, December 10.

Murdock, George Peter. 1949. *Social structure*. New York: Macmillan.

Murdock, George Peter, and Douglas R. White. 1969. The standard cross-cultural sample. *Ethnology* 8:329–69.

National Guidelines Task Force. 2004. *Guidelines for comprehensive sexuality education*. 3rd ed. New York: Sex Information and Education Council of the U.S.

National Institute of Allergy and Infectious Disease. 2001. *Workshop summary: Scientific evidence on condom effectiveness for sexually transmitted disease (STD) Prevention*, Herndon, VA, July 20.

Newcomer, Susan F., and J. Richard Udry. 1985. Oral sex in the adolescent population. *Archives of Sexual Behavior* 14:41–46.

Olds, Sally Wendkos. 1985. *The eternal garden: Seasons of our sexuality*. New York: Times Books.

Ortner, Sherry B., and Harriet Whitehead, eds. 1981. *Sexual meanings: The cultural construction of gender and sexuality*. Cambridge, UK: Cambridge University Press.

Popper, Karl R. 1959. *The logic of scientific discovery*. New York: Science Editions.

Proctor, Robert N. 1991. *Value-free science? Purity and power in modern knowledge*. Cambridge, MA: Harvard University Press.

Rains, Prudence. 1971. *Becoming an unwed mother*. Chicago: Aldine-Atherton.

Reiss, Ira L. 1948. Premarital sexual relations. Unpublished college paper available in the Kinsey Institute Archive Library's collection of my work.

Reiss, Ira L. 1956. The double standard in premarital sexual intercourse: A neglected concept. *Social Forces* 34 (March): 224–30.

Reiss, Ira L. 1957. The treatment of pre-marital coitus in "Marriage and the Family" texts. *Social Problems* 4 (April): 334–38.

Reiss, Ira L. 1960a. *Premarital sexual standards in America.* Glencoe, IL: Free Press.

Reiss, Ira L. 1960b. Toward a sociology of the heterosexual love relationship. *Marriage and Family Living* 22:139–45.

Reiss, Ira L. 1963. Personal values and the scientific study of sex. In *Advances in Sex Research,* ed. Hugo Beigel, 3–10. New York: Harpers, 1963.

Reiss, Ira L. 1964a. The scaling of premarital sexual permissiveness. *Journal of Marriage and the Family* 26:188–98.

Reiss, Ira L. 1964b. Premarital sexual permissiveness among negroes and whites. *American Sociological Review* 29:688–98.

Reiss, Ira L. 1965a. Social class and premarital sexual permissiveness: A re-examination. *American Sociological Review* 30:747–56.

Reiss, Ira L. 1965b. The universality of the family: A conceptual analysis. *Journal of Marriage and the Family* 26:443–53.

Reiss, Ira L. 1967. *The social context of premarital sexual permissiveness.* New York: Holt, Rinehart and Winston.

Reiss, Ira L. 1970. Premarital sex as deviant behavior: An application of current approaches to deviance. *American Sociological Review* 35:78–87.

Reiss, Ira L. 1971. *Family systems in America.* New York: Holt, Rinehart and Winston.

Reiss, Ira L. 1976. *Family systems in America.* 2nd ed. New York: Holt, Rinehart and Winston.

Reiss, Ira I. 1977. Changing sociosexual mores. In *Handbook of sexology,* ed. John Money and Herman Musaph, 311–25. Holland: Elsevier.

Reiss, Ira L. 1980a. *Family Systems in America.* 3rd ed. New York: Holt, Rinehart and Winston.

Reiss, Ira L. 1980b. Sexual customs and gender roles in Sweden and America: An analysis and interpretation. In *Research on the Interweave of Social Roles: Women and Men,* ed. Helena Lopata, 191–220. Greenwich, CT: JAI Press.

Reiss, Ira L. 1981. Some observations on ideology and sexuality in America. *Journal of Marriage and the Family* 43:271–83.

Reiss, Ira L. 1984. Human sexuality in sociological perspective. In *Sexually transmitted diseases,* ed. King Holmes, Per-Anders Mardh, P. Frederick Sparling, and Paul J. Wiesner, 39–50. New York: McGraw-Hill.

Reiss, Ira L. 1986. *Journey into sexuality: An exploratory voyage.* Englewood Cliffs, NJ: Prentice-Hall.

Reiss, Ira L. 1993. The future of sex research and the meaning of science. *Journal of Sex Research* 30 (February): 3–11.

Reiss, Ira L. 1998a. Reiss male and female premarital sexual permissiveness scales. In *Handbook of Sexuality-Related Measures*, 2nd ed., ed. Clive M. Davis, William L. Yarber, Robert Bauserman, George Schreer, and Sandra L. Davis, 496–98. Thousand Oaks, CA: Sage Publications.

Reiss, Ira L. 1998b. Reiss extramarital sexual permissiveness scales. In *Handbook of Sexuality-Related Measures*, 2nd ed., ed. Clive M. Davis, William L. Yarber, Robert Bauserman, George Schreer, and Sandra L. Davis, 226–28. Thousand Oaks, CA: Sage Publications.

Reiss, Ira L. 1999. Evaluating sexual science: Problems and prospects. *Annual Review of Sex Research* 10:236–71.

Reiss, Ira L. 2001a. The autobiography of a sex researcher: Short version. *Marriage and Family Review* 31:57–91.

Reiss, Ira L. 2001b. Sexual attitudes and behavior. In *International Encyclopedia of the Social and Behavioral Sciences*, ed. Neil J. Smelser and Paul B. Baltes, vol. 21, 13969–73. New York: Elsevier Science.

Reiss, Ira L. 2004. An introduction to the many meanings of sexological knowledge. In *International Encyclopedia of Sexuality*, ed. Robert T. Francoeur, 21–30. New York: Continuum Publishing. (Orig. pub. 1997)

Reiss, Ira L. 2005. *Selected professional letters of Ira L. Reiss.* (This manuscript and many more of my materials can be found in the Kinsey Institute Library Archives at Indiana University.)

Reiss, Ira L., Ron Anderson, and G. C. Sponaugle. 1980. A multivariate model of the determinants of extramarital sexual permissiveness. *Journal of Marriage and the Family* 42:395–411.

Reiss, Ira L., Albert Banwart, and Harry Foreman. 1975. Premarital contraceptive usage: A study and some theoretical explanations. *Journal of Marriage and the Family* 37:619–30.

Reiss, Ira L., and Albert Ellis. 2002. *At the dawn of the sexual revolution: Reflections on a dialogue.* Walnut Creek, CA: AltaMira Press.

Reiss, Ira L., and Frank F. Furstenberg, Jr. 1981. Sociology and human sexuality. In *Sexual Problems in Medical Practice*, 53–70. Chicago: American Medical Association.

Reiss, Ira L., and Gary R. Lee. 1988. *Family Systems in America.* 4th ed. New York: Holt, Rinehart & Winston.

Reiss, Ira L., and Robert K. Leik. 1989. Evaluating strategies to avoid AIDS: Number of partners vs. use of condoms. *Journal of Sex Research* 26:411–33.

Reiss, Ira L., and Brent Miller. 1979. Heterosexual permissiveness: A theoretical analysis. In *Contemporary Theories about the Family*, vol. 1, ed. Wesley Burr, Reuben Hill, Ivan Nye, and Ira L. Reiss, 57–100. New York: Free Press.

Reiss, Ira L., and Harriet M. Reiss. 1990. *An end to shame: Shaping our next sexual revolution.* Amherst, NY: Prometheus Books.

Reiss, Ira L., and Harriet M. Reiss. 1997. *Solving America's sexual crises.* Amherst, NY: Prometheus Books. (Orig. pub. 1990)

Reiss, Ira L., Robert H. Walsh, Mary Zey-Ferrell, William L. Tolone, and Ollie Pocs. 1980. Research in heterosexual relationships. In *Methodology in Sex Research: Proceedings of the Conference Held in Chevy Chase, Maryland, November 18 and 19, 1977*, ed. Richard Green and Jack Weiner, 1–66. Rockville, MD: U.S. Department of Health and Human Services Publication ADM-80-766.

Rind, Bruce, and Philip Tromovitch. 1997. A meta-analytic review of findings from national samples on psychological correlates of child sexual abuse. *Journal of Sex Research* 34:237–55.

Roos, Patricia. 1985. *Gender and work: A comparative analysis of industrial societies.* Albany: State University of New York Press.

Rosen, Raymond C., and Kevin E. McKenna. 2002. PDE-5 inhibition and sexual response: Pharmacological mechanisms and clinical outcomes. *Annual Review of Sex Research* 13:36–88.

Rosenbaum, Maj-Britt. 1991. Review of Reiss's 1990 book. *Journal of Sex and Marital Therapy* 17:59–62.

Ross, Marc H. 1983. Political decision making and conflict: Additional cross-cultural codes and scales. *Ethnology* 22:169–92.

Rostosky, Sharon S., Mark D. Regnerus, and Margaret L. C. Wright. 2003. Coital debut: The role of religiosity and sex attitudes in the Add Health survey. *The Journal of Sex Research* 40:358–67.

Rubin, Gayle. 1984. Thinking sex: Notes for a radical theory of the politics of sexuality. In *Pleasure and Danger: Exploring Female Sexuality*, ed. Carole S. Vance, 267–319. Boston: Routledge & Kegan Paul.

Rutter, Michael. 2002. Nature, nurture, and development: From evangelism through science toward policy and practice. *Child Development* 73:1–21.

Sanday, Peggy Reeves. 1981. The socio-cultural context of rape: A cross-cultural study. *Journal of Social Issues* 37:5–27.

Schlegel, Alice. 1972. *Male dominance and female autonomy.* New Haven, CT: Human Relations Area Files Press.

Schlegel, Alice. 1977. Toward a theory of sexual stratification. In *Sexual Stratification: A Cross-Cultural View*, 1–40. New York: Columbia University Press, 1977.

Schlegel, Alice. 1979. Sexual antagonism among the sexually egalitarian Hopi. *Ethos* 7:124–41.

Schwartz, Israel, and Ira L. Reiss. 1995. The scaling of premarital sexual permissiveness revisited: Test results of Reiss's new short form version. *Journal of Sex and Marital Therapy* 21:78–86.

Schwartz, Pepper, and Virginia Rutter. 1998. *The gender of sexuality: Exploring sexual possibilities.* New York: Rowman & Littlefield.

Scott, Jacqueline. 1998. Changing attitudes to sexual morality: A cross-national comparison. *Sociology* 32:815–45.

Shilts, Randy. 1987. *And the band played on: Politics, people and the AIDS epidemic.* New York: St. Martin's Press.

SIECUS Fact Sheet. 2004. Public support for comprehensive sexuality education. *SIECUS Report* 32:39–41.

Simon, William. 1996. *Postmodern sexualities*. New York: Routledge.

Simon, William. 1999. Sexual conduct in retrospective perspective. *Sexualities* 2:126–33.

Simon, William, and John H. Gagnon. 1984. Sexual scripts: Permanence and change. *Society* 22:53–60.

Singh, Susheela, and Jacqueline E. Darroch. 1999. Trends in sexual activity among adolescent American women 1982–1995. *Family Planning Perspectives* 31:212–19.

Smith, Bradley. 1978. *The American way of sex: An informal illustrated history*. New York: Two Continents Publishing.

Smith, Tom. 1994. Attitudes toward sexual permissiveness: Trends, correlates and behavioral connections. In *Sexuality across the Life Course*, ed. Alice Rossi, 63–97. Chicago: University of Chicago Press.

Society for the Scientific Study of Sexuality. 1980, 1981. Board Meeting Minutes Archive. Sept. 5 and 6, Nov. 15 and 16, 1980; Apr. 9 and 10, Nov. 19 and 22, 1981.

Strossen, Nadine. 2000. *Defending pornography: Free speech, sex and the fight for women's rights*. New York: Scribner.

Studor, Marilyn, and Arland Thornton. 1987. Adolescent religiosity and contraceptive usage. *Journal of Marriage and the Family* 49:117–28.

Suggs, David N., and Andrew W. Miracle, eds. 1993. *Culture and human sexuality: A reader*. Pacific Grove, CA: Brooks/Cole Publishing.

Suggs, Robert C. 1966. *Marquesan sexual behavior*. San Diego, CA: Harcourt Brace Jovanovich.

Symons, Donald. 1979. *The evolution of human sexuality*. New York: Oxford University Press.

Terman, Lewis M. 1938. *Psychological factors in marital happiness*. New York: McGraw-Hill.

Union of Concerned Scientists. 2004. Scientific integrity in policymaking: An investigation into the Bush administration's misuse of science. www.ucsusa.org/global_environment/rsi/index.html.

Udry, J. Richard. 2000. Biological limits of gender construction. *American Sociological Review* 65:443–57.

Voorhies, Barbara, and Kay Martin. 1975. *Female of the species*. New York: Columbia University Press.

Wallen, Kim. 1996. Nature needs nurture: The interaction of hormonal and social influences on the development of behavioral sex differences in rhesus monkeys. *Hormones and Behavior* 30:364–78.

Wallen, Kim, and Julia L. Zehr. 2004. Hormones and history: The evolution and development of primate female sexuality. *Journal of Sex Research* 41:101–12.

Waxman, Henry. 2003, August. The state of science under the Bush administration. Committee on Government Reform, Minority Office. www.house.gov/reform/min/politicsandscience.

Waxman, Henry. 2004. April 13, 2004, letter to Honorable John H. Marburger, director of the Office of Science and Technology Policy. www.house.gov/reform.

Weiderman, Michael W. 1998. The state of theory in sex therapy. *Journal of Sex Research* 35:88–89.

Weis, David, ed. 1998a. Special issue: The use of theory in research and scholarship on sexuality. *Journal of Sex Research* 35:1–124.

Weis, David. 1998b. The use of theory in sexuality research. *Journal of Sex Research* 35:1–9.

Westermarck, Edward. 1891. *The history of human marriage.* New York: Allerton Book, 1922.

Whyte, Martin K. 1978. *The status of women in pre-industrial societies.* Princeton, NJ: Princeton University Press.

Wilson, Edward O. 1975. *Sociobiology: The new synthesis.* Cambridge, MA: Harvard University Press.

Wilson, Edward O. 2000. *Sociobiology: The new synthesis.* 25th anniversary ed. Cambridge, MA: Harvard University Press.

Zelnik, Melvin, and John F. Kantner. 1980. Sexual activity, contraceptive use and pregnancy among metropolitan-area teenagers: 1971–1979. *Family Planning Perspectives* 12:230–37.

Zetterberg, Hans L. 1969. Om Sexuallivet I Sverige [On sexual life in Sweden]. Stockholm: Statens Offentiliga Utredningar [State Public Report].

Zucker, Kenneth J. 1999. Intersexuality and gender identity differentiation. *Annual Review of Sex Research* 10:1–69.

Zucker, Kenneth J. 2002. Evaluation of sex and gender assignment decisions in patients with physical intersex conditions: A methodological and statistical note. *Journal of Sex and Marital Therapy* 28:269–74.

Name Index

Abarbanel, Albert, 47
Abma, Joyce C., 31, 125, 145
Abraham, Carolyn, 175
Abramson, Paul R., 137, 210
Anderson, Ronald, 83, 87, 115–16
Aristotle, 202

Bachofen, J.J., 134
Bailey, J. Michael, 181
Baltimore, David, 123
Bancroft, John, 136, 154, 192–93, 196–98, 200
Banwart, Albert, 83, 116
Barbach, Lonnie, 148
Beach, Frank A., 27, 127
Bearman, Peter S., 35, 146, 181
Beigel, Hugo, 49
Bem, Daryl J., 180–81
Benjamin, Harry, 199
Blau, Peter, 53
Blanchard, Ray, 199
Bonner, E.J., 148
Borgatta, Edward, 53
Bourdieu, Pierre, 35, 178
Brandt, Allan M., 140

Brecher, Edward M., 47
Brewster, Karin L., 35, 146
Broderick, Carl, 50
Broude, Gwen J., 128
Bruckner, Hannah, 35, 146, 181
Bullough, Vern, 102, 107, 112–13, 150, 154, 190, 199
Burgess, Ernest W., 15–16, 25–26
Bush, George W., 174
Byne, W., 199

Calderone, Mary, 50–52
Capellanus, Andreas, 27
Caplowitz, David, 53
Carlson, Ruth, 158
Casanova, 46
Cates, William Jr., 143
Chafetz, Janet, 127, 133
Chandler, Alvin, 16–17
Chall, Leo, 58
Chernick, Berl A., 153
Chilgren, Rick, 63, 67
Chivers, Meredith, 183
Cohen, Al, 53
Coleman, Eli, 67–68, 117, 198–99

227

Coleman, James, 53–54
Coles, President, 14
Collins, Randall, 136, 154, 210
Cooksey, E.C., 35, 146
Coutu, Walter, 9–11
Crenshaw, Theresa L., 142
Cuber, John F., 23–24

Darroch, Jacqueline E., 72, 145
Darrow, William, 139
Davis, Clive, 103–4, 106, 109–11
Davis, James A. 43, 53, 72, 205–6
Davis, Katherine B., 27
DeLamater, John D., 137, 175, 193, 198
Demareth, Nick, 58
Deven, Fred, 137
Diamond, Lisa M., 183
Diamond, Milton, 178, 185
Donnerstein, Edward, 94–98
Drescher, Jack, 199
Durham, Lewis, 188
Dusek, Ron, 18
Dworkin, Andrea, 93, 95, 97, 99, 147

Ehrhardt, Anka A., 177–78
Ehrmann, Winston H., 26
Einstein, Albert, 37, 39
Eisenhower, Dwight, 26
Elias, James, 190
Ellis, Albert, xiii, 47–48, 52, 164–67
Ellis, Havelock, 134
Elwin, Verrier, 130
English, Deirdre, 93

Falwell, Jerry, 40
Farley, Frank, 193
Fisher, Martha, 18
Fithian, Marilyn, 102
Follet, Wilson, 24
Ford, Clellans, 27, 127
Foreman, Harry, 83, 116
Forrest, J.D., 46
Francoeur, Robert T., 137, 205
Fraser, Don, 93–96, 99

Freud, Sigmund 57, 164
Friedan, Betty, 75, 90–91
Fulton, Robert, xiii
Furstenberg, Frank, 92

Gagnon, John H., 53, 59, 61, 128–29, 172
Garfinkel, Harold, 53
Gathorne-Hardy, Jonathan, xii, 122, 187
Gebhard, Paul, 23, 69
Gendel, Eve, 148
Goldman, N., 46
Goleman, Daniel, 202
Goodale, Jane C., 130
Goode, William J., 53–54, 92
Gordon, Sol, 153
Gorer, Geoffrey, 130
Graham, Cynthia A., 193, 197–98
Green, Arnold, 9–10
Green, Richard, 49–50, 52, 86–88, 101–2, 199
Greene, Sarah J., 128
Gribble, Jessica, xiv
Groves, Ernest, 50
Groves, Gladys, 25, 50
Guilkey, D.K., 35
Guttman, Lewis, 70

Haeberle, Erwin J., 47, 210
Harlow, Harry, 120
Hartman, William, 102–5, 112
Hatfield, Elaine, 137, 179
Hearst, Norman, 145
Hefner, Hugh, 52–54
Heiman, Julia R., 183, 198
Henshaw, S., 46
Herdt, Gilbert, 36, 190
Herzog, Daniel, 103
Hill, Reuben, 16
Himmelhoch, Jerome, 22
Hitler, Adolph, xii, 2, 6, 47
Hofferth, Sandra L., 72, 208
Hollinbaugh, Amber, 93

Holmes, King, 123–24
Hooker, Evelyn, 86
Hopkins, Kenneth, 74, 83, 208
Houdek, P.K., 59
Hoyt, Charlee, 95–96
Hubbard, Sergeant, 6, 7
Hudson, Rock, 139
Hulley, Stephen B., 145
Hupka, Ralph B., 128, 135
Huxley, Aldous, 16
Hyde, Janet S., 137, 184

Ibsen, Henrik, 16
Infeld, Leopold, 37, 39
Inglehart, Ronald, 205–7, 209

James, Henry, 16
Jefferson, Thomas, 176
Jewson, Ruth, 106
Jocher, Kathleen, 22
Johnson, Magic, 140
Johnson, Virginia, 44, 57–60, 102,
    116–22, 141–43, 147
Jones, Elise F., 46
Jones, James H., xii

Kallman, Franz, 58
Kantner, John, 116, 145
Kaplan, Esther, 32
Kaplan, Helen Singer, 141–42
Kaplan, Jeremiah, 27
Kephardt, William M., 27, 74
Kernodle, Ruth, 19
Kernodle, Wayne, 17, 19
Keverne, E.B., 199
Kinsey, Alfred C., xi–xiii, 8, 14–17,
    22–26, 41, 45, 48, 59–60, 69, 122,
    187–88, 192
Kirby, Douglas, 34, 51, 146, 175
Klassen, Albert D., 43, 72, 206
Kleinplatz, Peggy, 121, 199
Klerman, Gerald, 88–89
Koestler, Arthur, 16
Kolodny, Robert C., 44, 141

Koop, C. Everett, 140, 152, 203
Krich, Aron, 47
Kuhn, Thomas, 38

Ladas, Alice K., 148
Lange, Heide, 148–49
Laumann, Edward O., 136–37, 152,
    176, 199, 208
Lehfeldt, Hans, 111
Lehrman, Hannah, 106, 110
Leiblum, Sandra R., 199
Leif, Harold, 62, 91–92
Leik, Robert, 93, 125, 143–44
Leik, Shelia, 93, 96
Leshner, Alan I., 175
Levay, Simon, 179
Levitt, Eugene E., 43
Libby, Roger, 153
Lieberson, Stanley, 183
Lincoln, R., 46
Lindensmith, Alfred, 53
Lippa, Richard A., 179
Locke, Harvey J., 16, 26
Longino, Helen, 30, 38
Lynn, Freda B., 183

MacKinnon, Catherine, 93, 95–99, 147
Maddock, James, 67
Maier, Patty, 158–59
Malinowski, Bronislaw, 27
Marshall, Donald, 129, 151
Martin, Clyde, 69
Martin, Kay, 86, 127, 185
Massey, Douglas S., 183, 202
Masters, William H., 44, 57–60, 102,
    116–22, 141–42, 147
Mattison, Andrew M., 136
DeMaupassant, Guy, 16
Di Mauro, Diane, 192, 198
McBride, Mary Margaret, 28
McCarthy, Joe, 14
McHale, John, 53
McIlhaney, Joseph, 175

McIlvenna, Ted, 61, 63–64, 67, 187–89
McKenna, Kevin E., 183
McKeon, Richard, 202
McWhirter, David P., 136
Meredith, Philip, 137
Merton, Robert K., 27, 171, 174
Messenger, Sheldon, 53
Meyer-Bahlburg, Heino, 185
Meyers, Lonny, 66
Miller, Arthur, 16
Miller, Brent, 70, 74, 83, 115
Miner, Michael, 199
Miracle, Andrew W., 137, 210
Modigliani, Amedeo, 58
Money, John, 47–49, 57, 174, 177–78, 185
Montague, D.J., 19
Moser, Charles, 148, 199
Mosher, William D., 31, 125, 145
Moses, 4
Murdock, George P., 27, 127–28
Musaph, Herman, 47

Nelson, Joel, xiii
Nemec, Jenn, xiv
Newcomer, Susan F., 129
Nimkoff, Meyer, 23
Noonan, Raymond J., 137, 205

O'Brien, Kathy, 94, 96
Olds, Sally, 44
O'Neill, Eugene, 16
Ortner, Sherry B., 127
Ozarin, Lucy, 57

Paik, Anthony, 199
Parsons, Talcott, 27
Perry, John D., 148
Petersen, C.G., 74–75
Peterson, William D., 31
Piccinino, L., 31
Pinkerton, Steven D., 137, 210
Pitts, George, 18
Pocs, Ollie, 88
Pogrebin, Letty Cottin, 147–48

Pomeroy, Wardell, 69, 188
Popper, Karl R., 34
Porter, Spence, 149
Proctor, Robert N., 31, 171

Rains, Prudence, 116
Rapson, Richard L., 137
Read, W.M., 24
Regnerus, Mark D., 35
Reagan, Ronald, 139, 142
Reiss, Albert J., 53
Reiss, Harriet M., xiii, 20, 24, 46, 62, 64, 66, 74–75, 79–80, 83, 117–22, 146–51, 155, 202–3, 209
Reiss, Ira L., 8, 11, 14–15, 17, 20–22, 25, 27, 29, 34–35, 41–43, 46–49, 62, 64, 69–70, 72–75, 82–83, 87, 90, 96–97, 107–8, 115–16, 123, 125, 129–30, 134–36, 144, 146, 150–51, 155, 162, 164–65, 169–71, 174, 180–81, 184, 188, 202–3, 205, 207–9
Reitman, Robert, 103–4, 106–8, 111
Renshaw, Domeena, 92
Rindfuss, R.R., 35
Robbins, Eli, 58
Roos, Patricia, 127, 133
Rosen, Raymond C., 183, 199
Rosenbaum, Maj-Britt, 153
Ross, Marc H., 128
Rossi, Peter, 53
Rosoff, J., 46
Rostosky, Sharon S., 35
Rubin, Gayle, 93, 154
Runden, Charity, 103
Ruppel, Howard, 189
Russell, Diana, 148
Russell, Seth, 9–10
Rutter, Michael, 179
Rutter, Virginia, 184

Sacks, Judith, 199
Saghir, Marcel, 86
Sanday, Peggy, 128
Sanders, Stephanie, 192–93, 197–98

Satterfield, Sharon, 117
Sarah (biblical character), 4
Schaeffer, Leah, 102–4, 107, 112
Schiller, Patricia, 51–52
Schlegel, Alice, 127, 134
Schuessler, Karl, 53
Schwartz, Israel, 83
Schwartz, Pepper, 123, 184
Scott, Jacqueline, 43, 72, 205–6
Seabloom, William, 157, 161
Seale, W. Holt, 24–25
Shilts, Randy, 140
Shirey, Richard, 18
Sigmundson, H. K., 178
Silverman, Merv, 148
Simon, William, 53, 128–29, 154, 172
Singh, Susheela, 72
Smigel, Irwin, 53
Smith, Bradley, 44
Smith, M. Brewster, 23
Smith, tom W., 43, 72, 205–6, 208
Sponaugle, G.C., 83, 87, 115–16, 207
Staples, Robert, 148
Stein, T.S., 199
Stephenson, C. Bruce, 43
Stephenson, John, 18, 21
Stewart, J. Jones, 108, 111–12
Stokes, Walter, 48
Stone, Abraham, 25
Stryker, Sheldon, 53
Studor, Marilyn, 146
Suggs, David N., 137, 210
Suggs, Robert C., 129, 151
Summerlin, John, 103, 107, 111
Sutton, Laird, 61, 189
Symons, Donald, 128

Tan, Francisco D., 179
Tanfer, Koray, 89
Taylor, Burt, 14
Terman, Lewis, M., 16, 26
Thornton, Arland, 146
Tinsley, Lieutenant, 6–7
Tolone, William, 88

Tolstoy, Leo, 17
Trost, Jan, 75–76

Udry, J. Richard, 129, 182

Vincent, Clark, 53
Voorhiers, Barbara, 86–87, 127, 185

Waller, Williard, 16
Wallin, Paul, 15–16, 25–26
Walsh, Robert, 87
Waxenberg, Sheldon, 57
Waxman, Henry, 32, 174–75
Weiderman, Michael W., 199
Weiner, Jack, 85–89
Weinstein, Debbie, 110–12
Weis, David, 69, 200, 209
Westermarck, Edward, 134
Westerveldt, Frank, 103, 105, 108, 110–11
Westerveldt, Mary, 103, 105, 108, 110–11
Westoff, C., 46
Wheeler, Connie, 102–5, 108
Whipple, Beverly, 148
White, Douglas, 128
Whitehead, Harriet, 127
Whyte, Martin K., 127–28, 133
Williams, Collin J., 43
Williams, Tennessee, 16
Wilson, Edward O., 128, 182–83
Winer, Julius, 111
Winokur, George, 57
Wright, Margaret , 35
Wulf, D., 46

Yarber, William, 193, 197
Young, Robert, 199

Zehr, Julia L., 179
Zelnik, Melvin, 116, 145
Zetterberg, Hans, 77–78
Zey-Ferrell, Mary, 87
Zucker, Kenneth J., 178, 199

Subject Index

abstinence: abstinence only sex
    education, 32, 35–36, 51, 146, 175;
    as one choice, 150–53; risks
    involved, 35–36, 145–46. *See also*
    contraception, HIV/AIDS, politics
    and sex, pluralism theory
American Association of Sex Educators,
    Counselors, and Therapists
    (AASECT): and importance to
    sexual science, 52; and Patricia
    Schiller, 51. *See also* sex therapy
American Medical Association (AMA):
    and gender language 92–93; and
    value of joint writing, 92. *See also*
    sexual science PhD
anti-Semitism: in the army, 6–7; in
    public schools, 2. *See also* bias
attitudes and behaviors: how they relate,
    41, 207–9. *See also* sexuality trends
assumptions about society: pluralism vs.
    traditionalism, 201–4; rational vs.
    emotional views, 36–37. *See also*
    religion, science, theory
autonomy theory: explaining autonomy,
    69–71; fit with linkage and pluralism

theories, 155, 209–10; importance of
    affection, 20–21; national 1963
    sample, 21, 42–43, 70–71;
    proposition one explained, 71;
    research in the 1950s, 17–21;
    responses to autonomy theory,
    74–75; in Sweden, 82–83; testing
    proposition one, 72–73. *See also*
    contraception, linkage theory,
    pluralism theory, sexual
    permissiveness, sexual revolution,
    Sweden

behavior. *See* attitudes and behaviors
bias: family textbooks, 14–16; and
    values, 1, 26, 34–36. *See also*:
    pluralism theory, politics and sex,
    science, values
biology and social science: clash on
    defining gender, 128, 183–85;
    examples of bio/social interaction,
    179–83; John-Joan Case and
    "scientific evangelism", 177–79; on
    Sexnet, 176–79. *See also* linkage
    theory, sexual science PhD

child and adolescent sexual well-being: forming a committee on, 157; issues with Department of Health, 158–62; and sexual pluralism, 160. *See also* autonomy theory, pluralism theory

Consortium of Sexual Science Associations, (COSSA), 33. *See also* politics and sex

contraception: condom effectiveness, 35, 142–45, 171, 175; increased condom usage, 31, 125, 140; older contraceptive methods, 46–47; role of pill in sexual revolution, 43–47; a theory predicting contraceptive usage, 116. *See also* abstinence, politics and sex, premarital sexual permissiveness, sexual revolution, Sweden

cross cultural research and theory. *See* linkage theory, SCCS, sexuality trends

double standard: critiquing the double standard, 22; and female sexuality, 13–14; and linkage theory, 132–34; in sexuality, 4–5; in Sweden, 80–81. *See also* assumptions about society, gender, pluralism theory, sexual ethics

extramarital sexual permissiveness: extramarital scales, 115–16; a theory and predictors, 87, 115–16; world wide trends, 206–10. *See also* autonomy theory, linkage theory, pluralism theory, sexual revolution

family: influence on sexuality, 115; textbook treatment of sexuality, 14–16. *See also* autonomy theory, gender roles, linkage theory, pluralism theory, religion, values

gender roles: conflicting definitions of, 183–85; cross cultural gender studies, 127, 133–34, 137; equality in Sweden, 75, 80–81; first PhD degree in gender studies, 198; gender factors in Sweden, 81–82; and premarital sexual permissiveness, 72–73; and prostitution, 2–3; trends in employment of women, 13–14, 46–47, 74. *See also* double standard, linkage theory, pluralism theory, SCCS, Sweden

Groves Conference, 50–51, 59–61

HIV/AIDS: abstinence and risk, 145–46; condoms and risk, 143–45; epidemiological approach, 123–25; lack of Federal support, 139–40; sex therapists reactions, 140–43. *See also* autonomy theory, contraception, linkage theory, pluralism theory, politics and sex

homosexuality: American Psychiatric Association 1973 decision, 86; debates on homosexuality, 199; EBE theory, 180–82; Hooker's research, 86; linkage theory, 134, 136; trends in attitudes, 129, 204–7. *See also* autonomy theory, pluralism theory, politics and sex

International Academy of Sex Research, (IASR): Richard Green, 49–50; value to our field, 52

intersex, 177–79, 185, 198–200. *See also* pluralism theory, politics and sex, sexual science PhD

linkage theory: building a theory, 127–28; defining sexuality, 129–30; fit with autonomy and pluralism theories, 155, 209–10; gender linkage, 132–34; ideology linkage,

134; jealousy linkage, 134–36; pleasure and disclosure and social bonding, 130–32; response to linkage theory, 136–37; role of reproduction, 129–31; and sexual scripts, 129; and social bonding, 130–32; societal ideology linkage, 134; summation, 136–37. See also assumptions about society, autonomy theory, pluralism theory, SCCS

National Organization for Women (NOW): and feminine mystique, 75; and politics, 90–91. See also autonomy theory, double standard, gender, linkage theory, pluralism theory, Sweden
North American Federation of Sexuality Organizations (NAFSO), 210. See also politics and sex

Playboy, Hefner's sociology party, 52–55. See also pluralism theory, Sexual Attitude Reassessment
pluralism theory: defining sexual pluralism, 150–53; fit with autonomy and linkage theories, 155, 209–10; HER sexual pluralism, 150–53; reaction in USA, 85; researching sexual pluralism, 146–50; responses to pluralism theory, 153–55; in Sweden, 79–81; traditional sex standards and sexual problems, 150. See also autonomy theory, linkage theory, politics and sex
politics and sex: Bush Administration anti-science actions, 32–34, 174–76; in graduate school, 8–11; lack of social science input, 123–25; lack of government support, 85–89, 139–40; politics of publication, 23–24; problem solutions from scientists, 149, 154–55, 210–11; at

William & Mary, 16–17. See also abstinence, bias, pluralism theory, pornography, science, sexual science PhD, values
pornography: Canadian law, 99; debate in Minneapolis, 93–99; erotica vs. pornography, 96; experimental studies, 98; author's view of, 93; National Commission on Pornography, 97; research on pornography and gender equality, 97. See also assumptions about society, autonomy theory, double standard, gender, linkage theory, pluralism theory, politics and sex, power
premarital sexual permissiveness: impact of contraceptive pill, 43–47 ; premarital scale, 20–21; premarital sexual standards, 19–20, 41–43; problems in publishing, 24–27; rates of non virginity by age, 145–46; revolution in 1960s and 1970s, 41–43; writing a college paper, 7–8. See also autonomy theory, linkage theory, pluralism theory, sexual revolution, sexuality trends
prostitution, in Scranton, 2–3

Rational Emotive Behavior Therapy (REBT): Albert Ellis's contribution, 164–65; qualifying REBT philosophy, 165–67. See also sex therapy
religion: orthodox Judaism, 3–4; orthodox views on sex, 82, 204; relation to gender equality, 75–83; relation to sexual attitudes, 71–72. See also abstinence, autonomy theory, double standard, gender, linkage theory, pluralism theory, science, Sweden
retirement, author's view of, 162–64
revolution. See sexual revolution

science: and advocacy, 33–34; ancient
roots, 29–30; clash with religion, 30;
clash with politics, 332–33;
description vs. explanation, 39;
Einstein's views on tentativeness,
37–38; ethics, 31–32; in seventeenth
century, 30–32. See also bias, politics
and sex, sexual science PhD, social
constructionism, values

sex education: abstinence only sex
education, 32, 35–36, 51, 146, 175;
Koop's educational proposals, 203;
new graduate grants, 192; PhD
minor at Indiana University,
198–200; taskforce for PhD in sexual
science, 191–97. See also AASECT,
autonomy theory, contraception,
politics and sex, SAR, science,
sexual science PhD, SIECUS

Sex Information and Education Council
of the US (SIECUS): and Mary
Calderone, 50–52; and sex education,
34; and value to our field, 52. See also
abstinence, contraception, pluralism
theory, politics and sex, sex
education, values

sex therapy: assumptions of Master's and
Johnson's (M&J) approach, 58–59;
Chair in Sexual Health in PHS,
67–68; M&J's early work on, 57–58;
M&J's first book and, 59–61;
observing the M&J organization,
118–23; as part of a PhD in sexual
science, 198–99; PHS at University
of Minnesota, 62–63, 116–18; sexual
attitude reassessment, 61–68;
therapists and HIV/AIDS, 140–43.
See also AASECT, assumptions
about society, pluralism theory,
politics and sex, sexual science PhD

sexual attitude reassessment (SAR):
early development, 61–62; 1972 San

Francisco SAR, 63–67; at University
of Minnesota, 62–63, 68. See also sex
education, sex therapy

sexual ethics, and ethics of pluralism,
150–53. See also assumptions about
society, politics and sex, pluralism
theory

sexual organizations. See AASECT,
IASR, SIECUS, SSSS

sexual pluralism theory. See pluralism
theory

sexual revolution: and changes in
females, 72; comparison in
premarital, homosexual, and
extramarital sex, 204–10; overlooked
early studies, 42–43; role of the
contraceptive pill, 43–47; prediction
by author, 27, 42. See also autonomy
theory, contraception, gender,
homosexuality, linkage theory,
pluralism theory, premarital sexual
permissiveness

sexual science Ph.D: including subfields,
198–200; older programs in sexuality,
187–90; progress toward PhD at
Kinsey Institute, 197–98; taskforce
for PhD in sexual science, 191–97.
See also autonomy theory, linkage
theory, pluralism theory, politics and
sex, science

sexuality trends: defining sexuality,
129–30; explaining worldwide
trends, 209–10; premarital,
homosexual, and extramarital cross
cultural trends, 72, 204–7. See also
autonomy theory, linkage theory,
pluralism theory

social constructionism: clash with
science, 171; confusion of relativism
and tolerance, 173; outsider
and insider views, 170; radical
branch, 170; reasons for social

constructionism, 172–74; supporters of radical sexual constructionism, 172–74. *See also* politics and sex, science, values

Society for the Scientific Study of Sexuality (SSSS): and Albert Ellis, 47–9; crisis in 1980 about executive director, 101–13 ; other 1980 organizational problems, 103–5, 108–9; value to our field, 52. *See also* science

Standard Cross Cultural Sample (SCCS): explained, 128; and female power, 132–34. *See also* linkage theory

Sweden: autonomy of children in, 76–77; "erotic peace," 77; fit with autonomy theory, 82–83; key causes of gender equality, 81–82; premarital sexual attitudes, 77, 79–81; privacy norms, 76, 78. *See also*: autonomy theory, contraception, gender, linkage theory, pluralism theory

theory, overview, 37–39. *See also*: autonomy theory, linkage theory, pluralism theory, science

transsexual, 198–200. *See also* pluralism theory, politics and sex, sexual science PhD

trends. *See* sexuality trends

values: and assumptions about people, 36–37; of author, 1–11; contrasted to bias, 26, 34–36; and value aware, 34–36; and value fair, 34–36. *See also* bias, pluralism theory, politics and sex, science

~

About the Author

Ira L. Reiss's primary effort has been to improve the scientific credibility of sociological explanations concerning human sexuality. For over fifty years, he has developed and tested explanations of how society shapes our sexual customs and has used these explanations to develop possible resolutions of the myriad of controversial social problems related to these areas. His work has raised public and professional respect for professors, therapists, social workers, public health workers, and others engaged in sexual-science work. He has made it easier for this generation of sexual scientists to be willing to investigate these highly sensitive areas in which emotion so often blocks our understanding. He is now professor emeritus in sociology at the University of Minnesota and is a former president of the International Academy of Sex Research, the Society for the Scientific Study of Sexuality, the National Council on Family Relations, and the Midwest Sociological Society. He has received numerous awards for his professional work and is the author of 14 books and 150 professional papers. He has given hundreds of talks at universities, in the media, and in other forums in the United States and abroad.